Noble Beauty, Transcendent Holiness

Why the Modern Age Needs the Mass of Ages

PETER KWASNIEWSKI

Noble Beauty, Transcendent Holiness

Why the Modern Age Needs the Mass of Ages

Foreword by
Martin Mosebach

First published in the USA
by Angelico Press 2017
© Peter Kwasniewski 2017
Foreword © Martin Mosebach 2017

For information, address:
Angelico Press
4709 Briar Knoll Dr.
Kettering, OH 45429
angelicopress.com
info@angelicopress.com

ISBN 978 1 62138 284 3 pb
ISBN 978 1 62138 285 0 cloth
ISBN 978 1 62138 286 7 ebook

Cover photograph of the Rood in the Holy Cross
Priory Church, Leicester, by Fr. Lawrence Lew, O.P.
Cover design: Michael Schrauzer

CONTENTS

TABLE OF PHOTOGRAPHS

Photographs are listed according to the chapter before which they appear.

1 Main door, Cathedral of S. Rufino, Assisi, by Julian Kwasniewski
2 Bell tower,* Norcia, by Julian Kwasniewski
3 Wood carving of Calvary, in the Cloisters, New York, by Peter Kwasniewski
4 Wood carving of a saint, the Cloisters, New York, by Julian Kwasniewski
5 St. Benedict of Nursia, in St. Germain des Prés, Paris, by Julian Kwasniewski
6 Stained glass, Our Lady of the Blessed Sacrament Chapel, Marytown, Illinois, by Julian Kwasniewski
7 Sculpture on the wall of the courtyard of the Cathedral of S. Rufino, Assisi, by Julian Kwasniewski
8 Church of St. Winifride, Holywell, North Wales, for a Latin Mass Society Pilgrimage, courtesy of Dr. Joseph Shaw
9 Co-Cathedral of Norcia,* by Julian Kwasniewski
10 Church of St. Gallus, Gestratz, by Fr. Alban Cras, FSSP, © Priestly Fraternity of St. Peter
11 Chapel, Silverstream Priory, County Meath, Ireland, © Paweł Kula, used with permission
12 Lion, Palazzo Comunale, Norcia, by Julian Kwasniewski

* The places in these photographs were destroyed by the earthquakes in Norcia in the second half of 2016.

IN GRATEFUL MEMORY OF

Michael Davies (1936–2004)
László Dobszay (1935–2011)
Msgr. Klaus Gamber (1919–1987)

and others of their generation,
who fought the good fight in a time of great darkness,
and without whom no such book as this
could ever have been written.
May the Lord crown their labors
in the heavenly fatherland.

"The memory of you will go with me all my life, to comfort
and encourage me. You were a flame burning in darkness, and
the fire which consumed you was the love of Mass."
Michael Kent, *The Mass of Brother Michel*

Thus saith the Lord: Stand ye on the ways, and see and ask for the old paths which is the good way, and walk ye in it: and you shall find refreshment for your souls.

Jeremiah 6:16

The first characteristic of the anti-liturgical heresy is hatred of tradition as found in the formulas used in divine worship. One cannot fail to note this special characteristic in all heretics, from Vigilantius to Calvin, and the reason for it is easy to explain. Every sectarian who wishes to introduce a new doctrine finds himself, unfailingly, face to face with the Liturgy, which is Tradition at its strongest and best, and he cannot rest until he has silenced this voice, until he has torn up these pages which recall the faith of past centuries.

Dom Prosper Guéranger, O.S.B.

Repudiated by the Modernists, the beauty of the Catholic liturgy, with its plainsong and its polyphony, with its noble prayers inherited from Christian Rome, with its harmonious reverence and its sure appeal to the human heart, is a cultural as well as a spiritual treasure. The traditional faith preserves not only the fabric of ancient churches but their meaning, the worship for which they were built and beautified. The works of the European past, in poetry, in painting, in music, reach out to the Catholic tradition for their interpretation; the same tradition guides the mind by a universal philosophy, one taken from the clarity of Greece and refined by the highest minds in the European intellectual tradition. If we would rise above the barbarism of modern society, we must turn to these things to rediscover what it has thrown aside.

H. J. A. Sire

Acknowledgments

THE CONTENT of this book is woven out of previously published essays and articles, rewritten and reorganized around the question: Why is the traditional understanding and practice of liturgical worship right in itself, and therefore crucial to recover in our day, when it has been largely abandoned?

Chapter 1 derives from a lecture delivered at the Franciscan University of Steubenville on September 7, 2015; chapter 2 from a lecture at the Premonstratensian Abbey of Strahov in Prague for the launch of the Czech edition of *Resurgent in the Midst of Crisis* on October 14, 2016; and chapter 3 from my plenary address at the Annual General Meeting of the Vancouver Traditional Mass Society on November 12, 2016. Part of Chapter 7 was published at the blog *OnePeterFive*. Chapter 9 was published in *Latin Mass: The Journal of Catholic Culture and Tradition*. Most of the other chapters contain material that first appeared at *Rorate Caeli*, *New Liturgical Movement*, or *Views from the Choir Loft*.

Passages of Sacred Scripture quoted in this book are generally drawn from the Douay-Rheims translation. Citations of the Psalms follow the traditional Vulgate numbering.

I express my gratitude to all the conference organizers who gave me the opportunity to develop my thoughts in writing and to the various editors who, over the years, have improved my work with their criticisms and counsel. In particular, this manuscript benefited from the astute eye of Michael Martin. I thank the friends, young and old, who have read my essays, corrected my errors, and forced me to go deeper and further. Deserving of special thanks for the handsome black and white photographs that adorn the chapters are Fr. Alban Cras, F.S.S.P., Dom Mark Kirby, O.S.B., Paweł Kula, Dr. Joseph Shaw, and my son Julian.

Martin Mosebach's incisive writings on the liturgy have influenced me greatly. It is therefore a special joy for me to be able to include, as the Foreword of this book, a translation of the lecture Mr. Mosebach delivered at the Kölner Internationale Liturgische Tagung, April 1, 2017. This lecture is published herein with Mr. Mosebach's gracious consent, for which I am most grateful.

I would be remiss not to mention John Riess, an ideal publisher to work with, and James Wetmore, an expert typographer. In my opinion, John and James have built up Angelico Press into the most thoughtful and creative Catholic publishing house in the English-speaking world.

Lastly, I wish to thank the many priests and bishops who, down through the years, have served as faithful ministers of Christ and stewards of the mysteries of God (cf. 1 Cor 4:1–2), transmitting the blessed inheritance of our traditional Roman liturgy and through it bestowing abundant graces upon me and those dear to me. Without the zeal, perseverance, and generosity of these *viri Dei,* the longed-for renewal of the postconciliar Church would never have begun. May Our Lord grant them, both living and dead, the reward of good and faithful servants (cf. Mt 25:21).

Foreword

For Pope Benedict XVI, On His Ninetieth Birthday

by Martin Mosebach[1]

O NE SHOULDN'T CALL a "cult of personality" the papal devotional items that are offered to the hordes of pilgrims and tourists round about Saint Peter's in Rome: postcards and calendars, coffee cups and silk cloths, plates and plastic gadgets of every kind, always with the picture of the currently happily reigning Holy Father—and next to them also those of Popes John Paul II, John XXIII, and even Paul VI. There is only one pope you will not find in any of the souvenir shops—and I mean in none, as if there were a conspiracy here. To dig up a postcard with the picture of Benedict XVI requires the tenacity of a private detective. Imperial Rome knew the institution of *damnatio memoriae*: the extinction of the memory of condemned enemies of the state. Thus, Emperor Caracalla had the name of his brother Geta—after he had killed him—chiseled out of the inscription on the triumphal arch of Septimius Severus. It seems as if the dealers in devotional goods and probably also their customers (for the trade in rosaries also obeys the market laws of supply and demand) had jointly imposed such an ancient Roman *damnatio memoriae* on the predecessor of the current pope.

It is as if, on this trivial level, should be accomplished that which Benedict himself could not resolve to do after his resignation (disturbing to so many people, profoundly inexplicable and still unexplained)—namely, to become invisible, to enter into an unbroken silence. Those especially who accompanied the pontificate of Bene-

---

1. Translated by Stuart Chessman; annotated by Peter Kwasniewski.

dict XVI with love and hope could not get over the fact that it was this very pope who, with this dramatic step, called into question his great work of reform for the Church. Future generations may be able without anger and enthusiasm to speak about this presumably last chapter in the life of Benedict XVI. The distance in time will place these events in a greater, not yet foreseeable order. For the participating contemporary, however, this distance is not available because he remains defenseless in the face of the immediate consequences of this decision. To speak about Benedict XVI today means first of all trying to overcome these feelings of pain and disappointment.

All the more so, because during his reign this pope undertook to heal the great wounds that had been inflicted on the visible body of the Church in the time after the Council. The party that had assembled against tradition at the Council viewed the compromise formulas that had settled the conflict in many conciliar documents only as stages in the grand war for the future shape of the Church. The "spirit of the Council" began to be played off against the literal text of the conciliar decisions. Disastrously, the implementation of the conciliar decrees was caught up in the cultural revolution of 1968, which had broken out all over the world. That was certainly the work of a spirit—if only of a very impure one. The political subversion of every kind of authority, the aesthetic vulgarity, the philosophical demolition of tradition not only laid waste universities and schools and poisoned the public atmosphere but at the same time took possession of broad circles within the Church. Distrust of tradition, elimination of tradition began to spread in, of all places, an entity whose essence consists totally of tradition—so much so that one has to say the Church is nothing without tradition. So the postconciliar battle that had broken out in so many places against tradition was nothing else but the attempted suicide of the Church—a literally absurd, nihilistic process. We all can recall how bishops and theology professors, pastors and the functionaries of Catholic organizations proclaimed with a confident victorious tone that with the Second Vatican Council a new Pentecost had come upon the Church—which none of those famous Councils of history which had so decisively shaped the development of the Faith had ever claimed. A "new Pentecost" means nothing less than a new illumination, possibly one that would surpass that received two thousand years ago; why not advance immediately to the "Third Testament" from the *Education of the Human Race*[2] of Gotthold Ephraim Lessing? In the view of these people, Vatican II meant a break with the Tradition as it existed up till then, and this breach was salutary. Whoever listened to this could have believed that the Catholic religion had found itself really only after Vatican II. All previous generations—to which we who sit here owe our faith—are supposed to have remained in an outer courtyard of immaturity.

To be fair, we should remember that the popes attempted to counter this—with a weak voice and above all without the will to intervene in these aberrations with an organizing hand as the ruler of the Church. Only a very few individual heresiarchs were disciplined—those who with their arrogant insolence practically forced their own reprimand. But the great mass of the "new-Pentecostals," unrestrained and protected by widespread networks, could continue to exercise a tremendous influence on the day-to-day life of the Church. So, for outside observers, the claim that with Vatican II the Church had broken with her past became ever more probable. Anyone accustomed to trusting his eyes and ears could no longer convince himself that this was still the Church that had remained faithful for thousands of years, through all the changes of the ages. The German Catholic legal scholar Carl Schmitt made the following scornful rhyme: "Heraclitus taught that all things flow; the rock of Peter—it's flowing too."[3] An iconoclastic attack like the worst years of the Reformation swept through the churches; in the seminaries the "demythologizing of Christianity" *à la* Bultmann was propagated; the end of priestly celibacy was celebrated as something imminent; religious instruction was largely abandoned, even in Germany, which had been highly favored in this regard; priests gave

2. A work of the Enlightenment, published in 1780, that asserted a threefold development or "education" of mankind through the successive stages of the Old Testament, the New Testament, and the Modern Age.

3. "Alles fließt, lehrt Heraklit. / Der Felsen Petri, der fliesst mit." Schmitt is likely alluding to a well-known aphorism by W. Busch: "Einszweidrei, im Sauseschritt / Läuft die Zeit; wir laufen mit."

up clerical attire; the sacred language—which the liturgical consti-tution of the Council had just solemnly confirmed[4]—was aban-doned. All this happened, so it was said, to prepare for the future, otherwise the faithful couldn't be kept in the Church. The hierarchy argued like the proprietors of a department store, who didn't want to sit on their wares and so tossed them out to the people at throw-away prices. Regrettably the comparison isn't exact, for the people had no interest in the discounted products. After the "new Pente-cost" there began an exodus out of the Church, the monasteries, and the seminaries. The Church, unrestrainedly pushing ahead with her revolution, continued to lose both attractiveness and retentive capacity.

She resembled that baffled tailor who, looking at a badly cut pair of trousers while shaking his head, muttered: "I've cut you off three times and you're still too short!" It is claimed that this exodus from the Church would also have happened without the revolution. Let's conditionally accept for the moment this claim. If that had really been the case, however, the great revolution would not have been necessary at all. On the contrary, the flock remaining in the Church would have been able to persevere in faith under the "sign that will be contradicted" (Lk 2:34). There's not one argument in favor of the post-conciliar revolution; I certainly haven't encountered any yet.

Pope Benedict could not and would never allow himself to think in that way, even if in lonely hours it may have been difficult for him to defend himself against an assault of such thoughts. In no way did he want to abandon the image of the Church as a harmoniously growing organism under the protection of the Holy Spirit. With his historical consciousness it was also clear to him that history can never be turned back, that it is impossible as well as reckless to try to make what has happened "unhappen." Even the God who for-gives sins does not make them "undone," but in the best case lets them become a *felix culpa*. From this perspective, Benedict could not accept what the progressives and traditionalists expressed equally and with the best reasons: that in the post-conciliar era a decisive break with Tradition had indeed occurred; that the Church

---

4. Constitution on the Sacred Liturgy *Sacrosanctum Concilium*, §36, §54, §101.

before and after the Council was not the same institution. That would have meant that the Church was no longer under the guidance of the Holy Spirit; consequently, she had ceased to *be* the Church. One cannot imagine the theologian Joseph Ratzinger as laboring under a naive, formalistic faith. The twists and turns of ecclesiastical history were very familiar to him. That in the past, too, there had been in the Church bad popes, misguided theologians, and questionable circumstances was never hidden from him. But, while contemplating ecclesiastical history, he felt borne up by the indisputable impression that the Church, in constant development, had again and again overcome her crises not simply by cutting off mistaken developments but by making them, if possible, even fruitful in the succeeding generations.

It thus appeared to him imperative to combat the idea that this rupture had really occurred—even if all the appearances seemed to argue for it. His efforts aimed at attempting to remove from men's minds the assertion of such a rupture. This attempt has an air of legal positivism[5] about it, a disregarding of the facts. Please do not understand it as irony when I quote in this context the famous lines of the great absurdist poet Christian Morgenstern: "what may not be, cannot be!"[6] The Church can never exist in contradiction to itself, to tradition, to revelation, to the doctrines of the Fathers and to the totality of the Councils. This she cannot do; even when it appears as if indeed she has done so, it is a false appearance. A more profound hermeneutic will finally always prove that the contradiction was not a real one. An inexhaustible confidence in the action of the Holy Spirit resides in this attitude. A cynical outside observer could speak of a "holy slyness." In any case, this standpoint can be justified from both perspectives: that of trust in God and that of Machiavellianism. For a glance at ecclesiastical history shows that

---

5. *Etwas Dezisionistisches.* "Decisionism" is a legal philosophy which determines the validity of an act or law solely from the fact that the proper authority has decided it. This may be traced back to the voluntarism of William of Ockham and the political theory of Thomas Hobbes; it is most clearly formulated by Carl Schmitt.

6. "Nicht sein kann, was nicht sein darf!"

the continuation of the Church was always connected with a firm faith (or at least a fearlessly asserted fiction) that the Holy Spirit guided the Church in every phase. What Pope Benedict called the "hermeneutic of rupture"—whether asserted by the traditionalist or progressive side—was for him an attack on the essence of the Church, which consists of continuity without a rupture. Therefore he would always talk of the concept of a "hermeneutic of continuity." That was not so much a theological program nor a foundation for concrete decisions but an attempt to win others over to an attitude of mind—the only one from which a recovery of the Church could arise. When, finally, all would have understood that the Church does not and cannot rely on ruptures and revolutions, then the hierarchy and theologians would, of their own accord, find their way back to a harmonious development of Tradition.

From these thoughts speaks an almost Far Eastern wisdom, a principled distrust of all manipulations and the conviction that decrees issued from a desk cannot end a spiritual crisis. "*Les choses se font en ne les faisant pas.*"[7] No Chinese said that but the French foreign minister Talleyrand, who after all was a Catholic bishop. "Things get done by doing nothing"—that's an everyday experience; everyone may have encountered it once. But it is also a profound insight into the course of history, in which great developments remain uninfluenced by the plans of men—however excitedly the political protagonists in the foreground of the present day may gesticulate. That was what Benedict, as Cardinal and Prefect of the Congregation for the Doctrine of the Faith, had already criticized in Paul VI's reform of the Mass. Here organic growth, the development shaped by the imperceptible hand of time, had been interrupted by a bureaucratic act, a "*dictatus papae.*" It appeared to him to be not just hopeless but even forbidden to try to heal through another dictate this wound that Pope Paul's attack against Tradition had inflicted. A gradual transformation of thought, proceeding from the contemplation of the model that Benedict gave

---

7. In another version: *La plupart des choses se font en ne les faisant pas* (most things get done by doing nothing).

the world, would create a frame of mind in which the return of Tradition would ensue almost by itself. He trusted in the power of
images arising out of his public appearances, where, for example, he
employed the Roman Canon or distributed communion on the
tongue to the kneeling faithful. To allow truth to act only through
"the gentle power" of truth itself, as is stated in the conciliar Declaration on Religious Liberty[8]—this maxim corresponded both to his
temperament and to his conviction.

A characteristic expression of his approach was his care for overcoming the many aberrations in the liturgy that obscured the
Eucharistic mystery. He hoped to be able to eliminate the abuses
through a "reform of the reform." "Reform"—now that's something
the justification for which is completely understandable. Everyone
demands, after all, continuous economic, political, and social
reforms. Indeed, wasn't "reform of the reform" well-nigh an intensification of this positive word, an expression of the maxim *ecclesia
semper reformanda*? And wasn't an evaluation and reassessment of
the *ad experimentum* phase which the liturgy had gone through
since its revision by Paul VI also necessary? The progressives, however, were not deceived regarding the innocuousness of this
"reform" initiative. They recognized even the first ever-so-cautious
steps of the Cardinal and even more so those of the Pope as a danger
for the three great objectives of the revolution in the Mass (even
though the popes had already contested all three). What Benedict
wanted to achieve would stand in the way of the desacralization, the
Protestantizing, and the anthropomorphic democratization of the
rite. What struggles were involved just in eliminating the many
errors in the translations of the missal into modern languages! The
philologically absolutely clear falsification of the words of institution, the well-known conflict over the *pro multis* of the consecration, which even with the best (and worst) of wills cannot mean *pro*

---

8. The phrase Mosebach has in mind is *Dignitatis Humanae* §1: *nec aliter veritatem sese imponere nisi vi ipsius veritatis, quae suaviter simul ac fortiter mentibus ill-
abitur.* In Prof. Michael Pakaluk's translation: "Nor is there any other way for truth
to impose itself except by the force of truth itself, which penetrates sweetly and yet
at the same time strongly into the human mind."

omnibus, has not yet been resolved in Germany.[9] The English-speaking and Romance worlds had submitted, more or less gnashing their teeth, while for the Germans, the theory of universal salvation, one of the dearest offspring of the post-conciliar era, was endangered! That at least a third of the Gospel of Matthew consists of proclamations of eternal damnation so terror-inducing that one can hardly sleep after reading them was a matter of indifference to the propagandists of the "new mercy"—regardless of the fact that they had justified their struggle against Tradition by the desire to break through historical overgrowth and encrustation to the sources of the "authentic" Jesus.

The same thing happened to another central cause of Benedict's—one that really didn't touch Pope Paul's reform of the Mass. As is well known, that reform did not require a change in the direction of the celebration. The liturgical scholar Klaus Gamber, admired by Pope Benedict, had given the scholarly proof that in no period of the Church's history had the liturgical sacrifice been made facing the people instead of facing East, together with the people, to the returning Lord. Already as Cardinal, Pope Benedict had pointed out again and again how greatly the Mass had been distorted and its meaning obscured by the celebration's false orientation. He said that Mass celebrated facing the people conveyed the impression that the congregation is not oriented towards God, but celebrates itself. This correct insight, I admit, never made it either into a binding document of the Congregation for the Doctrine of the Faith or into papal legislation. Here too, truth was supposed to prevail through the "gentle power" of truth—so appeared the rule of the "Panzerkardinal" or "God's Rottweiler" (or whatever other compliments public opinion dreamed up for Pope Benedict). The consequences of the effects of this "gentle power" are today apparent to everyone. The unique hope of the present Curia, the Prefect of the Congregation for Divine Worship, Cardinal Sarah, who teaches and acts in

9. This, in spite of the April 14, 2012 letter that Pope Benedict XVI addressed to Archbishop Robert Zollitsch (and through him, the German Bishops' Conference) explaining why *pro multis* must be translated "for many" in all vernacular liturgical books.

Benedict's spirit, has nothing in his hands with which to turn into reality the mission he inherited from Benedict. "Reform of the reform," which always was just a set phrase instead of a policy, is now even forbidden as a phrase.[10]

Is it then still worthwhile to ask, how, realistically, the "reform of the reform" might have looked? In any case, Pope Benedict did not think of calling into question the use of the vernacular. He considered this to be irreversible, even if he might have greeted the spread of occasional Latin Masses. Correcting the incorrect orientation of celebrating the Mass was very important for him, likewise the reception of communion on the tongue (likewise not abolished by the missal of Paul VI). He favored the use of the Roman Canon—also not prohibited today. If he had, moreover, thought of putting into the new missal the extremely important offertory prayers of the traditional rite, one could say that the reform of the reform was nothing but a return to the post-conciliar missal of 1965 which Pope Paul himself had promulgated before his drastic reform of the Mass. In regard to the 1966 edition of the Schott missal,[11] the Cardinal Secretary of State at that time, Amleto Giovanni Cicognani, specifically wrote: "The singular characteristic and crux of this new edition is its perfected union with the Council's Constitution on the Sacred Liturgy."[12] What drove Pope Paul to disregard the missal he himself

10. See, e.g., Holy See Press Office Communiqué of July 7, 2016: "New liturgical directives are not expected from next Advent, as some have incorrectly inferred from some of Cardinal Sarah's words, and it is better to avoid using the expression 'reform of the reform' with reference to the liturgy, given that it may at times give rise to error." Pope Francis made similar remarks in an interview with Fr. Antonio Spadaro, S.J. that was published as the preface of *Nei tuoi occhi è la mia parola* (Rizzoli, 2016), a collection of his main talks and homilies as archbishop of Buenos Aires.

11. The "Schott" is a well-known German-Latin daily missal for the use of the faithful. It has gone through many editions.

12. *Eigenart und Kernpunkt dieser Neubearbeitung ist der vollzogene Anschluß an die Liturgiekonstitution des Konzils.* This statement, in a letter addressed to the Abbot of Beuron by Cardinal Cicognani on behalf of Pope Paul VI, was later printed as a foreword to the Schott missal, before it was rendered obsolete by the march of events.

had promulgated and shortly thereafter to publish a new missal—one which no longer corresponded to the task set by the Council—is among the great puzzles of recent Church history. One thing is certain: if things had remained as they were in the 1965 version, which although inflicting many senseless sacrifices, left the rite as a whole untouched, the rebellion of the great Archbishop Lefebvre would never have occurred. But one other thing is also true: even today nothing prevents a priest from including in his celebration of the Mass the most important components that could have been anticipated from a "reform of the reform": *ad orientem* celebration, communion on the tongue, the Roman Canon, the occasional use of Latin. According to the books of the Church this is possible even today, although in an individual congregation it requires considerable courage and authority to find the way back to this form without support from Rome. I want to say that the reform of the reform would not have been a tremendous achievement; it would not have won back many spiritual treasures of the old Rite. But it certainly would have led to a change in the atmosphere—it would have allowed the spirit of adoration and of sacred space to arise again. When an individual priest undertakes this in a parish alone and on his own account, he risks an exhausting struggle with his superior and trouble with his liturgy committee. Thus, that which is possible and permitted quickly becomes practically impossible. How helpful would be a single papal document that recommended *ad orientem* celebration!

While entertaining (perhaps pointless) thoughts regarding "what would have happened, if...," it may be appropriate to recall what would have been more important still than work on ritual details. Anyone who has dealt more thoroughly with the great crisis of the liturgy in the twentieth century knows that it didn't simply fall down from heaven or rise up out of hell. Rather, there were developments reaching into the far past that finally led to the catastrophe: a mindset which, looked at in isolation, doesn't seem dangerous at first, cannot be understood as simply anti-liturgical and anti-sacral, and can be found even today among some friends of the traditional rite. One could call it Roman-juristic thought or misunderstood scholastic analytic thought. In any case, it was a manner of thinking and perceiving that was completely foreign to the first Christian millennium that formed the rite. According to this view, some parts in the rite are essential and others less important. For the mindset influenced by this theology of the Mass, the concept of "validity" is critical. It is a concept derived from the realm of civil law, which inquires into the prerequisites that have to be present for a legal action to be valid, and those things that do not contribute to this validity. This perspective necessarily leads to a reduction, a formal minimalism that only wants to know whether the minimal prerequisites for the validity of a certain Mass exist. Under the influence of this understanding, reductive forms of the rite were created early on, for example, the "low Mass." We can certainly love it, but we cannot forget that it represents a conceptual impossibility for the Church of the first millennium, which continues to live in the various Orthodox churches. Choral music is prescribed for the Orthodox celebrant even when he celebrates alone. For the liturgy moves man into the sphere of the angels, the angels who *sing*. And the men who sing the songs of the angels, the Sanctus and the Gloria, take the place of the angels, as the Eastern liturgies expressly state. The low Mass developed when, in monasteries, several priests celebrated at the same time at different altars. Easily understandable practical considerations sought to avoid musical chaos. But you only have to have been in the Church of the Holy Sepulcher in Jerusalem to experience that in the spiritual world of the first millennium practical considerations had no legitimacy in matters of the *opus Dei*, the liturgy. Greek Orthodox, Egyptian Copts, and Armenians sing at different altars each in their own chant, until a holy noise fills the space. Admittedly, that may confuse, perhaps even repel people of the North in their search for Protestant inwardness and contemplation—especially when from a nearby mosque the call of the muezzin gets mixed into the whole. What interests us here is that even in the face of such jarring consequences, the Eastern liturgies could not even imagine a minimalization, a "reduction to the essentials," the omission of elements that do not concern the consecration, etc.

To summarize, the essential distinction between the thought of the ancient Church and the more recent Western Latin conceptions consists in the understanding of the consecration of the offerings. Ancient Christian belief understood the entire liturgy in all its parts as "consecrating." The presence of Christ in the liturgy is not centered only on the words of consecration in the strict sense, but runs through the entire liturgy in different forms till it experiences its summit in the form of the sacrificial death made present in the consecration.

Certainly, whoever understands the Mass in this way does not think of reduction and even less of arbitrary interventions, for, from the outset, the presence of Christ excludes any arbitrary arranging and staging by man. It was the new Western way of perceiving the "real" sacred act as narrowed down to the consecration that handed over the Mass to the planners' clutches. But liturgy has this in common with art: within its sphere there is no distinction between the important and the unimportant. *All* parts of a painting by a master are of equal significance, none can be dispensed with. Just imagine, in regard to Raphael's painting of St. Cecilia, wanting only to recognize the value of the face and hands, because they are "important," while cutting off the musical instruments at her feet because they are "unimportant."

What is decisive, however, is that the Latin world reached this opinion against the facts of its own liturgy, which spoke a totally other, increasingly incomprehensible language. Not only the Orthodox but also the Roman liturgy consists of a gradual increase of the Lord's presence, culminating in the consecration. But this is precisely not in the form of a division separating the parts before the consecration from those afterwards—just as the life of Christ is not separated from its climax, the sacrificial death, but logically leads up to it. Christ recalled and made present is the theme of the Latin liturgy from is first moments; the language of its symbols permits no other interpretation. The liturgy had taken over from the court ceremonial of the pagan emperors the symbolic language for the presence of the supreme sovereign: candles, which preceded the em-peror, and the thurible. Whenever candles and incense appear in the liturgy, they indicate a new culmination of the divine presence. The priest himself, as he enters upon his liturgical function, is an *alter Christus,* a part of the great work of theurgy, "God-creation,"[13] as the liturgy has been called. He represents the Christ of Palm Sunday, who festively enters into Jerusalem, but also Christ come again on the last day, surrounded by the symbols of majesty. At the reading of the Gospel the candles of the Gospel procession and the incensing of the Gospel book as well as of the celebrating priest once more indicate the presence of the teaching Christ. The readings are not simply a "proclamation" but above all the creation of a presence. Then the offertory gifts, hidden by the chalice veil, are brought to the altar and are reverently received and incensed. The prayers that are recited at this moment can be understood to mean that these gifts, even though unconsecrated, just by reason of their having been set aside already have the role of representing Christ preparing for his sacrificial death. Thus, the liturgical understanding of the first millennium interpreted the removal of the chalice veil on the altar as a representation of the moment in which Christ was stripped of his garments.

The traditional offertory was a particular thorn in the side of the reformers of the Mass. Why these prayers, why these signs of reverence, if the gifts have not yet even been consecrated? A theology of the Mass of the second millennium had stolen in, from whose perspective this offertory had suddenly become incomprehensible, a detail that had been dragged along which only produced embarrassment. Now just appreciate the spirit of reverence of, say, the epoch of the Council of Trent. It had revised the liturgy, but of course did not think at all of changing a liturgical rite because it had been found to be theologically inconsistent. But when this offertory reached the desks of the unfortunate twentieth century, it could finally be eliminated. One senses the satisfaction of the reformer with having eliminated the nonsense of millennia with one stroke of the pen. It would have been so easy, on the other hand, to recognize the offertory as a ritual of re-presentation if one had glanced over at the Orthodox ritual. But Roman arrogance preserved us from such digressions. It haughtily ignored the fact that one cannot make any competent statement concerning the Roman rite unless

13. *Gottesschöpfung*, in the sense that the priest and the liturgy make God become present or appear.

one also keeps an eye on the Orthodox rite. In it, the offertory is celebrated in a far more festive and detailed way, precisely because it is considered part of the consecration. Why did no one [at the time of the reform] wonder why the *epiclesis,* the invocation of the Holy Spirit at the consecration of the gifts, is part of the offertory in the Latin rite?[14] That the liturgy thus contains a clear sign that the consecration has already begun at that point? But the more profound understanding of the liturgical process had already been so largely lost that one felt able to throw away that which one could no longer understand as if it were a meaningless frill. It must have been an exalted feeling, as a member of a future generation, to be able so blithely to cut down to size the greatest pope in history, St. Gregory the Great! Allow me here to cite an atheistic writer, the brilliant Stalinist Peter Hacks, who said regarding the question of revising classic plays: "the best way to revise classic plays is to understand them." A principle already heeded in literature—how much more so should it be when it involves the liturgy, the greatest treasure we possess? Among the greatest achievements of Pope Benedict was directing the Church's attention once more to Orthodoxy. He knew that all the striving towards ecumenism, however necessary, must begin not with attention-grabbing meetings with Eastern hierarchs but with the restoration of the Latin liturgy, which represents the real connection between the Latin and Greek churches. Now, in the meantime, we have realized that all such initiatives were in vain—especially because it wasn't death that interrupted them, but a capitulation long before one was sure that irreversible facts had been created.

The disappointment over the shocking end of the Benedictine pontificate is all too understandable, but threatens to obscure a sober view of the facts. Just imagine what the liturgical reality would be if Pope Bergoglio had immediately succeeded John Paul II. Even if the dearest cause of Pope Benedict, the reform of the

14. Mosebach is referring to this prayer of the old offertory: *Veni, Sanctificator omnipotens aeterne Deus: et benedic hoc sacrificium, tuo sancto nomini praeparatum* (Come, O Sanctifier, almighty and eternal God, and bless this sacrifice, prepared for the honor of Thy holy Name).

reform, has failed, he remains a pope of the liturgy, possibly, hopefully, the great savior of the liturgy. His *motu proprio* truly earned the designation "of his own volition." For there was nobody—or very, very few—in the curia and in the world episcopacy who would have stood at the side of the Pope in this matter. Both the progressive side and regrettably also the "conservative" side (one has grown accustomed to putting this word in quotation marks) implored Pope Benedict not to grant the traditional rite any more freedom beyond the possibilities created unwillingly by John Paul II. Pope Benedict, who with his whole being distrusted isolated papal decisions, in this case overcame himself and spoke an authoritative word. And then, with the rules of implementation for *Summorum Pontificum,* he created guarantees, anchored in canon law, that secured for the traditional rite a firm place in the life of the Church. That is still just a first step, but it was a conviction of this pope, whose spiritual seriousness cannot be denied, that the true growth of liturgical consciousness cannot be commanded. Rather, it must take place in many souls; faith in tradition must be proved in many places throughout the world. Now it is incumbent on every individual to take up the possibilities made available by Pope Benedict. Against overwhelming opposition he opened a floodgate. Now the water has to flow, and no one who holds the liturgy to be an essential component of the Faith can dispense himself from this task. The liturgy IS the Church—every Mass celebrated in the traditional spirit is immeasurably more important than every word of every pope. It is the red thread that must be drawn through the glory and misery of Church history; where it continues, phases of arbitrary papal rule will become footnotes of history. Don't the progressives secretly suspect that their efforts will remain in vain so long as the Church's memory of her source of life survives? Just realize in how many places in the world the traditional rite is celebrated since the *motu proprio*; how many priests who do not belong to traditional orders have meanwhile learned the old rite; how many bishops have confirmed and ordained in the old rite. Germany—the land from which so many impulses harmful to the Church have issued—regrettably cannot be listed here in first place. But Catholics must think universally! Who would have believed it possible twenty years ago that there would be held in St. Peter's, at the Cathedra Petri, a pontifical Mass in the old rite? I admit that that is little, far too little—a small phenomenon in the entirety of the world Church. Nevertheless, while soberly contemplating the gigantic catastrophe that has occurred in the Church, we do not have the right to place little value on exceptions from the sorrowful rule. The totality of the progressive claims has been broken—that is the work of Pope Benedict XVI. And whoever laments that Pope Benedict did not do more for the good cause, that he used his papal authority too sparingly, in all realism let him ask himself who among the cardinals with realistic chances to become pope would have done more for the old rite than he did. And the result of these reflections can only be gratitude for the unfortunate pope, who in the most difficult of times did what was in his power. And his memory is secure, if not in evidence among the items of devotional kitsch at the pilgrims' stores around St Peter's. For whenever we have the good fortune to participate in a traditional Mass, we will have to think of Benedict XVI.

Collect for the Pope

O GOD, the Shepherd and Ruler of all the faithful, graciously look upon Thy servant N., whom Thou hast been pleased to appoint pastor over Thy Church: and grant, we beseech Thee, that by both word and example he may edify those over whom he is set, and, together with the flock committed to his care, may attain to eternal life. Through Our Lord Jesus Christ Thy Son, who liveth and reigneth with Thee, in the unity of the Holy Ghost, God, for ever and ever. Amen.

Collect for the Hierarchy of the Church

ALMIGHTY AND EVERLASTING GOD, by whose Spirit the whole body of the Church is sanctified and governed: hear our supplications for all the orders thereof, that by the gift of Thy grace, all in their several degrees may do Thee faithful service. Through Our Lord Jesus Christ Thy Son, &c.

Collect for Prelates and Their Flocks

ALMIGHTY AND EVERLASTING GOD, who alone workest great marvels, send down upon Thy servants and upon the flocks entrusted to them the spirit of Thy saving grace, and that they may please Thee in truth, pour forth upon them the continual dew of Thy blessing. Through Our Lord Jesus Christ Thy Son, &c.

Collect for Priests

O GOD, who for the glory of Thy Majesty and the salvation of the human race didst establish Thine only-begotten Son as the supreme and eternal Priest: grant that those He has chosen to dispense His mysteries may be found faithful in fulfilling the ministry they have received. Through the same Our Lord Jesus Christ Thy Son, &c.

Ego sum ostium. Per me si quis introierit, salvabitur:
et ingredietur, et egredietur, et pascua inveniet.

I am the door. By me, if any man enter in, he shall be saved:
and he shall go in, and go out, and shall find pastures.

GOSPEL OF JOHN 10:9

1

Why the New Evangelization Needs the Old Mass: Beyond the Long Winter of Rationalism

A
LLOW ME TO BEGIN with some facts. The attendance of Catholics at Mass has been in steady decline, one might even say freefall, since about 1965—the year when huge changes began to be made to the way in which the Mass had been celebrated for centuries.[1] On the other hand, since the year 1984, when Pope John Paul II first asked bishops to be generous in allowing and appointing priests to celebrate the *usus antiquior* or older use of the Roman Rite, and particularly since the year 2007, when Pope Benedict XVI's *motu proprio Summorum Pontificum* dispensed with the last vestiges of restriction, the number of traditional Latin Masses available to the faithful, the number of clergy offering them, and the number of Catholics attending them have steadily increased. As of 2013, over 1,000 clergy in North America had completed a formal training program for celebrating the classical Roman Rite.[2] In 1988, there were only about 20 places in the United States where one could find a traditional Latin Mass on Sundays; by

---

1. See Susan Benofy, "The Day the Mass Changed," in *Adoremus* 15, n.10 (February 2010), and 16, n.1 (March 2010), available at https://adoremus.org/2010/02/15/The-Day-the-Mass-Changed/ and https://adoremus.org/2010/03/15/The-Day-the-Mass-Changed/.

2. For some thoughts on the use and abuse of the terms "Extraordinary Form" and "Ordinary Form," see Chapter 6. In this book I will employ *usus antiquior* and *usus recentior*, "traditional Latin Mass" and "Novus Ordo," and similar turns of phrase.

2013 that number had risen to almost 500.[3] In response to an obvious demand on the part of students, faculty, and staff, a good many Catholic colleges and universities now include Extraordinary Form Masses in their chaplaincy schedules. Religious orders have incorporated the *usus antiquior* into their way of life or even adopted it exclusively, with the result of a surge in vocations. The average age of Catholics attending traditional Latin Mass parishes or chaplaincies is lower than the national average, while the average family size is higher.[4] It is a vibrantly youthful, flourishing, and expanding movement. As Pope Benedict XVI observed in 2007:

> Immediately after the Second Vatican Council it was presumed that requests for the use of the 1962 Missal would be limited to the older generation which had grown up with it, but in the meantime it has clearly been demonstrated that young persons too have discovered this liturgical form, felt its attraction and found in it a form of encounter with the Mystery of the Most Holy Eucharist, particularly suited to them.[5]

Antonio Cardinal Cañizares Llovera, when still Prefect of the Congregation for Divine Worship, wrote in a similar vein in 2013:

> The *motu proprio* [*Summorum Pontificum*] also produced a phenomenon that is for many astonishing and is a true "sign of the times": the interest that the Extraordinary Form of the Roman Rite elicits, in particular among the young who never lived it as an ordinary form, [an interest] that manifests a thirst for "languages" that are not "more of the same" and that call us towards new and, for many pastors, unforeseen horizons. The opening-up of the liturgical wealth of the Church to all the faithful has made possible the discovery of all the treasures of this patrimony for those who

---

3. See http://reginamag.com/update-latin-mass-america-today/, accessed January 4, 2017.

4. Moreover, anecdotal evidence as well as actual research suggests that the ratio of men and women in traditional Latin Mass communities is more balanced than in Ordinary Form communities, where women outnumber men by a sizeable margin. For more on this subject, see the FIUV Position Paper 26, "The Extraordinary Form and the Evangelisation of Men," and resources available at the weblog of Dr. Joseph Shaw.

5. Benedict XVI, Letter to Bishops *Con grande fiducia*, July 7, 2007.

had not known them—among whom this liturgical form is stirring up, more than ever, numerous priestly and religious vocations throughout the world, willing to give their lives to the service of evangelization.[6]

Why is all this happening? Why did the liturgical reform of the 1960s and 1970s fail to produce a new springtime in the Church? What, in contrast, is the secret of the old Latin Mass's appeal—the reason or reasons for its surprising resurgence in our day, when most of the people who celebrate or attend it were born *after* 1970? And how is this development good for the Church and for the New Evangelization?[7]

In order to begin answering these questions, we need to orient ourselves correctly with respect to what the New Evangelization means and how the liturgy fits into it. One could give a number of valid formulations, but I find Bishop Dominique Rey's the most succinct:

> The New Evangelization is not an idea or a program: it is a demand that each of us comes to know the person of Christ more profoundly and, by doing so, become more able to lead others to Him. The only way to begin to do this is through the sacred liturgy, and if the liturgy is somehow not as it should be, or I am not properly prepared, this encounter with Christ will be impeded, the New Evangelization will suffer.... The history of evangelization throughout the centuries shows how the great missionaries were great men of prayer, and more specifically of authentic devotion. It also shows the correlation between the quality and depth of liturgical life and apostolic dynamism.... The New Evangelization

---

6. For full text, see http://rorate-caeli.blogspot.com/2014/07/supreme-liturgical-authority-says.html, accessed January 4, 2017.

7. See Tracey Rowland, "The *Usus Antiquior* and the New Evangelisation," in *The Sacred Liturgy: Source and Summit of the Life and Mission of the Church,* ed. Alcuin Reid (San Francisco: Ignatius Press, 2014), 115–37. This volume contains a number of papers relevant to our topic. See also Athanasius Schneider, "The Extraordinary Form and the New Evangelization," a lecture given on January 15, 2012, to the Parisian association Réunicatho, the English translation of which was first published as Paix Liturgique's Letter 26, March 12, 2012. It is available at a number of places online.

needs to anchor itself in profound Eucharistic and liturgical renewal.[8]

In the propositions issued by the XIII Ordinary General Assembly of the Synod of Bishops, held in October 2012, we find a lofty acknowledgment of these truths:

> The worthy celebration of the sacred liturgy, God's most treasured gift to us, is the source of the highest expression of our life in Christ (cf. *Sacrosanctum Concilium*, 10). It is, therefore, the primary and most powerful expression of the New Evangelization. God desires to manifest the incomparable beauty of his immeasurable and unceasing love for us through the sacred liturgy, and we, for our part, desire to employ what is most beautiful in our worship of God in response to his gift. In the marvelous exchange of the sacred liturgy, by which heaven descends to earth, salvation is at hand, calling forth repentance and conversion of heart (cf. Mt 4:17; Mk 1:15). Evangelization in the Church calls for a liturgy that lifts the hearts of men and women to God. The liturgy is not just a human action but an encounter with God which leads to contemplation and deepening friendship with Him. In this sense, the liturgy of the Church is the best school of the Faith.[9]

Taking what Bishop Rey and the Synod say, we can formulate a thesis. If the old Mass helps people to "come to know the person of Christ more profoundly," if it helps us become "great men of prayer and authentic devotion," if it provides superior "quality and depth," if it can "manifest the incomparable beauty" of the Lord and "leads to contemplation and deepening friendship with Him," then it is, and will continue to be, one of the most important elements of the New Evangelization.

---

8. Bishop Dominique Rey, "Introduction," in Reid, *Sacred Liturgy,* 15–16. Canon Francis Altiere offers this elegant single-sentence definition of evangelization: "Evangelisation concretely means helping practicing Catholics to grow in holiness and become apostles; helping lapsed or non-practicing Catholics to return to the sacraments; and helping non-Catholics to become Catholics" (*Mass of Ages,* issue 185 [Autumn 2015], 10).

9. Proposition 35.

The Old Mass Newly Encountered

It will be most helpful to take an experiential or inductive approach by looking at what Catholics themselves say when asked what struck them about the traditional Latin Mass the first time they attended it. Personal testimonies are abundantly available.[10] Let us begin with several from young adults:

> I took more notice of what the priest was doing, which surprised me. His facing away from us was refreshing, because I liked the fact that he is one of us, looking towards God, representing us. . . . The smell of the incense, kneeling for Communion, wearing of the mantilla, quiet prayer . . . all focused on God with reverence and humility, and I was not distracted by the priest or altar servers.[11]

Here is another report:

> It was a Missa Cantata, a sung Mass. All I had known [before] was folk Masses, people singing "Kumbaya," and the first thing that struck me was the seriousness of it. . . . I was just amazed at the solemnity of the people and the priest. . . . I felt really focused for the first time in a Mass. . . . The main thing I like is the silence. . . . It is an opportunity to meditate and contemplate. I like to think of myself at the foot of the Cross.[12]

And a third reaction:

> It was here [in Oxford] where I first experienced the Mass in Latin. It was a Solemn High Mass, and it was perhaps the most beautiful

10. For more examples of this burgeoning genre, see Carl Wolk, "The Flight to Eternal Rome and the Mass of the Revolution," *OnePeterFive,* June 11, 2015; James Kalb, "What the Traditional Mass Means to Me," *Crisis,* December 4, 2014; "Finding What Should Never Have Been Lost: Priests and the Extraordinary Form," *The Catholic World Report,* August 19, 2014; Anne M. Larson, ed., *Love in the Ruins: Modern Catholics in Search of the Ancient Faith* (Kansas City: Angelus Press, 2009). It is a fertile field for research for someone looking to identify subjective or experiential factors in the resurgence of the traditional Latin Mass.

11. Maile Hanson, *Mass of Ages* 185 (Autumn 2015), 9. In the magazine of the Latin Mass Society of England and Wales, *Mass of Ages,* there is a feature in which Catholics are asked to attend the *usus antiquior* and then give their honest-to-goodness reactions. Some are attending for the very first time, while others are older Catholics who have not been to this Mass in decades or may not even be practicing their faith any more.

12. Philip Dillon, *Mass of Ages,* issue 182 (Winter 2014), 8.

experience I have ever had. Though now I know the liturgy, understand what is happening upon the altar, and am familiar with the replies in Latin, in my ignorance on that happy day in Oxford I was able to experience that Mass as a blind child, imagining the angels singing from on high, as I was too embarrassed in this foreign place to turn my head back to get a glimpse of the choir loft.... There is an unsurpassed solemnity that the "old" rite carries.[13]

A student of the Franciscan University of Steubenville, Mary Bonadies, talks about her experience of singing in the choir at the first Extraordinary Form Mass she attended:

It opened up a whole new world to me. At the end of the liturgy, I broke down and cried because I had never experienced such beauty.[14]

A young couple preparing for their wedding at St. Walburge's in Preston, Lancaster, had this to say about their journey:

Coming from an atheist background, my fiancé and I have been attracted to the Catholic faith this year through the beauty of the Extraordinary Form of the Mass. We were taken in by the liturgical music, tradition, and reverence of everyone that attended. It sparked a curiosity in the Faith that led to us being received into the Catholic Church.[15]

To show that such reactions are not limited to the young, here are two testimonies from elderly people:

I was focused during the whole of the service. It felt more spiritual and I felt much more connected to the service because it wasn't in English. It seemed a lot more profound ... there was no shaking of hands or anything. We were all focused on the Mass rather than the priest. Often, at Mass it's all about the character of the priest and this wasn't like that.... I felt myself listening intently.... It

---

13. Written under the pen name Zita Mirzakhani: "An Atheist's Conversion to Catholicism, the Traditional Liturgy, and Young Adults," published at *New Liturgical Movement*, accessed August 20, 2015.
14. Emily Stimpson, "Singing for God," *Franciscan Way*, Summer 2015, 5.
15. *Mass of Ages*, issue 185 (Autumn 2015), 11.

felt really special in a way I hadn't thought about Mass being special in 40 years.[16]

I came by chance to discover the [Institute of Christ the King] Shrine Church in New Brighton and the Extraordinary Form of the Mass. I was immediately transported to another realm. The obvious spirituality, respect, and devotion that I saw amongst the people and clergy moved me to such a degree that I was transfixed and knew immediately that I had found what I never knew I was looking for. . . . Being given this wonderful chance to draw close to God for the first time in many years, and to engage with him at a far deeper level than I ever believed possible, is something that I could only have found in the Traditional Mass.[17]

As these first-person reports bear witness, people find something special in the traditional Latin Mass, something they may never have experienced or encountered elsewhere. Allowing for differences of emphasis or vocabulary, all of the writers seem to be expressing a threefold perception. First, the old Mass is *theocentric*, focused on God, "vertical," evocative of the transcendent. Second, it is *Christocentric*, bringing out the priesthood of Christ and His supreme sacrifice on Calvary, and throwing into high relief the ministerial priest's acting *in persona Christi*, while downplaying his idiosyncratic self. Third, it is *hagiocentric*, emphasizing the holiness of the ritual, the piety and reverence that should characterize our approach to God, the peculiar modes of addressing the tremendous and fascinating mystery that God is, with hushed awe and holy fear, and a heightened awareness of one's own interiority—one's capacity for recollection, meditation, and contemplation.[18]

In other words, the *usus antiquior* Mass follows the great sacramental principle of doing what it looks like, and looking like what it is. In scholastic language, we say a sacrament effects what it signi-

---

16. Timothy Whitebloom, *Mass of Ages*, issue 180 (Summer 2014), 8.

17. J. Mackenzie, *Mass of Ages*, issue 183 (Spring 2015), 7. The writer describes himself as a convert from Anglicanism.

18. Note how these features line up with what is most needed, most neglected, and even most derided in our times.

fies. Water cleanses dirt from the body; therefore baptism, which is for cleansing sin from the soul, is done with water, and that water, together with the words, really cleanses the soul. Similarly, bread and wine nourish the body and bring joy to the heart of man; therefore the Eucharist, which is for nourishing the soul with God, the source of our joy, is given to us under the forms of bread and wine. Thus, if the Holy Sacrifice of the Mass is indeed *the* mystery of faith,[19] a reality so awesome and divine that we cannot possibly wrap our finite minds around it but can only yield ourselves to it and be carried away by it, then it should *come across* that way to us. Our encounter with the transcendent God should *look* and *feel* both sacred and transcendent. It should signify what it is, and be what it signifies. John Paul II forcefully argued this truth:

> The celebration of the Liturgy is an act of the virtue of religion that, consistent with its nature, must be characterized by a profound sense of the sacred. In this, man and the entire community must be aware of being, in a special way, in the presence of Him who is thrice-holy and transcendent. Consequently, the attitude of imploring cannot but be permeated by reverence and by the sense of awe that comes from knowing that one is in the presence of the majesty of God. ... [The Mass] has, as its primary aim, to present to the Divine Majesty the living, pure, and holy sacrifice offered on Calvary once and for all by the Lord Jesus, who is present each

---

19. A truth underlined by the very words *mysterium fidei* embedded into the heart of the consecration of the chalice, which is how they were always uttered for as far back as we have written records of the Mass. As Jungmann explains: "The most striking phenomenon in the Roman text is the augmentation of the words of consecration said over the chalice. ... The phrase is found inserted in the earliest texts of the sacramentaries, and mentioned even in the seventh century. ... What is meant by the words *mysterium fidei*? Christian antiquity would not have referred them so much to the obscurity of what is here hidden from the senses, but accessible (in part) only to (subjective) faith. Rather it would have taken them as a reference to the grace-laden *sacramentum* in which the entire (objective) faith, the whole divine order of salvation is comprised. The chalice of the New Testament is the life-giving symbol of truth, the sanctuary of our belief" (*The Mass of the Roman Rite: Its Origins and Development,* trans. Francis A. Brunner [Notre Dame, IN: Christian Classics, 2012], 2:199–201).

time the Church celebrates Holy Mass, and to express the worship due to God in spirit and truth.[20]

If the liturgy does its work well, we will be humbled in its midst, provoked to prayer, stirred by singing, brought to silence, caught up in things invisible, turned inward to the depths of our soul, turned outward to the absolute primacy of God. The *usus antiquior* does all these things exceedingly well. The question may then be asked: *Why* is it so efficacious? How does it work?

A Common Objection—and Fallacy

We can answer this question by considering one of the most common objections to the revival of the traditional Latin Mass: "This Mass is in an ancient language that no one speaks any more. It's often very quiet, so we can't hear what the priest is saying. The ceremonies are complex and hard to follow. The chants are in a strange style that has no connection with today's popular culture. All of these things make the old Mass hard for modern people to relate to or enter into. By the time of the Second Vatican Council, the Mass had become inaccessible, and so it needed to be put into the vernacular, simplified, and adapted to modern ways of thinking and acting."

That is the objection one will often hear, as well as the justification for most of the changes that were made. Under the influence of rationalism, the architects of the modern Roman Rite did their utmost to make the liturgy more (as they saw it) intelligible, transparent, and accessible—and this, ironically, has meant a tremendous *decrease* in the liturgy's power to convey and communicate the mystery of the Eternal and Infinite God and the mysteries of Christ in His divine humanity. As just about everyone has noted at one point or another in the past fifty years, the "mysteriousness" of the

20. Address to the Plenary Assembly of the Congregation for Divine Worship and the Discipline of the Sacraments, September 21, 2001. This truth was dear to John Paul II and could be seen in the earnestness of his *ars celebrandi*, emerging out of a deep Polish piety, even if the effective manifestation of this piety was limited by the Novus Ordo liturgies "planned out" by Virgilio Cardinal Noè, Archbishop Piero Marini, and countless committees around the world.

Mass has evaporated. This is not merely an incidental problem; it is a problem that strikes at the very essence and purpose of liturgy as divine worship.[21] "Without faith, it is impossible to please God" (Heb 11:6). As Msgr. Ronald Knox says: "Faith is the first duty of the Christian, and mystery is the food of faith."[22]

The most basic fact of our existence is that we are in need of God—not a god of our own making, who fits into our mental categories, but a God who transcends all we can ever think and imagine.[23] The liturgy has to introduce us to *this* God, the real one, in order to satisfy our neediness of Him. "Thou didst touch me," says St. Augustine, "and I have burned for Thy peace."[24] If the liturgy is to bring us into the real presence of the sovereign mystery of God, accessed by faith alone, it will have to make serious demands on us, in God's name; in keeping with the logic of the Cross, it will try us as gold in the fire, to see whether we are worthy and to render us less and less unworthy. The believer, for his own good, needs the liturgy to be dense, elusive, and fascinating. The "thickness" of the old liturgy[25] better expresses and inculcates the mysteries of the Faith; its layers of prayer, symbolism, ceremony, and chant, even in their apparent foreignness, have the power to speak more directly to the soul and to call forth an interior response. This interior response is the *primary* element of active participation—the most properly

21. For an excellent treatment of this problem, see Aidan Nichols, O.P., *Looking at the Liturgy: A Critical View of Its Contemporary Form* (San Francisco: Ignatius Press, 1996), esp. ch. 2, "The Importance of Ritual," 49–86; Uwe Michael Lang, *Signs of the Holy One: Liturgy, Ritual, and Expression of the Sacred* (San Francisco: Ignatius Press, 2015), 17–41.

22. Ronald Knox, *The Hidden Stream* (New York: Sheed & Ward, 1953), 184.

23. As St. Augustine said in his lapidary way: *Si comprehendis, non est Deus*—"If you grasp it with your mind, it's not God" (*Sermon* 117, PL 38:663).

24. *Confessions*, trans. Frank Sheed, ed. Michael P. Foley (Indianapolis: Hackett, 2006), Bk. 10, ch. 27, 210.

25. The language of "thickness" is borrowed from C.S. Lewis, who contrasted "thick" and "clear" religions, and argued that the true religion has to be thoroughly both: see "Christian Apologetics," in *God in the Dock: Essays on Theology and Religion*, ed. Walter Hooper (Grand Rapids: William B. Eerdmans, 1970), 101–3. For further discussion, see Thomas Storck, "Catholicism: The Perfection of Religion," in *Homiletic & Pastoral Review*, 99.11–12 (August/September 1999): 7–12, available at http://www.thomasstorck.org/theological-topics.

human kind of action. When the interior response is vividly present, it needs little in the way of external expression, although it will often benefit therefrom. When it is lacking, however, all the external actions in the world cannot substitute for it.

Transparency and Opacity

Traditional liturgies, Eastern and Western, have a certain inherent density of content and meaning that demands a response from us, yet our response is never fully adequate, satisfactory, or exhaustive: we can always have prayed better, we are always being outstripped by the reality. We never get to the bottom of it, shrug our shoulders, and say: "Well, that was nice, what's next?" In contrast, a liturgy that attempts to be totally "intelligible," in the sense of having no opacity, impenetrability, or beyondness, is ill-suited and off-putting to man as an intellectual being. It gives him nothing to sink his teeth into; it leaves his highest faculties in the lurch; it gives precious little exercise even to his lower faculties.[26]

The truth of the matter is quite different from what the liturgical reformers thought. To them, the liturgy had to be transparent so that we could see through it. But total transparency equals total invisibility. A window that is perfectly clean and clear is one that birds kill themselves flying into, because it has ceased to appear *as* a window, as a paradoxical barrier that lets the light through. In this life, we do not have full possession of the divine light, but this purifying, illuminating, and unifying light flows to us through the liturgy's prayers, ceremonies, and symbols. If we wish to compare the liturgy to a window, it would be a *stained glass* window, where the colors and shapes of the glass, the stories it tells or the mysteries it evokes, are both what is seen and that through which the light is seen.

Christ appears in our midst through the liturgy, and it is vitally important that we *come up against* the liturgy to experience, in a palpable way, His physicality, His resistance to our pressure, His

---

26. It may give plenty of exercise to them quantitatively, but it is not well-structured and ordered to a definite goal; it is exercise for the sake of exercise, rather than for the sake of producing a certain physique.

otherness, precisely as the condition of our union with Him. You cannot marry an idea or a concept, you can only marry a person of flesh and blood who is different from you: the precondition for oneness is otherness. This is why it is extremely dangerous for human beings to think of themselves as the creators or modifiers of the liturgy and to act accordingly—whether before or after the coming of Christ.

Speaking of the golden calf, which is the nation of Israel's collective fall, parallel to the fall of Adam, Joseph Ratzinger writes:

> The people cannot cope with the invisible, remote, and mysterious God. They want to bring him down into their own world, into what they can see and understand. Worship is no longer going up to God, but drawing God down into one's own world. He must be there when he is needed, and he must be the kind of God that is needed. Man is using God, and in reality, even if it is not outwardly discernible, he is placing himself above God. This gives us a clue to the second point. The worship of the golden calf is a self-generated cult. When Moses stays away for too long, and God himself becomes inaccessible, the people just fetch him back. Worship becomes a feast that the community gives itself, a festival of self-affirmation. Instead of being worship of God, it becomes a circle closed in on itself: eating, drinking, and making merry.... Then liturgy really does become pointless, just fooling around. Or still worse it becomes an apostasy from the living God, an apostasy in sacral disguise.[27]

To the extent that we think and act that way, we are in serious danger of hugging ourselves rather than encountering Christ, of gazing into a pool like Narcissus and falling in love with our own reflection. One cannot truly be obedient to something he himself has instituted, since it emanated from his will and remains ultimately within his power.[28] The teacher is not docile to himself, the king is not submissive to his own will. As Ratzinger often says, the true liturgy is

---

27. Joseph Ratzinger, *The Spirit of the Liturgy*, trans. John Saward (San Francisco: Ignatius Press, 2000), 22–23.

28. One is reminded of the conversation in which Fr. Louis Bouyer said he would never pray the second Eucharistic Prayer, and when asked why, responded: "Because I *wrote* it!"

one that comes down to us along the stream of tradition, dictates to us our (relative) place, impresses us with its own form and shapes us according to its mind—the mind of the Church collectively, not of any particular committee or even any particular pope.[29]

Doorway to the Sacred

Let me suggest a different example.[30] A door is a useful thing: it enables us to pass from one space into another, while keeping the outside out and the inside in. As such, a door can be ignored apart from its functionality; we do not typically think about common-place doors, the ones we use every day at home or at work. You might say we give them our peripheral attention, enough not to walk into them like one of the Three Stooges.

But there are at least two situations in which our experience of a door is different. First, if we are going to an important place for the first time—the office of a prominent person such as a bishop or a president, or the family home of a boyfriend or girlfriend. *This* door can be rather intimidating, because it represents something to us: it is a barrier, a threshold, a test, a point of no return. Such a door seems to have a personality: it challenges us, dares us to go in, per-haps whispers that we are not ready to go in and had better turn around. This door becomes *more* than a door; it is a symbol of the unknown, a sign of an unknown person. The second situation is when we see a massive, elaborate, richly-decorated door, as one finds on the great cathedrals and even in many humbler churches from ages past. Notice what has happened. The door, in its origin a purely utilitarian thing, has now become a reality in its own right: it

29. The old Mass is certainly not "the Mass of" St. Gregory the Great, St. Pius V, or St. John XXIII in the same way that the new Mass is the Mass *of* Paul VI. More-over, there was never a time in the Church's history prior to the invention of the *Consilium* when the Roman liturgy was sliced into discrete portions that were farmed out to subcommittees (the many *Coetus*) for redactions and spliced back together, with the ragged joints still showing.

30. I am indebted to Romano Guardini's masterful treatment of the metaphysi-cal-psychological language of signs: see his *Sacred Signs,* trans. Grace Branham (St. Louis: Pio Decimo Press, 1956).

is Christ, who *is* the door, the gate, the entrance. This door is something more than a door, something meaningful and beautiful in itself. With wonderful strangeness, it is not merely something we go *through*, but something we take into ourselves as we pass through it, something we give ourselves over to as it receives us. If, as in the great entrances of the medieval churches, the image of Christ is integrated into the doorway, He embraces us and we embrace Him. Here it is no longer possible to say that the door is just a door. It is a sign and a reality that transcends its usefulness, as a true friend is not only useful but also pleasant and virtuous.

How does all this relate to the liturgy? The liturgy is not merely a means to an end, but an end in its own right: a sign and a reality, like the door, that demands and deserves our devout attention and our surrender to its own language as we pass through it to the heavenly Jerusalem. When we pass through the liturgy, we do not leave it behind or forget about it, much less denigrate it; we take it into ourselves and it takes us into itself. It may be fanciful to say it, but we could think of the entire church as one great door to heaven, and, in that sense, we never finish passing through the door; we are *always* passing through it. The liturgy is the same way. That is why, like those magnificent old church doors, the liturgy, too, should be massive, elaborate, and richly-decorated. It is not trying to get out of the way, but to get *in* the way, because it *is* the way. We speak, eloquently in my opinion, of "going to Mass," as if the goal of our going were the Mass. This is quite true: we should be going *to the Mass*, and once we are *within* it, then we are joined to the mysteries it carries and conveys. It has to be *not* transparent in order to serve as a connection to God. In this way, a church door is like the stained glass window, and the liturgy is like both—not like a modern minimalist door of industrial manufacture or a plate glass window with no differentiation.

The English language has the poignant idiom "seeing *through* something," meaning, exposing its emptiness or uncovering its imposture. If we can "see through" the liturgy, if it does not interpose signs and symbols like the stained glass window or the grand doorway, we cease to *see* it; we take it for granted, and, soon enough, *we* are the ones who take center stage, as in Ratzinger's analysis of the golden calf. In the ensuing vacuum, we need to invent something creative to occupy ourselves and our audience, or we need to play heavily on the emotions, since we are not wrapped up in the fullness and thickness of traditional theocentric liturgy.[31] The message conveyed by one-dimensional texts and ceremonies comes across as superficial. Whether it *is* superficial or not, the *manner* of its communication is what counts: "the medium is the message." The natural human reaction to superficiality on a serious occasion is to attempt to elicit or inject more content, more meaning, more feeling, more earnestness. It is precisely in such environments that we find the invasion of foreign practices like chronic ad-libbing, secular readings, liturgical dancing, rock or pop music, special lights, video screens, and pseudo-symbols (e.g., the unity sand ceremony at weddings), interwoven with more or less invasive methods of cajoling active participation. None of this "enhancement" would be necessary if the liturgy was doing its own work well, so that worshipers could be brought into the presence of God and abide in it.

As surely as night follows day, this filling-in of the gaps or filling up of dead space fails to entertain the people, and they go away, sometimes forever. To the hopeful but misguided liturgical planners and activists might be said the words: "Be confounded, O tillers of the soil, wail, O vinedressers, for the wheat and the barley; because the harvest of the field has perished" (Joel 1:11). It was never meant to be *our* harvest, the work of *our* hands, but the Lord's, in His own time and in His own way—the way of tradition. In His justice, He permits us to be deprived of the fruits we audaciously promised ourselves. Such is the tragic consequence of failing to respect the grandeur, strangeness, and singularity of the liturgy as received and attempting to shift it into more familiar categories that are, nevertheless, foreign to it.

---

31. As Ratzinger has remarked: "If the Liturgy appears first of all as the workshop for our activity, then what is essential is being forgotten: God. For the Liturgy is not about us, but about God. Forgetting about God is the most imminent danger of our age. As against this, the Liturgy should be setting up a sign of God's presence" (Preface to Alcuin Reid, *The Organic Development of the Liturgy: The Principles of Liturgical Reform and Their Relation to the Twentieth-Century Liturgical Movement Prior to the Second Vatican Council,* 2nd ed. [San Francisco: Ignatius Press, 2005], 13).

Accessibility and Elusiveness

Next, let us consider the phenomenon of boredom. It is not difficult to see that total accessibility equals boredom. One of the reasons modern Western man is so unhappy is that he has too much of everything too easily available to him. We are awash in food and drink, laden with clothes, living in comfort; sexual titillation is suffocatingly omnipresent; we can get where we are going quickly and easily, but we do not really know where we are going or why we should go there. What do we have to strive for, to hope for, to suffer for, to *sacrifice* ourselves for? The value of our goals decreases in proportion to their triviality and ease of acquisition. Does modern man have a transcendent Other to whom he can surrender himself, an elusive quarry that fascinates him, beckons him onwards, and is always just around the corner but never in his grasp? No, modern man is trapped in the quotidian, the pedestrian (or should we say, the automotive), the predictable, the endless bestirring and satisfaction of finite needs. It all gets rather wearisome. No wonder chronic boredom has become a psychological epidemic. We are seeing what happens when a creature, created from an eternal idea and destined for eternity, created by the Infinite for the infinite, has bound itself by chains to the finite and the temporary.

What are the liturgical implications of this point? A liturgy, to be true to God and true to man made in God's image, cannot be totally "accessible"—and the attempt to make it so will only result in its degradation. To make the liturgy obvious, easy, simple, is to make it cease to be the liturgy. If it becomes proportionate to man in his temporality and finitude, it becomes, to that same extent, disproportionate to God and to man's immortal intellectual soul, created in God's image. This principle affects *every* aspect of liturgy.

For example, sacred music should not be a music that emphasizes temporality by a heavy regular beat, and finitude by catchy and simplistic melodic phrases. Gregorian chant is supremely fitting for the liturgy and serves as the supreme model of sacred music *because* its lack of the straightjacket of accentuated metricality, its free-floating rhythm and graceful, sinuous melodies, intimately wedded with the words in a one-flesh union, leave behind the predictable patterns of this world and carry us into the heavenly realm, the world of supernal beauty. The vestments worn by the ministers must *not* look like polyester drapes that could be hung on a curtain rod in a house designed by Frank Lloyd Wright. In their rich colors and embroidered symbols, their splendor and set-apartness, liturgical vestments should be pushing at the limits of what clothing can be—signs of the invisible clothing of the beauty of sanctifying grace. The sacred vessels placed on the altar of sacrifice should be resplendent precious metals, and the chalice ornamented with gems, engravings, filigree, whatever can set it apart as "this glorious chalice" that Our Lord will take into His holy and venerable hands, to fill with His most precious Blood, "whereof a single drop has power to win / All the world forgiveness of its world of sin."[32] Everything in the liturgy must bespeak the sacred, the transcendent, the holy, the beautiful, the noblest offerings of love and thanksgiving.

It is sometimes said that the loss of all these treasures, these evocations of mystery, was simply the result of an unfortunate series of misunderstandings, a hostile scrambling of the code of Vatican II, and the interference of the culture of the 1960s and 1970s, which prevented the successful implantation of the embryonic Novus Ordo. Sadly, such noble-minded attempts at diffusing the blame for the liturgical debacle cannot be squared with the hard facts of history. The engineers of novelty knew what they wanted; reverence for existing rites rarely held back their minds or hands; their pursuit of a rational and modern liturgy would be all-encompassing and ruthless. The overall vision found eloquent expression in a pastoral letter published in 1958 by none other than Giovanni Battista Montini, Archbishop of Milan, the future Paul VI:

> The Latin is not the only obstacle [to modern man's participation]. The difficulty arises principally from the way in which the liturgy expresses the prayer of the Church and the divine mysteries. The variety of its forms, the dramatic progression of its rites, the hieratic style of its language, the continual use of sign and symbol, the theological depth of the words and the mysteries ful-

32. From Gerard Manley Hopkins' translation of St. Thomas Aquinas's *Adoro te devote.*

filled—all seem to conspire to impede the understanding of the liturgy, especially for the modern man, accustomed to reducing everything to an extreme intelligibility. . . . [The faithful] will find themselves excluded from its inner spiritual precincts, whereas the progress of culture has accustomed them to understanding and knowing all about everything in their environment and field of interest. We must transform the difficulty posed by the liturgical rite into a help for the penetration of the hidden meaning contained in Catholic worship.[33]

All of Montini's pastoral overtures were premised on the conviction that modern circumstances demanded a radical simplification in the outward expressions of the Faith, which would involve stripping off layers of accumulated culture, as one might scrape off rust or barnacles from a ship's keel. As Henry Sire recounts:

In his Lenten pastoral of 1962 Cardinal Montini outlined to the Milanese faithful what he saw as the new direction of Catholicism, pointed out by his friend John XXIII: "The Church will divest itself, if need be, of whatever royal cloak still remains on its sovereign shoulders, so that it may put on the simpler forms modern taste demands."[34]

To such a drift, G.K. Chesterton had already responded: "[Catholicism] is the only thing that frees a man from the degrading slavery of being a child of his age."[35] "We do not want, as the newspapers say, a Church that will move with the world. We want a Church

33. Giovanni Battista Montini, "Liturgical Formation: Pastoral Letter to the Archdiocese of Milan for Lent 1958," English translation in *Worship* 33 (1958–59), 136–64; at 153–54.

34. H.J.A. Sire, *Phoenix from the Ashes: The Making, Unmaking, and Restoration of Catholic Tradition* (Kettering, OH: Angelico Press, 2015), 364. Let it be said plainly that these texts exude the atmosphere of Enlightenment rationalism; they are pervaded with the anti-traditional reformism of the Synod of Pistoia. Martin Mosebach is unsparing: "In the ancient world, if a ruler broke a tradition he was regarded as having committed an act of *tyrannis*. In this sense Paul VI, the modernizer with his eyes fixed on the future, acted as a tyrant in the Church" (*The Heresy of Formlessness: The Roman Liturgy and Its Enemy*, trans. Graham Harrison [San Francisco: Ignatius Press, 2006], 24).

35. G.K. Chesterton, "Why I Am a Catholic," in *The Collected Works of G.K. Chesterton* (San Francisco: Ignatius Press, 1990), 3:127.

that will move the world."[36] Robert Speaight, initially an enthusiastic supporter of the Second Vatican Council, echoes G.K. Chesterton in his sober assessment of the situation in 1970:

> We were concerned to sacralise the world, not to secularise the Church. We may have wished to simplify the altar, in so far as we bothered about such things at all; we had no desire to displace it for a kitchen table. The Latin of the Mass was not only familiar but numinous, and we had no wish to barter it for a vernacular which has justified our worst fears. We did not wish priests to dress like parishioners, any more than we wished judges to dress like jurymen. We were anti-modernist and even, except in aesthetics, *anti-modernes*; radical only in the sense that we wanted to get down to roots, not in the sense that we wanted to pull them up. We were more anxious to preserve the values of an ancient civilisation than to set about the construction of a new one.[37]

The ancient civilizations out of which the Church's traditional liturgies emerged were neither primitive nor simplistic; on the contrary, they tended towards artistic intricacy and luxuriance, architectural grandeur, and great depth of thought, expressed in paradox and poetry. It is not by chance that these were the cultures out of which the Lord drew forth the sacred writings and the substance of our sacred Tradition. Writing about Scripture's "innumerable obscurities and ambiguities," St. Augustine says that Divine Providence has willed the text to be, in some places, "dense and dark ... in order to break in pride with hard labor, and to save the intelligence from boredom, since it readily forms a low opinion of things that are too easy to work out."[38] He observes that Scripture prefers to say things in a poetic or parabolic vein rather than in plain expository language, and that we ourselves find it more delightful and more memorable to listen to poetry than to a didactic lesson. He then embellishes his earlier observation: "Magnificent and salu-

---

36. Quoted in Maisie Ward, *Gilbert Keith Chesterton* (London: Sheed & Ward, 1944), 398.

37. Robert Speaight, *The Property Basket: Recollections of a Divided Life* (London: Collins and Harvill, 1970), 164.

38. Augustine, *Teaching Christianity* [*De Doctrina Christiana*], trans. Edmund Hill, O.S.A. (Hyde Park, NY: New City Press, 1996), Bk. 2, ch. 7, 131.

tary, therefore, is the way the Holy Spirit has so adjusted the Holy Scriptures, that they ward off starvation with the clearer passages, while driving away boredom with the obscurer ones."[39]

The very same line of reasoning applies to the liturgy and, indeed, to our faith as a whole. One commonly hears the claim that our religion should be "contemporary," should meet us where we are and respond to our modern concerns. Of course, the true religion has to be relevant and offer real answers to our real problems. But there is a deeper sense in which the true religion will also often seem frustratingly *irrelevant,* precisely because it is immutably true, because it deals with the transcendent God, the Eternal and the Infinite, who stands totally beyond us and our fallen subjectivity. A sign of its truth is that it seems *strange* to us, and we will find ourselves strangers to it, estranged from the ultimate reality—and desperately in need of salvation to *make* us new and save us from our time, our age, our self-enclosure. Christ came into this world not to merge Himself with the world but to break it open to the divine, working its matter in a new way, pulling out of it His masterpieces of grace, like a potter drawing vases from dense clay, all the while preparing it for eventual destruction and recreation. The world as it stands, and we, and our concerns, are so small compared to Him, and He is strangely beautiful, past all domesticated words of ours. Religion is not a form of therapeutic deism or a self-help seminar.

Let me summarize my argument against liturgical rationalism. Liturgy that is totally intelligible is irrelevant, because it no longer summons forth from us the leisurely labor of the deepest and fullest response we can give, with our senses, imagination, memory, intellect, will. Liturgy that is totally transparent is invisible and thus ignored, because it does not catch our attention at the very point where the invisible God becomes visible in otherworldly signs and symbols, like light becoming narrative in the stained glass window. Liturgy that is totally accessible is boring, because it is too easy. As the mystics tell us, God is our sovereign Lover, and He woos mankind with a lengthy and perilous courtship. We, in return, chase

39. Ibid., Bk. 2, ch. 8, 132.

after Him with sighs, groans, and tears, ever on the trail, catching now and again a glimpse that sets our hearts ablaze. If we have any clue about what we are doing, there is nothing quick, easy, or boring about it: the liturgy is a lifelong courtship, an exhilarating chase, the exploration of a new world in which we are not the conquerors but the captives; the liturgy is our wedding feast, anticipated and somehow already present. Such metaphors fall so far short of the reality that they strain the bounds of language, they clash and meld. This, too, should be our experience of liturgy: it is a mystery that strains the bounds of our language, our thoughts, our feelings, beckoning us to go "further up and further in."

The traditional liturgies of the Church, Eastern and Western, most perfectly express and fulfill these inherent requirements and human needs. They are not readily intelligible but opaque, multi-layered, cosmic in scope, rich in paradox, proclaiming the ineffable divine sacrifice; they are not transparent but, like a rood screen or an iconostasis, stand before us and between us, mediating the unapproachable Light; they are not easily accessible, but exacting, requiring self-discipline,[40] demanding our conversion to something objective, outside of us, prior to us, higher than us, and normative of us. A traditional liturgy dictates the terms of our engagement with it; we are not in the position of telling it what to be or what to do. In all these ways, the great liturgies of the Christian tradition— the Mass of St. Gregory as codified by St. Pius V, the Ambrosian rite, the Mozarabic rite, the Divine Liturgies of St. John Chrysostom or of St. Basil—are supreme gifts given by God to His Church on earth, by which our profound neediness of God is stirred up and quenched, and God's mysterious "longing" for man reaches down

---

40. Historically, of course, the Holy Sacrifice of the Mass was not for outsiders, nor even for catechumens, but for the fully initiated: it was the culminating thing Christians did, not the first thing they did—a holy rite guarded with strictest secrecy. With the gradual Christianization of the European world, it was inevitable that the liturgy came to be celebrated more and more publicly, without such restrictions—and that, in subsequent ages, from the time of the Protestant revolt onwards, it has been able to function as a major incentive to conversion, as Pope Benedict XVI reminded us in his address of November 10, 2012 to participants in the National Congress of *Scholae Cantorum*, noting the example of Paul Claudel.

and calls forth from us the response *He* desires, one that is as simple as Himself and as complex as ourselves.

One can therefore see the fatal flaw in such a statement as this: "Before the evils or problems of the Church it is useless to seek solutions in conservatism and fundamentalism, in the restoration of obsolete practices and forms that even culturally lack the capacity to be meaningful."[41] First, it is false as a simple matter of fact; there are plenty of people with whom the old traditions have always resonated and, when reintroduced, begin to resonate anew, affording them spiritual nourishment. But more deeply, the traditional practices and forms speak to us, wake us up, nourish us, precisely *because* they are not modern, "more of the same."[42] It is their radically different spirit that grabs our attention and fixes it on the "strangeness" of God, His absolute primacy, and His supernal beauty, which is to be our everlasting joy when this mortal life is past.

Simplicity and Complexity, Revisited

Earlier I spoke of the danger of simplicity and the attraction of complexity. But we need to be more precise, because there is good simplicity and bad, good complexity and bad. If, because of the way things are being done, one can see at a glance that the Mass is a sacrificial action in which our Lord and God is present for our adoration, that is a good simplicity—something the tiniest child can perceive and the oldest person still relish as the awe-inspiring wonder it is. If, on the other hand, one thinks the Mass is a Bible study with a communion service, one might have been exposed to a bad simplification of it. Similarly, if you become immersed and a bit dizzy in the richness of the Mass as it invades all your senses and thoughts, that is a good complexity; no analysis could ever do it jus-

---

41. Pope Francis, Address to the Fifth Convention of the Italian Church, Cathedral of Santa Maria del Fiore, Florence, Tuesday, November 10, 2015. On the fairly recent phenomenon of using "fundamentalism" as a pejorative term for Catholicism based on defined doctrine and the repository of tradition, see my article "Thoughts on 'Catholic Fundamentalism,'" *The Latin Mass*, 24, n. 2 (Summer 2015): 14–18.

42. See the words of Cardinal Cañizares quoted near the top of this chapter.

tice. But if there is a lot of disjointed and distracting stuff going on at Mass and you can hardly pray and cannot wait to get out, that is a bad complexity.

Again, the key to making such distinctions is to ponder the difference between rationalism, which brings everything down to our level, and mysticism, which elevates us to the divine. Rationalism seeks the linguistification of reality in order to control it, seeks to capture transcendent mystery in handy formulas, speaks on and on as though one could create an image of eternity if one only talks long enough. The old liturgy knows better:[43] the priest praying at the altar, primarily addressing God on behalf of all; the schola chanting antiphons and psalms; the incense rising and bells ringing; the people following their missals or praying rosaries, singing the Creed, or just watching, letting their souls be led by images, sounds, motions—everyone is glued together by the complex simplicity and simple complexity of the divine mysteries, which are always far beyond us and yet right there before us and inside us, at once transcendent and immanent.

Many Catholics today, however, are harassed with a simplistic simplicity (the banality of all-too-human activity, unskilled and redolent of the marketplace) combined with a complex complexity (since language, especially when it attempts to be "self-explanatory," is often a distraction, a barrier, to the apprehension of inward meaning). Thus modern liturgical praxis re-instates unintelligibility by insisting overmuch on intelligibility. Verbosity cancels out the ineffable *Verbum*; "undisciplined squads of emotion" cloud over the

---

43. Indeed, Paul VI occasionally seems to have known better. He writes in the Apostolic Exhortation *Evangelii Nuntiandi:* "We are well aware that modern man is sated by talk; he is obviously often tired of listening and, what is worse, impervious to words. We are also aware that many psychologists and sociologists express the view that modern man has passed beyond the civilization of the word, which is now ineffective and useless, and that today he lives in the civilization of the image." This he said in 1975—five years after the introduction of a rite whose verbose didacticism and elimination of much non-verbal symbolism is by now as painfully out of date as the architecture of the same period, much of which has been torn down by the swifter intelligence of secular entrepreneurialism.

deifying light.[44] Contrary to the stated intentions of the reformers ("simplify, simplify"), the complexity is never actually reduced to an aesthetic and spiritual simplicity. Ratzinger puts his finger on this very problem:

> More and more clearly we can discern the frightening impoverishment which takes place when people show beauty the door and devote themselves exclusively to "utility." Experience has shown that the retreat to "intelligibility for all," taken as the sole criterion, does not really make liturgies more intelligible and more open but only poorer. "Simple" liturgy does not mean poor or cheap liturgy: there is the simplicity of the banal and the simplicity that comes from spiritual, cultural, and historical wealth.[45]

Or, as Dom Mark Kirby observes:

> There is a cold, reasonable, and altogether too "grown-up" form of religion that fails to address the needs of the heart. Chilly and cerebral, it is foreign to the spirit of the Gospel because it is so far removed from things that children need and understand. In many places, the past fifty years saw the imposition of a new iconoclasm, an elitist religion without warmth, a religion for the brain with precious little for the heart, a religion stripped of images and devoid of the sacred signs that penetrate deeply those places in the human person where mere discourse cannot go.[46]

The classical liturgy is already simple in a profound way that comprises complexity of word, image, gesture, song, silence; it is simple in the way that a living animal is simple, in spite of an inconceivable multitude of parts, because it is a single holistic, articulated, organic whole, a unified center of action and suffering.

The New Evangelization

All this may sound rather speculative, but it has decisive practical consequences for the everyday life and mission of the Church in the

---

44. The phrase in quotation marks is from T.S. Eliot's *Four Quartets,* East Coker, V; for "deifying light," see the *Rule* of St. Benedict, Prologue: "Let us open our eyes to the deifying light."

45. *The Ratzinger Report,* trans. Salvator Attansio and Graham Harrison (San Francisco: Ignatius Press, 1985), 128.

46. Dom Mark Daniel Kirby, O.S.B., *Vultus Christi,* May 21, 2008.

modern world. "The way the liturgy is treated determines the fate of the Faith and the Church," said then-Cardinal Ratzinger.[47] The humanism, rationalism, archaeologism, utilitarianism, modernism, and other -isms on the basis of which the reformers worked in the sixties and seventies have yielded a liturgy inadequate to its own theological essence, unequal to its ascetical-mystical vocation, and estranged from its cultural inheritance. This modern liturgy, in the manner in which it is commonly celebrated and experienced today, reflects and inculcates an anthropocentric view of worship that is spiritually damaging, since it deviates from the evidently theocentric, Christocentric, and hagiocentric worship bequeathed by tradition. This, in turn, will continue to weaken the Church's internal coherence, mar the external beauty of her face, deplete her doctrinal fidelity, limit the extension and intensity of her holiness, and diminish the efficacy of her missionary efforts. As Cardinal Burke laments:

> If the sacred liturgy is celebrated in an anthropocentric way, in a horizontal way in which it is no longer evident that it is a divine action, it simply becomes a social activity that can be relativized along with everything else—it doesn't have any lasting impact on one's life.[48]

Conversely, as the traditional liturgical rites and their spirituality are recovered and come to occupy an ever-greater place in the lives of the faithful, to that extent the damage of the past fifty years will be able to be reversed, fortitude can be developed for persecutions yet to come, and tremendous energies of evangelization can be nurtured and released.[49]

---

47. Joseph Ratzinger, *A New Song for the Lord: Faith in Christ and Liturgy Today,* trans. Martha M. Matesich (New York: Crossroad, 1997), ix. The translation here, which is from Athanasius Schneider's "The Extraordinary Form and the New Evangelization," differs slightly from Matesich's.

48. *"The Wanderer* Interviews His Eminence Raymond Cardinal Burke," February 2, 2015.

49. I would not say that the modern Roman Rite, or some kind of "reform of the reform," has no part whatsoever to play in this process of repentance and restoration, but I am convinced it will not have the leading role. While it is true that anything short of the beatific vision can admit of improvements, the Tradition was not

Bishop Athanasius Schneider has given eloquent expression to the real priorities that face the Church today:

> Only on the basis of adoring and glorifying God can the Church adequately proclaim the word of truth, that is, evangelize. . . . Everything about the liturgy of the Holy Mass must therefore serve to express clearly the reality of Christ's sacrifice, namely the prayers of adoration, of thanks, of expiation, and of impetration that the eternal High Priest presented to His Father. . . . How can we call others to convert while, among those doing the calling, no convincing conversion towards God has yet occurred, internally or externally?[50]

Bishop Dominique Rey, whom I quoted at the start of this chapter, puts it well: "I wish to say very clearly that the New Evangelization must be founded on the faithful and fruitful celebration of the sacred liturgy as given to us by the Church in her tradition—Western and Eastern."[51]

This is good news: God, having loved us first, has given us, in various traditions, optimal ways to make our response to Him in love—a work that we can do, but only through Him, with Him, and in Him. That is the great gift of the sacred liturgy. That is why the rediscovery of the traditional Latin Mass, with all of its special qualities, is vital *both* for the re-evangelization of Catholics and the sharing of the Gospel with non-believers: it is at the very heart of the good news that we seek to share, it is itself a powerful agent of conversion, and without it, we are in danger of talking *about* the good news rather than initiating people *into* it, as a living communion with Christ.

Think of it this way: an atheist, out of curiosity, goes to church. What will he find there? Will he be shattered out of complacency by the "shock of the beautiful"?[52] Or a Protestant wonders what the Catholic Mass is all about, and she decides to attend one Sunday.

---

broken and did not need fixing; the reformed liturgy was broken from the start and needs all the help it can get. Bouyer does not hesitate to call it "the abortus we brought forth": see *The Memoirs of Louis Bouyer,* trans. John Pepino (Kettering, OH: Angelico Press, 2015), 224, n.100.

50. Athanasius Schneider, "The Extraordinary Form and the New Evangelization," Paix Liturgique, Letter 26, March 12, 2012.

51. "Introduction," in Reid, *Sacred Liturgy: Source and Summit,* 15–16.

52. See Benedict XVI's *Address to Artists,* November 21, 2009.

Will she be overwhelmed by her confrontation with the majesty and mystery of Christ in his holy sanctuary, an existential contact with undiluted sacredness? It is sad to have to say that, if our atheist and our Protestant happen to pick a Catholic church at random, they run a great risk of being turned off by the banality or puzzled as to how such a religion can survive its moribundity. Or let us say that we have shared the word of truth with our neighbor; with God's help, we have rekindled the spark of faith in a fallen-away Catholic, or started a promising exchange with an unbeliever. What is it, ultimately, that we are inviting them to share? Our faith is far more than belief in a book or a set of propositions, far more than a plan of life or a social network. We want them to come fully alive in Jesus Christ, the Word made flesh; we want them to behold the glory of the only-begotten Son of God, full of grace and truth; we want them to *experience* "the divine, holy, most pure, immortal, heavenly, life-creating, and awesome mysteries of Christ."[53] Where and how is that going to happen? Do we have something truly wonderful, truly satisfying, to invite them to? Something that can make their hearts burn within them and their minds rise up to heaven, as it does for us? If our liturgy is not as it should be, evangelization has no real end in view.

Where Does This Leave Us?

Msgr. Ignacio Barreiro writes these sobering words:

> Only the man who has roots has a future. Part and parcel of the problems of modern man are that because he has cut his roots with his own past, he can no longer project himself to the future. Man, without an inherited and objective frame of reference, cannot even make sense of the present in which he lives. To attempt to achieve freedom by escaping from the burdens of tradition tends to result in a new enslavement to a chaotic present.[54]

Yet there is hopefulness in this observation, too, if we take it to heart. "Only the man who has roots has a future": we must regain our roots, get reconnected with them, in order to bear much fruit.

---

53. As chanted in the Divine Liturgy of St. John Chrysostom.

54. Msgr. Ignacio Barreiro Carámbula, "Sacred Liturgy and the Defense of Human Life," in Reid, *Sacred Liturgy: Source and Summit*, 384.

It is, of course, extremely disturbing that leaders in the Church have created or permitted a situation as disastrous as the one that still surrounds us on all sides. But we would be guilty of great naiveté if we did not recognize how much confusion has afflicted the Church at certain times in her 2,000-year pilgrimage: the treason of bishops during the Arian crisis; the moral degradation of the papacy in the Dark Ages; the worldliness of Renaissance Rome with its princely pontiffs; the colossal mistakes made at the time of the Protestant revolt; and the surrender to Enlightenment seductions. All of these are prominent episodes in Church history that teach us just how much ignorance, error, and sin God in His inscrutable Providence may allow for the testing of the saints.[55]

Serious confusion is possible among believers, as we see in the famous scene in the Acts of the Apostles when St. Paul asks a band of disciples at Ephesus: "Did you receive the Holy Spirit when you believed?" They replied: "No, we have never even heard that there is a Holy Spirit."[56] Obviously, whoever had preached the Good News to them not done a thorough job of catechizing. The same can be true today: "Did you receive the Holy Tradition when you believed?" "No, we have never even heard that there *is* a Catholic tradition—no one ever told us about it. We did not know there was a great, rich, solemn, prayerful form of the Mass prior to the Second Vatican Council—no one ever showed it to us." It is the role of apostles today to bring to men, believers and unbelievers alike, *all* the riches of Christ and of the Church's long and fruitful life in Christ. We do not need to judge the erring or the ignorant; we need to have mercy on them by loving them enough to care that they hear, touch, taste, smell, and see the beautiful. Indeed, as St. Augustine says, we need to start the works of mercy by showing mercy to *ourselves.*[57] We are the poor and hungry, the lame, blind, and deaf, for whose benefit Christ has lavished upon His Church vast stores of spiritual nourishment. It is therefore our *duty* to immerse our-

---

55. The best overall account I have seen of the crisis moments in the history of the Catholic Church, with particular attention to the crisis of the past sixty years, is Sire's *Phoenix from the Ashes.*

56. See Acts 19:1–7.

57. See *City of God,* Bk. 10, ch. 6; *Sermon* 106 on Luke 11:39, n. 4.

selves in those stores and, once we have become strengthened by the food of kings, to lead others to the same banquet.

Those who already attend the traditional Latin Mass should take pains to know the liturgy better. We should follow along (at least sometimes) with a hand-held missal: when it comes to vocal and mental prayer, nothing richer or more worthy of meditation will ever be found than the very prayers of the Mass, including those the priest says silently and privately. If one's main or exclusive exposure has been to the Low Mass, one should make an effort to find a High Mass or a Solemn High Mass. We need both the Low Mass for its peacefulness and the High Mass for its glory—they capture both aspects of the song of the angels: "*Glory* to God in the highest, and *peace* on earth to men of good will"—but the Roman liturgy is fully itself only when clothed in its full ceremonial and musical splendor.[58] We should read good books about the Mass. There are such wonderful authors to get to know: Ratzinger, Guardini, Fortescue, Davies, Mosebach, Dobszay, Mahrt, Lang, Reid.[59] We who have received the grace of loving the liturgy should never be bashful about inviting friends and family to the *usus antiquior,* so that they, too, may come to know this treasure of our faith.

The New Evangelization begins with *my* conversion and *your* conversion. As Archbishop Alexander Sample of Portland says: "If we are transformed by the sacred liturgy, then we, as believers, can help transform the culture."[60] Let us place ourselves in the school of the old Mass, the school of countless saints, so that it can shape our minds and hearts, nourish us, and equip us for the work God is calling us to do. The traditional Latin Mass has an irrepressible power to make Our Lord *Rex et centrum omnium cordium,* the king and center of all hearts. As it did for so many centuries, the Church's hallowed worship creates a culture of life and love in which the Catholic Faith will blossom anew in the midst of our modern wasteland.

58. See Chapter 10.

59. My book *Resurgent in the Midst of Crisis: Sacred Liturgy, the Traditional Latin Mass, and Renewal in the Church* (Kettering, OH: Angelico Press, 2014) goes more deeply into a number of the points mentioned in this chapter. See the bibliography below for further reading suggestions.

60. "Bishop Sample: 'Transformed by the Liturgy, Transforming the Culture,'" Anna Abbott, *National Catholic Register,* online edition, March 8, 2013.

Memento dierum antiquorum, cogita generationes singulas.
Remember the days of old, think upon every generation.
DEUTERONOMY 32:7

Ne transgrediaris terminos antiquos quos posuerunt patres tui.
Pass not beyond the ancient bounds which thy fathers have set.
PROVERBS 22:28

2

Reverence Is Not Enough: On the Importance of Tradition

I N THE LAST FEW MONTHS of 2016, the Catholic world was shocked to see the enormous destruction visited upon Umbria by a series of powerful earthquakes. This region of Italy includes the town of Norcia, the birthplace of saints Benedict and Scholastica and the site (since the Jubilee Year of 2000) of a Benedictine monastery famous for Latin liturgy and delicious beer. The news was particularly distressing to me as an oblate of this monastery who had just spent two weeks there in July teaching a course on the Epistle to the Hebrews. As I looked at photos of the damage, I could not help thinking of two verses from that letter: "We have here no abiding city but we seek one that is to come" (13:14) and "Whom the Lord loveth, he chastiseth; and he scourgeth every son whom he receiveth" (Heb 12:6). The monks, true to the spirit of the Benedictine motto *succissa virescit*,[1] are rebuilding in earnest. Many people are coming to their aid, and, in due course, they will not only recover but, God willing, come out stronger than before. *Lignum habet spem: si praecisum fuerit, rursum virescit, et rami ejus pullulant.* "A tree hath hope: if it be cut, it groweth green again, and the boughs thereof sprout" (Job 14:7).

---

1. "Cut down, it grows back again." This motto seems to be derived from Job 14:7.

The damage in Norcia was substantial. The earthquakes happened suddenly, their magnitudes were considerable, and there have been powerful aftershocks. Beautiful churches throughout the town, including the medieval basilica over the ancient Roman crypt, are collapsed into ruins. In buildings that were still standing, huge cracks zigzagged down the walls. Experts carefully inspected building after building to assess problems and set priorities for reconstruction. Places once full of life were no longer inhabitable. Years of expensive repairs will be necessary before daily life can resume with any kind of fullness. Then there are the costs that are harder to speak about, because they are emotional, personal, spiritual: some people will be sanctified by these trials, while others may take occasion for sinning. Due to the upheavals of just a few separate days, Norcia became a place of distress, confusion, headaches and heartaches too numerous to count. It has also become a place of heroic charity and generosity, a summons to patience, hope, and determination, and a reminder of what is most important in life.

It seems to me that we can take this earthquake as a parable for the Church in our times. Something similar commenced about fifty years ago in the day-to-day life of the Catholic Church, namely, a series of sudden and sizeable changes in the manner in which the Holy Sacrifice of the Mass and the other liturgies and sacraments were celebrated, together with the often heretical meanings that were attached to those changes. The ground shifted underneath us as centuries-old liturgical rites and practices were replaced almost overnight with rapidly-constructed forms and unprecedented novelties. In Western Europe and America, there was an epidemic of unbridled experimentation; all certainties vanished; the map and compass of tradition were discarded, replaced by communal exercises in self-expression. The advent of the Novus Ordo Missae was like an earthquake in its suddenness as well as in the devastation that followed after it in so many places.[2] Local churches that had

2. It is true that the Novus Ordo Missae was prepared for by several years or even decades of "tremors," such as the Holy Week "reforms" of Pius XII and the bewildering series of changes emanating from the Vatican in the years between 1963

been thriving in numbers of faithful and in priestly and religious vocations collapsed, as millions of Catholics stopped practicing their faith and thousands of priests, monks, nuns, and sisters abandoned their holy calling. When the dust settled, instead of a renewal, there were huge cracks in the intellectual and spiritual structure; the walls and ceilings of artistic beauty had fallen apart; ecclesiastical structures were dangerous to inhabit, if not uninhabitable.[3]

Half a century later, however, many in the Church have yet to come to grips with the reports of our own "engineering inspectors," who were keenly aware of the magnitude of the earthquake and the scope of its damage—experts who know and love (or knew and loved) the Church's liturgy, theology, and tradition; experts familiar with human disciplines such as anthropology, psychology, and sociology.[4] There was Msgr. Klaus Gamber, who, seeing the vast difference between the classical Roman Rite and the reformed liturgy in every significant element, maintained that the new could not be viewed as a mere revision of the old but had to be treated as a dis-

and 1969, including an increasing trend of vernacularization and the adoption of the *versus populum* stance. As problematic as all these steps were (some more than others), they pale in comparison with the gutting of the rite itself and its replacement by the Consilium's fabrication, which would have been still more barren had it not been for last-minute augmentations insisted on by Paul VI. These augmentations, although still novelties, preserved something of the external structure of the rite: I refer to the depersonalized Confiteor with the abolition of the distinction between priest and people, and the quasi-Jewish offertory rite. When we consider at the same time the magnitude of changes to the Divine Office and all the sacramental rites, the comparison to a major earthquake is fully warranted.

3. I am well aware that the defection from priestly and religious life had already begun during and after the Second Vatican Council, prompted by the revolutionary impulses of the 1960s. Nevertheless, what began as a trickle swelled to a flood as the certainties and practices of the Catholic Faith crumbled, offering no resistance to the mindless euphoria for change and the casting off of restraints. The creation of a new liturgy was nothing less than an official validation of this irresponsible attitude of contempt for sacred tradition.

4. See Nichols, *Looking at the Liturgy*, 49–86; Lang, *Signs of the Holy One*, 17–41; Christopher M.J. Zielinski, O.S.B. Oliv., "Liturgy, Ritual and Contemporary Man: Anthropological and Psychological Connections," in Reid, *Sacred Liturgy*, 237–54.

tinct "modern rite."[5] There was Michael Davies, who demonstrated, in his book *Cranmer's Godly Order,* that the changes made to the Roman Catholic liturgy paralleled those made by Thomas Cranmer in his creation of the Protestant liturgy of the Church of England. There was László Dobszay, who painstakingly documented the ritual-musical incoherence of the new rites. There is Dom Alcuin Reid, who has shown that the liturgical reform of the 1960s cannot be considered to be in continuity with the Roman tradition by any historically-grounded and philosophically coherent understanding of "organic."[6] There is a host of authors, among whom could be named Aidan Nichols, Catherine Pickstock, Mary Douglas, and Anthony Archer, who, drawing on human disciplines such as the anthropology of religion, have exposed with embarrassing clarity how badly the revised liturgical rites assessed the *actual* needs of "modern man," and how they have not only failed to stem the tide of secularism and desacralization but have even contributed to it.

Natural disasters are responsible for many physical and cultural evils, but they also serve to bring out the best in people. Something similar is true of the liturgical and theological revolution that took place last century. Once it became clear that the great Catholic tradition was under attack and exposed to the risk of extinction, the Holy Spirit raised up many noble souls from all ranks, classes, and

5. Klaus Gamber, *The Reform of the Roman Liturgy: Its Problems and Background,* trans. Klaus D. Grimm (San Juan Capistrano, CA: Una Voce Press and Harrison, NY: The Foundation for Catholic Reform, 1993), 23–26, 91–95, et passim. Fr. John Parsons comments: "The result was not really a 'reform' at all. It was the creation of a new rite, loosely derived from the historic Roman rite, but differing from it as much as do some of the historic non-Roman rites, and a great deal more than, for instance, the rites of the Carthusians, Cistercians and Dominicans. Monsignor Gamber's terminology of a 'Roman Rite,' describing the ancient tradition still maintained in the Missal of 1962, and a 'Modern Rite,' describing the Missal and Lectionary of 1969, is scientifically accurate and just" ("A Reform of the Reform?," originally published in 2001 in *Christian Order* and republished as Appendix 6 of Thomas Kocik's *The Reform of the Reform? A Liturgical Debate: Reform or Return* [San Francisco: Ignatius Press, 2003], 211–56; here, 237–38).

6. See Reid's *Organic Development of the Liturgy.*

states of life, the famous as well as the humble, to oppose this forced march of modernization. A high-profile petition signed by many famous people from Great Britain, begging Paul VI for the continued allowance of the Tridentine liturgy, resulted in the so-called "Agatha Christie indult," whereby priests in England could obtain permission to celebrate the traditional rite. Pope John Paul II encouraged bishops to be "generous" in making room for Catholics attached to their liturgical tradition. Most notably, Pope Benedict XVI called the Church back to continuity with her glorious past, her faith-filled tradition, her unsurpassed culture of beauty in the service of the Word. In these decades of wandering in the wilderness, in this Babylonian captivity to contemporary Western fashion, the movement to rediscover and restore the fullness of the Church's worship has quietly grown. Clergy, religious, and laity dedicated to the *usus antiquior* are now found in every country and on every continent; their communities are characterized by large families and high numbers of vocations to the priesthood and consecrated life. Fully Catholic worship goes hand-in-hand with doctrinal integrity, a consistent witness of life, and a renewed thirst for holiness. This much is good news, amidst the rubble.

After this extended metaphor, an objection might be raised. "Why is tradition so important? Isn't it enough just to have a reverent liturgy? As long as we are sincere in our intentions and serious about our prayer, all these other things—the language of our worship, the type of music, the direction of the priest at the altar, the way people receive communion, whether or not we keep the same readings and prayers that Catholics used for centuries, and so forth—are just incidental or accidental features. They are 'externals,' and Jesus taught us that externals aren't the main thing in religion."

There is, of course, some truth to this objection. Our intentions are indeed fundamental. If a non-believer pretended to get baptized as part of a play on stage, he would not really become a Christian. No externals by themselves will ever guarantee that we are worshiping the Father in spirit and in truth (cf. Jn 4:23–24), and an attitude of reverence and seriousness is the most crucial requirement of the *ars celebrandi*. Nevertheless, I believe that the objection as stated is erroneous, and dangerously so, because it presumes, and thereby fosters, a radical transformation of the very nature of the Catholic religion under the influence of Enlightenment philosophy.

Prior to all arguments about which practice is better or worse is the overarching principle of the primacy of tradition, meaning the inherent claim that our religious inheritance, handed down from our forefathers, makes on us. We do not "own" this gift, much less "produce" it. Tradition comes to us from above, from God who providentially designed us as social animals who inherit our language, our culture, and our religion; it comes to us from our ancestors, who are called *antecessores* in Latin—literally, the ones who have gone before.[7] They are ahead of us, not behind us; they have finished running the race, and we stand to benefit from their collective wisdom. St. Paul states the principle in 1 Thessalonians 4:1: "We pray and beseech you in the Lord Jesus, that as you have *received* from us how you ought to walk and to please God, so also you would walk, that you may abound the more."[8]

The rejection of tradition and the cult of change embodies a peculiarly modern attitude of "mastery over tradition," which is the social equivalent of Baconian and Cartesian "mastery over nature." The combination of capitalism and technology has allowed us to abuse the natural world, treating it as raw material for exploitation in pursuit of the satisfaction of our selfish desires. In a similar way, the influence of rationalism and individualism has tempted us to treat Catholic tradition as if it were a collection of isolated facts from which we, who are autonomous and superior, can make whatever selection pleases us. In adopting this arrogant stance, we fail to recognize, with creaturely humility, that our rationality is socially constituted and tradition-dependent. By failing to honor our *antecessores*, we fail to live according to our political nature and our Christian dignity as recipients of a concrete historical revelation

7. The English word "ancestor" is derived from the Latin *antecessor*.
8. Emphasis added.

that endures and develops organically over time and space.[9] The psalm verse comes to mind: "Know ye that the Lord, he is God: he made us, and not we ourselves" (Ps 99:3). *Ipse fecit nos et non ipsi nos.* We do not make ourselves, nor do we make our religion or our liturgies; we *receive* our existence, we receive our faith, we receive our worship.[10] Tradition comes to us from outside ourselves, before and beyond us. It unambiguously expresses our dependence on God—as creatures, as Christians, as coheirs with the saints. An heir is one who inherits, not the "self-made man" of capitalism.

The reformed liturgy, moreover, like modern liberalism itself, exalts choice, spontaneity, and diversity, whereas the historic liturgies of Christianity, both Eastern and Western, present the worshiper with a fully articulated act of worship to which we gratefully yield ourselves, taking on its features as an icon panel receives layer after layer of prescribed color until the beautiful image stands forth.[11] The worshipers act according to roles and a script they have received, putting its words on their lips, wearing the mask (as it were) or *prosopon* of Christ, so that they may acquire His mind in this life and deserve to obtain His glory in the life to come. The liturgy is a continual putting on of Christ, which presupposes a putting off of the old man, with his warped desire for "authenticity,"

9. More specifically: the God whom we worship is no abstraction but, in Jesus Christ, a flesh-and-blood reality whose Incarnation is mystically continued in time and space.

10. See Ratzinger, *Spirit of the Liturgy,* 21–23, 159–70.

11. God writes Himself upon the tablets of our souls by means of a liturgy that is determinate and active, as He is. The art of the icon is essentially different from the Renaissance and post-Renaissance mentality of much of Western religious art. The iconographer does not seek self-expression through his art, or even the expression of his culture, people, place, or time. He humbles himself by following strict canons that aim at reproducing on his panel and in his soul the personal reality of the holy figure contemplated, so that when he is finished, the result draws the viewer directly to the holy figure. Even if icons will vary incidentally from writer to writer, they do not sign their names, because the goal is the veneration of the Other. The regimented process of writing an icon is exactly comparable to the regimented process of executing a liturgy: the point of departure is the Church's pre-existent tradition; the point of arrival is immediate contact with the Holy One. In between, the human agents do their work as well as they can, but they subordinate themselves to the canons and the goal; they "get out of the way."

originality, autonomy, recognition. The "inculturation" to which traditional liturgy aspires is best seen as a *re*-culturation into a common Christian patrimony accompanied by a *de*-culturation from the noxious errors and vices of our fallen condition and of the human societies we inhabit.[12] The liturgy is not simply a series of tasks, a holy agenda; it is a school of life, of thought, of desire, in which we are enrolled from our baptism until our death. In Dom Paul Delatte's definition, liturgy is "the sum of acts, words, chants, and ceremonies, by means of which we manifest our interior religion . . . a collective and social prayer, the forms of which have a character that is regular, definite, and determined."[13] How the liturgy understands human nature, how it asks us to behave, the axioms and aspirations it places on our lips and in our hearts, will shape us into an image of itself. Our participation in the earthly liturgy of the Church will prepare us well or poorly for our participation in the heavenly liturgy, depending on how well we have been educated in the school of Christian tradition. This is why it is such a grave problem if the curriculum and faculty of this school have been compromised by worldliness, corrupted by ideologies, diluted by a loss of confidence in the truth of the Gospel, or simply dis-

12. As John Paul II remarked: "The liturgy, though it must always be properly inculturated, must also be countercultural": *Ad Limina Address to the Bishops of Washington, Oregon, Idaho, Montana, and Alaska* (October 9, 1998), §4. The Church may borrow elements from a culture and give them a new Christian meaning or orientation, as when great missionaries seek to reach native peoples through a discriminating adoption of some of their customs and artifacts. But such inculturation presupposes the essential truth of the Christian faith and the rightness of its Catholic expressions, which serve as active and fertilizing principles for the ones receiving the word. The missionary brings the *Roman* or *Byzantine* liturgy to a pagan tribe and converts them to *it*. The existing liturgical rite is the solid rock on which inculturation is built, the magnet to which customs are attracted. In this way, a stable and preexisting Christian orthodoxy (which means "right worship" as well as "right belief") functions *counter*-culturally to whatever is sinful, unhealthy, unworthy, or ugly in the culture to which it comes. See my article "Is 'Contemporary' Church Music a Good Example of Inculturation?," published at *OnePeterFive* on May 11, 2016.

13. *The Rule of Saint Benedict: A Commentary by the Right Rev. Dom Paul Delatte*, trans. Dom Justin McCann, O.S.B. (Eugene, OR: Wipf and Stock, 2000), 132.

tracted by the whims and fads of their surrounding anti-Christian or semi-Christian society.[14]

St. Paul states to the Romans: "Do not be conformed to this world but be transformed by the renewal of your mind, that you may prove what is the will of God, what is good and acceptable and perfect" (Rom 12:2). Massively changing the liturgy to make it apparently more suited to "modern man" was, in fact, a form of yielding and conforming to the world rather than standing all the more firmly over against it with a supernatural alternative, holding fast what was already known to be "good and acceptable and perfect."[15] While earlier ages of the Church witnessed the enrichment of the liturgy with elements from the cultures through which it passed, there had never been, prior to the twentieth century, a systematic attempt to *reconfigure* the liturgy according to the pattern of a certain epoch or worldview. There had been pruning and adjustment, but never wholesale reconstruction and whole-cloth invention. The very ambition to attempt such an audacious feat could have arisen only in an age bedazzled by the Myth of Progress—a myth that played upon the well-known gullibility of rationalists and romantics alike. The liturgical reformers for the most part surrendered to the temptation without resistance, like springtime lovers in

14. I owe this comparison of the liturgy to a curriculum to Joel Morehouse, who compared the treasury of sacred music with a Great Books curriculum to which Catholics can profitably return again and again, with the benefit of an ever-deeper assimilation.

15. To the objection that the liturgy is never "perfect," I respond that there are two senses of the word. In one sense, only the heavenly liturgy is perfect, as enjoying a divine perfection. But the organically developed liturgy of the Church on earth, precisely as a work of the Holy Spirit, as Pius XII teaches in *Mediator Dei,* has a relative perfection and cannot be considered irrelevant, harmful, or corrupt. The theorists of the Novus Ordo, above all Josef Jungmann, S.J., held two false theories: the Corruption Theory (which maintains that the medieval liturgy departed more and more from its pristine ancient condition until it reached, in the Baroque period, a state antithetical to its original nature) and the Pastoral Theory (which holds that liturgy must be adapted to the mentality and condition of each age, and that modern man, being exceptionally different from his forbears, needs a radically different liturgy). The former has as its corollary antiquarianism or archaeologism, while the latter has as its corollary modernization. Both theories are false and must be rejected, and their poisons purged from the Mystical Body.

Paris. "Were they ashamed when they committed abomination? No, they were not at all ashamed; they did not know how to blush" (Jer 6:15). We could adapt what St. Paul says elsewhere in the Epistle to the Romans: "They became vain in their thoughts, and their foolish heart was darkened" (Rom 1:21).

In my book *Resurgent in the Midst of Crisis,* I speak often about my personal experience of discovering the old Roman liturgy and how much it has affected my family for the better—how it has awakened us to a deeper, broader, and loftier vision of God, man, and the world than anything we have ever encountered in the "updated" catechesis, preaching, or liturgies of the post-conciliar Church. At our wedding, my wife and I exchanged vows using the beautiful preconciliar ritual, and then assisted as a newlywed couple at a splendid *Missa cantata.* We had our children baptized and confirmed in the magnificent older forms, which put to shame their modern counterparts. We went to confession with priests who used the richer and more explicit traditional prayers of the sacrament. We began to pray the age-old Divine Office. Most importantly, the Mass came alive for us *as a holy sacrifice.*[16]

A certain verse from the Psalms has become for me a motto of this journey: *Et eduxit me in latitudinem,* "And he brought me forth into a large place" (Ps 17:20), or, as other translations have it, "he led me out into a broad area." This large place, this broad area, is Catholic tradition, which is immense beyond imagining, rich beyond reckoning, more colorful, diverse, and surprising than the humdrum uniformity of modern man's concocted religion, with its see-through rationalism, its superficial whims and fads. The Lord in His goodness led us out into the broad area of sublime sacred music; the unmatched eloquence of Latin orations; the moving spectacle of ceremonies rich with symbolism; the self-abnegating worship of the transcendent, thrice-holy God, expressed and aroused through gestures of humility, adoration, spiritual longing, and peaceful possession.

---

16. The new Mass is also a sacrifice, *in se,* but this dogmatic truth is phenomenologically obscured by the new rite's "table fellowship" model, which both follows from and further reinforces the anthropocentric distortion of liturgy, with its traits of informality, horizontality, and secularity.

Reverence Is Not Enough: On the Importance of Tradition

In this large place called Catholic tradition, we see beauty all around us, stretching off into the distance, further than the eye can see, far beyond what any individual man can master in his lifetime. We bask in the sunshine of the ancient world, we breathe freely the fresh air of man's medieval childhood, we meet with every generation of believers who have trodden the path of faith before us. For me, for my family, for our friends, it has been a liberating, exhilarating, and stabilizing experience—somehow like growing roots and wings at the same time. Traditional liturgy is our lifeline, not only to Our Lord but to the entire history, heritage, culture, theology, and identity of the Roman Catholic Church to which we belong. Without this, we are anybody and anywhere, that is, nobody and nowhere—modern-day orphans, illegitimate children of modernity, without honorable birth from a noble family.

The movement to restore the *usus antiquior* is therefore not merely an expression of personal taste, a "preference" or a "sensibility," as some people would have it, in their effort to co-opt the movement for the very project of liberalism and democratic pluralism that is our mortal disease. Traditionalism is—or should be, and has the potential to be—a principled rejection of modernity's fundamental assumptions so as to prepare the way for a new birth of Christendom out of the rubble and ashes of the rapidly crumbling post-Christian West. It is a movement for the restoration of identity, sanity, spiritual health, and vigor. It is about the rediscovery and re-assertion of the Catholic Faith in its highest and fullest expression. The sacred liturgy in all its fullness is the indispensable means for renewing the priesthood, marriage and family, and the missions—precisely because it is not merely a *means* to those ends, but because through it we are united with the end that endows everything else with its meaning, orientation, efficacy, and even desirability.[17]

Let me expand on that last point for a moment. What is it that

17. In light of what we learn from the last book of Scripture, namely, that our earthly sacramental worship is a real participation in the heavenly worship of the Lamb, we can understand better why it is false to say that the liturgy is a "means" to some further end: *it makes the end present to us, and us present to the end.*

makes lifelong indissoluble marriage and the begetting and educating of children *appealing* to fallen human beings, who are notable for their selfishness and impatience of hardship? It is nothing other than belief in God, first of all, and belief in the Real Presence of Jesus in the Eucharist. If there is a God, marriage is possible. If God has given Himself to the very end—as Jesus has done in the Incarnation, in His Passion and death—then the sacrificial love of parenthood is possible, and more than that, *desirable.* If you take away God, there is no reason whatsoever to love any other person "for better or for worse, for richer or for poorer, in sickness and in health"; take away the Eucharist, and there is no reason to pour out one's life to bring more life into the world. Without God, without the mystery of the Cross, without the divine food of the Eucharist, marriage and family would be irrational, insane, a delusion, an impossible and deceptive fantasy. But if He goes before us as our *antecessor,* if He clears the path for us, if He gives Himself to us as our daily bread, sacrificial love is a reality already present in our midst, accessible, inviting, compelling. "The charity of Christ presses us" (2 Cor 5:14).

Consequently, liturgy ought to be unambiguously focused on Our Lord's sacrifice on the Cross and the awesome reality of His Eucharistic presence—a focus obviously fostered by such practices as chanting, praying in silence, kneeling, and turning eastwards to offer the holy oblation in peace. When practices like these are absent, we are not confronted with the sovereign Mystery that redeems our fragmented lives, we are not prompted to surrender ourselves to the One who loves us beyond all that we can imagine or conceive. In this sense, the oft-remarked "verticality" of traditional worship is in service of the most intimate communion with the One who loves us from all eternity with an infinite love. In contrast, it is horizontal sociability, artistic banality, non-stop verbiage, and clerical showmanship that obstruct the soul's ascent to God and the immediate "mystical" contact between creator and creature, savior and sinner, lover and beloved.

Traditionalists are sometimes blamed for elevating their "personal preferences" over the reformed liturgy of Paul VI and over the common discipline of the Church. Why can we not "get with the program" and do what everyone else is doing? But the accusation is ironic and ill-placed. For it was the Novus Ordo that, for the first time in the history of the Church, elevated the preferences, tastes, and even whims of the "presider" and the "assembly" into a matter of principle by allowing an indefinite number of possible realizations of liturgy.[18] Many texts are optional; the music is optional (there are no strict rules for what constitutes a High Mass, which has arguably brought about its demise); the rubrics are minimal, at times open-ended. Some have even spoken of the "*vel* missal": you may use Latin *or* the vernacular. You may use chant *or* some other music. You may use this Penitential Rite *or* that one, this Eucharistic Prayer *or* that one. You may worship either *ad orientem* or *versus populum*. In all these ways, the mutable will and personality of the celebrant (and, perhaps, of the group over against him) is thrust to the fore, pushing the indissoluble and immutable marriage of Christ and the Church into the background. Every celebration is, in a sense, a new project, a new compilation, a new construct of the human agents involved. Even if the same "traditional" options were to be chosen as a rule, the very fact that they are *chosen* and could be otherwise makes the liturgy not so much an *opus Dei* as an *opus hominis*.[19] As Martin Mosebach acutely explains:

> Many people, too, concerned about these issues, will ask, "Isn't it still possible to celebrate the new liturgy of Pope Paul VI worthily and reverently?" Naturally it is possible, but the very fact that *it is possible* is the weightiest argument against the new liturgy. It has been said that monarchy's death knell sounds once it becomes necessary for a monarch to be competent: this is because the monarch, in the old sense, is legitimated by his birth, not his talent. This observation is even truer in the case of the liturgy: liturgy's death knell is sounded once it requires a holy and good priest to perform it. The faithful must never regard the liturgy as some-

---

18. I once saw an attempt to calculate the total number of distinct liturgies possible in the Novus Ordo, by means of choosing each option in combination with every other possible set of options. Since there are so many changeable pieces, the final number was astronomical—in the billions.

19. Joseph Ratzinger makes a similar point in his penetrating essay "The Image of the World and of Human Beings in the Liturgy and Its Expression in Church Music" in *A New Song*, 111–27.

thing the priest does by his own efforts. It is not something that happens by good fortune or as the result of a personal charism or merit. While the liturgy is going on, time is suspended: liturgical time is different from the time that elapses outside the church's walls. It is Golgotha time, the time of the *hapax,* the unique and sole Sacrifice; it is a time that contains all times and none. How can a man be made to see that he is leaving the present time behind if the space he enters is totally dominated by the presence of one particular individual? How wise the old liturgy was when it prescribed that the congregation should not see the priest's face— his distractedness or coldness or (even more importantly) his devotion and emotion.[20]

This voluntaristic malleability of the new liturgy, joined with an emphasis on local adaptation and continual evolution, is precisely the liturgical equivalent of the decades-long dispute between Walter Kasper and Joseph Ratzinger in the sphere of ecclesiology. For Ratzinger, the universal Church and its sole Lord and Savior take precedence[21]—and therefore the liturgy, which is the act par excellence of Christ and His Mystical Body, should embody, express, and inculcate exactly this universality, the faith of the "one, holy, catholic, and apostolic Church." Now, those who are familiar with it know that everything in the traditional Roman Rite fulfills this lofty requirement. As for unity, the liturgy offers us, year after year, the same rite, the same rubrics, the same texts, the same chants, as befits "one Lord, one faith, one baptism" (Eph 4:5).[22] As for holiness, the Council of Trent notes:

20. Mosebach, *Heresy of Formlessness,* 31–32.

21. Cf. Hebrews 13:8: "Jesus Christ is the same yesterday and today and forever."

22. During those periods in my life when no traditional liturgy, Eastern or Western, was available and I have been compelled to attend the *usus recentior,* I have often experienced a palpable, almost overwhelming sense of relief once I am able to go back to the *usus antiquior.* The words of St. Faustina could be my own: "When Mass began, a strange silence and joy filled my heart" (St. Maria Faustina Kowalska, *Diary: Divine Mercy in My Soul* [Stockbridge, MA: Marian Press, 2003], n. 608). It is not merely a sense of coming home or reaching port, but a sense of recovering one's sanity after a bout of madness. I can make my own the words of the psalmist: *Eripies me de contradictionibus populi,* "Thou wilt deliver me from the contradictions of the people" (Ps 17:44).

Holy things must be treated in a holy way, and this sacrifice is the most holy of all things. And so, that this sacrifice might be worthily and reverently offered and received, the Catholic Church many centuries ago instituted the sacred canon [that is, the Roman Canon]. It is so free from all error that it contains nothing that does not savor strongly of holiness and piety and nothing that does not raise to God the minds of those who offer.[23]

The Council of Trent then says something similar about *all* of the ceremonies of the Mass. With regard to the mark of catholicity, the same traditional liturgy is offered everywhere in the Roman Catholic world, from the rising of the sun even to its setting, offered by all men and for all men, with no distinction of nation, race, or sex.[24] Finally, the apostolicity of the Church is reflected in the principle of tradition spoken of earlier, which St. Paul enunciates with resounding clarity: "I commend you because you remember me in everything and maintain the traditions even as I have delivered them to you" (1 Cor 11:2); "For I received from the Lord what I also delivered to you" (1 Cor 11:23). "Brethren, stand fast, and hold the traditions which you have learned, whether by word, or by our epistle" (2 Th 2:14).

In contrast, we see Cardinal Kasper's group-based "ecclesiology from below" reflected in the localist Novus Ordo Missae—not in its abuses, but in its very essence as a matrix of possibilities destined to receive its "inculturated" form from priests and people at each celebration. It is a liturgy in a constant state of fermentation, re-visioning, re-invention, which is antithetical to orthodoxy in its original

---

23. Council of Trent, Session 22, ch. 4. In ch. 5 the Fathers continue: "Holy Mother Church ... has provided ceremonial, such as mystical blessings, lights, incense, vestments, and many other rituals of that kind from apostolic order and tradition, by which the majesty of this great sacrifice is enhanced and the minds of the faithful are aroused by those visible signs of religious devotion to contemplation of the high mysteries hidden in this sacrifice" (Denzinger, *Enchiridion Symbolorum: A Compendium of Creeds, Definitions, and Declarations of the Catholic Church,* 43rd edition, ed. Peter Hünermann [San Francisco: Ignatius Press, 2012], nn. 1745 and 1746).

24. This, in contrast to the Novus Ordo, which has been proved to attract more women than men, and which appeals more to modern Westerners than to others. See note 4 on page 4.

meaning of "right-worship-and-right-doctrine."[25] It is worth pointing out that proponents of Kasperian ecclesiology and liturgy also
tend to repudiate Constantinian Christianity and its universalizing
aspiration to "re-establish all things in Christ" (Eph 1:10). This is
because they hold, with Karl Rahner, than every man is already
Christian at some level, and that the world as such, the secular
world, is already holy. Thus there is no clear distinction between *ad
intra* and *ad extra*, between sanctuary and nave, between minister
and congregation, between tradition and innovation, or even
between sacred and profane. "Her priests have despised my law, and
have defiled my sanctuaries: they have put no difference between
holy and profane" (Ez 22:26). All things collapse into immanence,
into the choice of the moment, the quest for instant inculturation,
the transient emotional connection, the self-proclamation of the
group. It is a liturgy of the Enlightenment, ahistorical, sociable,
accessible, efficient, unthreatening. It is supposed to be pleasant,
convenient, thoroughly free of magic, myth, or menace. There must
not be any of that primitive or medieval *mysterium tremendum et
fascinans*, none of that groveling of slaves to their masters: we are
grown-ups who can treat with God as equals. As a matter of fact, we
will edit out "difficult" passages from Sacred Scripture and rewrite

---

25. Joseph Ratzinger writes: "We must remember that originally the word
'orthodoxy' did not mean, as we generally think today, right doctrine. In Greek, the
word *doxa* means, on the one hand, opinion or splendor. But then in Christian
usage it means something on the order of 'true splendor,' that is, the glory of God.
Orthodoxy means, therefore, the right way to glorify God, the right form of adoration" (*Spirit of the Liturgy*, 159–60). Geoffrey Hull develops this point at length in
The Banished Heart: Origins of Heteropraxis in the Catholic Church (London/New
York: T&T Clark, 2010), esp. 23–39. One is orthodox if one worships the right way,
the way expressive of the truth of the Gospels as handed down by the Church. The
emphasis is on giving glory to God by professing the truth *in liturgical worship*, not
"being in the right" by intellectually holding the correct formulas. This has been
lost sight of in Roman Catholicism, where the measure of fidelity has become
adherence to the content of a recently-promulgated *Catechism*, some of whose formulations are open to question, instead of adherence to the content of an age-old
Mass, none of whose formulations are open to question. In this way the theological
compilation of a committee has been placed over centuries of unanimous assent on
the part of the faithful.

"difficult" prayers so that offenses or challenges to our modern way of life will be, if not eliminated, then at least kept to a polite minimum.[26]

It should be obvious at this point that the traditionalist defense of the classical Roman Rite and all that goes along with it is not just a matter of aesthetics or personal preferences. It is an adherence to a *premodern* understanding of man, the world, and Christianity that is uncontaminated with modern errors[27] and therefore capable of saving modern men and women from the abyss into which they have hurled themselves from the time of the Protestant Revolt to the French Revolution, down to the Sexual Revolution and now the Gender Revolution. We believe that what modern people need the most is someone with a foothold *outside* of modernity, transmitting a wisdom which originated *before* its rebellion and which aims at goals *not* of this world—this political age of great violence and failed originality. The liturgical revolution was the ecclesiastical equivalent of these social revolts, as people threw off the rubrics of restraint, the formality of address, and the commitment to a way of life received rather than a utopian (and thus artificial) construct. The only way forward is to quit our dead end, reverse our steps, and go back to the more demanding narrow path, which, by a delightful divine paradox, leads us to the large place, the broad area, of tradition. Then we shall say with the psalmist: *Dilatasti gressus meos subtus me et non sunt infirmata vestigia mea.* "Thou hast enlarged my steps under me; and my feet are not weakened" (Ps 17:37).

26. See Peter Kwasniewski, "The Reform of the Lectionary," in *Liturgy in the Twenty-First Century: Contemporary Issues and Perspectives,* ed. Alcuin Reid (London/New York: Bloomsbury T&T Clark, 2016), 287–320; idem, "Not Just More Scripture, but Different Scripture," in Matthew P. Hazell, *Index Lectionum: A Comparative Table of Readings for the Ordinary and Extraordinary Forms of the Roman Rite* (N.p.: Lectionary Study Press, 2016), vii–xxix; idem, "The Omission that Haunts the Church—1 Corinthians 11:27–29," published at *New Liturgical Movement* on April 11, 2016; Matthew Hazell, "On the Inclusion of 1 Corinthians 11:27–29 in the Ordinary Form," published at *New Liturgical Movement* on April 22, 2016.

27. Exactly the errors, in other words, that are condemned in Pius IX's *Quanta Cura* and *Syllabus Errorum* and the great encyclicals of Leo XIII, Pius X, and Pius XI.

My conclusion, then, is that reverence is *not* enough. Good intentions are not enough. Following the official books is not enough. If we are to be Roman Catholics, if we are to be the heirs and recipients of our faith rather than promethean neo-Pelagians who shape it to ourselves, if we are to be imitators of the apostles and all the saints, then entering into the Church's traditional *lex orandi* is no less necessary, and no less important in our times.[28] If anything, rediscovering the rich, multifaceted, profound, undiluted symbolism and doctrinal fullness of the sacred liturgy—the fruit of the Holy Spirit's gentle brooding over *all* the centuries of our ecclesiastical life—has acquired a new and special urgency as the dictatorship of relativism clamps down on us with a vengeance. Even within the hierarchy of the Church, there are those who would barter away the primogeniture of the Gospels for a bowl of modern pottage. This is not what we shall do; we will take Christ as our King and the tradition of His Church as our strong support.

I am reminded of the words of the ancient martyr St. Genesius: "There is no King but Christ, and though I be slain a thousand times for Him, yet you cannot take Him from my mouth or my heart."[29] This, too, is how we feel about the traditional liturgy. It is our privileged access to Christ, who gives Himself to us not only by placing His Body and Blood in our mouths, but *also* by burying deep in our hearts the treasure of His Church's prayer. This joy, this pearl of great price, this glorious inheritance, no one can take away from us.

---

28. Without this continuity in orthodoxy (meaning both right worship *and* right belief), we risk inventing or drifting into a new religion that has certain appearances of the old but deviates in open or subtle ways into modernism.

29. *The Roman Martyrology,* 1956 ed., ed. Canon J.B. O'Connell (Westminster, MD: The Newman Press, 1962), under August 25.

Prayer for the Traditional Movement

O LORD, remember in Thy Kingdom *N.* and *N.*,
[*names of individuals or communities*]
and all religious, clergy, and laity throughout the world
who are dedicated to the *usus antiquior.*
Bless us, govern us, defend us, purify us, and multiply us
for the good of souls,
for the restoration of Thy Church,
and for the glory of Thy Holy Name.
Amen.

In amicitia illius delectatio bona, et in operibus manuum illius hones-
tas sine defectione, et in certamine loquelae illius sapientia, et prae-
claritas in communicatione sermonum ipsius.

There is great delight in her friendship, and inexhaustible riches in
the works of her hands, and in the exercise of conference with her,
wisdom, and glory in the communication of her words.

WISDOM 8:18

3

The Spirit of the Liturgy in the
Words and Actions of Our Lady

I N THE RECORD OF Sacred Scripture, the Blessed Virgin Mary is a
woman of few words and few appearances. But the words she
speaks and the role she plays are of such a depth that never in a
thousand centuries would their wisdom and fecundity be
exhausted, and for all eternity their echoes will sound and resound
in the heavenly places. It can be said, without exaggeration, that
Mary's words and actions summarize the entire Christian life. They
present the very pattern or archetype of that life; they are the whole
of ascetical-mystical theology *in nucleo*. If we had nothing but Our
Lady's sayings and deeds, we would still know from them how to be
perfect followers of Christ; we would have the pith or marrow of the
Gospel.[1] It is not to be wondered at, therefore, that we can also find
in them a guide to the spirituality of the liturgy—namely, to the
correct internal dispositions and external actions of the formal,
public, solemn prayer of the Church by which we most perfectly
exercise our baptismal share in Christ's priesthood and receive the
fruits of His redemption, becoming those "worshipers of God in
spirit and in truth" that the Father desires (cf. Jn 4:23–24).

Because of their very depth of meaning, Our Lady's words and
deeds are too vast a topic for one essay. I will limit myself to her
words at the Annunciation; her silent, interior, but supremely active

---

1. St. Thomas notes that *actio Christi fuit instructio nostra*, "the action of Christ
was our instruction" (*Summa theologiae* III, q. 40, a. 1, ad 3). The same may be said
of our Blessed Mother, because her actions, too, were sinless and perfect; she is the
most perfect image of the virtues of her Son.

participation at the foot of the Cross; and her poignant words at the wedding feast of Cana.

At the Annunciation

When the archangel St. Gabriel announces to the Blessed Virgin that she is to bear a son, her reaction indicates, without any doubt, that she had already consecrated herself to perpetual virginity: "How shall this be done, because I know not man?" (Lk 1:34). Pregnancy is impossible, it seems to Mary, for she has no intention of knowing a man; otherwise, she would have assumed that the angel was speaking about a son to be born from her wedlock with St. Joseph.[2] The angel replies: "The Holy Ghost shall come upon thee, and the power of the most High shall overshadow thee. And therefore also the Holy which shall be born of thee shall be called the Son of God" (Lk 1:35). In other words, this offspring will not be the result of a man's action, the son of a man, but will be formed by a direct action of the Holy Spirit, a fruit of the Creator's omnipotence, and therefore worthy to be called the offspring of God Himself.

In this exchange, there is a profound liturgical lesson for us. The Catholic Church is often spoken of as the Mystical Body of Christ, as the extension in space and time of the mystery of the Incarnation. Something similar can be said of the sacred liturgy: it is Christ among us, it is "the brightness of his glory and the figure of his substance" (Heb 1:3), as He is of the Father. Through it, the mysteries of the life, death, and resurrection of the Lord are made present and effective in our midst; the Lord Himself touches us, body and soul, to heal and elevate us. The liturgy, too, is the offspring of God in our midst, formed over long centuries by the brooding of the Holy Spirit upon the surface of human waters (cf. Gen 1:2). It is not a

2. The Catholic Tradition holds both that Our Lady made a vow of perpetual virginity, which was not rescinded by her betrothal to St. Joseph, and that St. Joseph understood and accepted her vow, which he had no intention of subverting. St. Thomas Aquinas discusses this point at great length; for texts and commentary, see John Saward, *Cradle of Redeeming Love: The Theology of the Christmas Mystery* (San Francisco: Ignatius Press, 2002), 217–31, and Matthias Joseph Scheeben, *Mariology*, trans. T.L.M.J. Geuker (St. Louis: B. Herder, 1946), 110–31.

mere construct of human hands, a product of man's initiative or labor or great ideas, but rather the unmerited gift of God, poured into our messy history as charity is poured into our sinful hearts (cf. Rom 5:5), and making something beautiful out of our nature, for our salvation. The liturgy is born from the womb of the Church, our Mother, by the power of the Most High overshadowing her. As we see in both Testaments, liturgy comes about primarily by God's intervention, impregnating His bride with the seed of the Word. The liturgy is born from the Church's virginal receptivity, and she retains her integrity and her honor in conceiving, giving birth, and mothering her child.

If this is true about the innermost essence of the liturgy, it follows that it is a fundamental error to think of the liturgy as if it were, first and foremost, the work of human hands, the offspring of our genius, our skills, our pastoral programs—as if we were the begetters of it, having the rights of a parent over it.[3] Rather, the liturgy comes from God, from the eternal liturgy of the heavenly Jerusalem;[4] it belongs to God alone, who entrusts it to our hands for safekeeping; it returns to God (and we return to Him through it), bearing our sheaves from the harvest, our increase of talents for His glory.[5] The Church as virgin bride says to God: "How shall my liturgy come forth, because I know not a man who can beget it?" And

---

3. It could be objected that Mary and Joseph *did* have the rights of a parent over Jesus, as indicated by Luke 2:51: "He was obedient to them." But this was a choice made by Our Lord, since naturally He was superior to them both in His divinity and in His humanity—something hinted at by His reaction to His Mother's words: "Son, why hast thou thus dealt with us? Behold, thy father and I have sought thee sorrowing" (Lk 2:48), to which He responds: "How is it that you sought me? Did you not know that I must be in my Father's house?" (v. 49), as if to say: The one to whom I am truly subject from all eternity is My Father; but I consent to be subject to you in the economy of salvation. Jesus says something similar to St. John the Baptist when the latter is surprised that Jesus would be baptized by him (Mt 3:13–15).

4. This is a point frequently made by Ratzinger in *The Spirit of the Liturgy* and other writings. It can be extrapolated from the Book of Revelation, many liturgical texts, Pius XII's Encyclical Letter *Mediator Dei*, and Vatican II's Constitution *Sacrosanctum Concilium.*

5. Ps 125:7; Lk 19:11–27.

answers her through Gabriel: "It is not for any man or any committee to form this liturgy; it is mine alone, in the hidden womb of the
ages—the fruit of countless holy men and women moved by the
Spirit of God, who first humbly receive, who, according to their
capacity, adorn and enrich this patrimony, and who then faithfully
transmit all the gifts they have received."[6] In truth, Holy Mother
Church never has the intention of "knowing a man," that is, treating
the liturgy as a "choice" made by partners in family planning, or
worse, as a man-made product that can be modified at will, decon-
structed and reconstructed as if it were a machine or a building or a
toy.[7] She rather conserves and preserves the holy seed entrusted to
her, utterly subordinating herself to it, treating it with the same reverence with which she would wash and anoint the Savior's very
body, as she lovingly and fearfully touches the flesh and blood of
God.[8]

Returning now to the scene of the Annunciation, we see Our Lady
giving her *Fiat*, on which the entire salvation of the world hinges.

6. This view does not ignore the fact that the liturgy, in its prayers, ceremonies,
processions, feast days, etc., was built up by human beings. What Christians contributed, however, they contributed to a given structure that preceded them, as if
adding ornaments to a Christmas tree. A better comparison would be the building
of a church. The fundamental plan of a Christian church is a given, not something
designed *ex nihilo*. The architects have to decide how the plan will be realized in
this place and in these circumstances; their final work will be more or less adequate
to the nature and purpose of a temple. Many people will contribute wealth to the
building of a church, and, over time, others will add *ex voto* offerings. The church is
therefore built by many and ornamented by many, but its basic plan preexists any
of their efforts, and its success, in the end, depends on how well it corresponds to
the "ideal temple" that is in the mind of God and descends from above, like a bride
adorned for her husband (Rev 21:2). One finds just such a neoplatonic conception
of church architecture among the Church Fathers.

7. Wherever this aberrant approach prevails, therefore, we can see that it is not
"the Church" acting, much less Christ, but churchmen who are abusing their
authority and, to the extent God permits it, obscuring and obstructing the activity
of the Church of Christ and stifling her maternal memory (cf. Lk 2:19).

8. The traditional Catholic's objection to laypeople receiving the Host in their
hands or distributing it to others has nothing to do with whether or not we deserve
to have Christ's Body touch our bodies. Whoever receives the Holy Eucharist is
physically touched by Our Lord, and no creature is worthy, absolutely speaking, of
this divine gift. The problem has rather to do with the understanding of *ministry*.

"Behold the handmaid of the Lord: be it done unto me according to Thy word" (Lk 1:38).

Note the double passivity of this statement. She does not say "*I* will do thus-and-such." She says: "Be it *done unto me*." Moreover, she does not say: "Be it done unto me according to my words" or "Be it done unto me as I understand it," as if she were entering into a contract between equals in which both parties have worked out a mutual formula of agreement. No, she says "according to *Thy* word." She does not grasp everything that this word contains or demands or portends. In fact, she knows that she is consenting to that which is absolutely beyond her understanding and surrenders to it.

In the words of Dionysius the Areopagite, the perfect theologian "not only learns, but *suffers* divine things."[9] The Blessed Virgin exemplifies this suffering of divine things. She lets them happen to her, she accepts, receives, embraces, and this is why she becomes pregnant with God. He is able to enter into her fully, *substantially,* because she gives herself, her humanity, her heart, soul, mind, and strength, to Him (cf. Mk 12:30). God does wonders in creation in proportion to the aptitude for wonders that He finds in the creature (cf. Mk 6:4–5). We may almost rephrase Mary's response: "Make me suffer according to Thy Word"; "Refashion me, transform me according to Thy Word."

The priest is a man set apart by God, metaphysically changed by the indelible character of Christ's priesthood, with a view to consecrating, handling, distributing, and caring for the sacramental Body of Christ and those things that directly pertain to It (such as absolving sins that prevent us from eating the bread of life). The priest's hands are specially anointed so that they may be worthy of performing these awesome tasks. The layman, in contrast, is empowered by his baptism to *receive* the Body of Christ, but not to have a ministerial power over It at the altar and the communion rail. To act otherwise is to arrogate to oneself an activity that is proper to Christ the High Priest, by His gift and choice, and therefore to insult Him by visibly undermining His determinations as well as the dignity of His ordained ministers.

9. *Summa theologiae* II-II, q. 45, a. 2: "Hierotheus est perfectus in divinis, non solum discens, sed et patiens divina." In his commentary on the *De Divinis Nominibus,* St. Thomas remarks: "he does not merely gather up knowledge of divine things in his intellect, but by loving them is united to them in his heart" ("idest non solum divinorum scientiam in intellectu accipiens, sed etiam diligendo, eis unitus est per affectum"): ch. 2, lec. 4, n. 191. Cf. *Summa theologiae* I, q. 1, a. 6, ad 3.

This formula illuminates the immensely powerful spirituality of the traditional liturgy of the Church, whether Eastern or Western. The liturgy, as such, is *given* to us as a word of infinite density, as the "pure emanation of the glory of the Almighty" (Wis 7:25), as a *Logos* to be embodied in our midst, in our churches, on our altars, in our souls, in our actions. In imitation of the *Theotokos*, we are to become bearers of this word, which we receive. We do not make or create or fashion this word, but, like Mary, we receive it from another, we suffer it and are thus transformed by it, as potency is fulfilled by actuality.

Hence, for the liturgy to *be* Marian, for it to change us into her image, it must not—I repeat, must not—be subject to the will of the celebrant. It cannot be full of options, variations, adaptations, extemporaneous utterances, improvisations. As Joseph Ratzinger has rightly said: "The greatness of the liturgy depends...on its unspontaneity."[10] The novelty of having options to choose from in the missal, as if one were partaking of a devotional buffet, the novelty of allowing celebrants to build from modules and to improvise at various points of the Mass—a malleability that some liturgists identify (and praise) as the single most characteristic feature of the reformed Roman liturgy[11]—changes the fundamental character of worship in a radical way. Instead of expressing the Marian stance, "be it done unto me according to Thy word," it expresses a distinctively modern stance of creativity, autonomy, and voluntarism: "I will do it according to my mind, my choice, and my words." When Lucifer cried out "I will not serve," he might just as well have said: I will not submit to a predetermined plan, I will not conform myself to a heavenly pattern (cf. Ex 25:9).

10. *Spirit of the Liturgy,* 166.

11. See, for example, Kevin W. Irwin, *Liturgy, Prayer, and Spirituality* (New York/Ramsey: Paulist Press, 1984), "Creativity and Option," 170–82. A sample: "The post-conciliar reform offers great latitude within the rites for flexibility and option. Hence, there is a wealth of text and option provided in each recently revised liturgical ritual in order that the particular worshiping community may derive maximum benefit from the experience of worship" (172). Cf. idem, *Responses to 101 Questions on the Mass* (New York/Mahwah: Paulist Press, 1999), 34–36, 93–95, 116, 144.

Lucifer's anti-Marian stance, epitomized in his rebellious cry "I will not serve," assumes many forms in the course of history. In the ecclesiastical sphere, it takes on the form of: "I will not *pre*serve, I will not *con*serve." Lucifer is the original liberal, inasmuch as he spurns order, discipline, rule, rubric, and tradition. He will not pass along something that came from another; everything has to be from himself, even if it is poor, banal, or ugly. What a stark contrast with Mary's *Ecce ancilla Domini*! She knows that she is not the master, she is the *ancilla*, the slave girl. So much for modern Catholics who take the words of Jesus out of context: "I no longer call you servants . . . but friends" (Jn 15:15) and conclude that we are not servants in any way. His Mother, the holiest of all human persons and the most intimate friend of Christ, calls herself an *ancilla*, because she knows more and loves more than those who do not wish to belong completely to another.

The word "demon" comes from a Greek word meaning "one who divides." Satan is a divider. One way he has lived up to this title is by dividing Catholics from our own heritage, our own tradition. This suits well his liberal agenda, which is to convince each generation that it is autonomous from past generations, and to convince each individual that he is autonomous from God, his fellow men, and his ancestors. The devil is permanently rootless, utterly without roots (that is why he goes "prowling about the world seeking the ruin of souls"), and he wants to uproot the rest of us. His greatest victory is not to hook us on pornography, alcohol, or drugs. Those things are wicked, to be sure, and have destroyed many lives and led to the damnation of many souls, but worse by far is cutting us off from the likelihood of conversion and contemplation by severing us from the Catholic tradition in which we will find all the medicine, the food and drink, the clothing, that we need for the healing of our sicknesses and the living of a godly life.

The liturgy, and therefore the Church herself, will not become healthy again—or, if she seems to be healthy in some places, will not be able to maintain that condition against the increasingly violent and demonic assaults of modernity—until the clergy have submitted to the *Logos* expressed in her traditional liturgical rites with their stability of form, soundness of formulas, inexhaustible treasury of holy prayers, thundering orthodoxy, transcendent orientation, and otherworldly beauty. This, too, is what St. Paul says: "Follow the pattern of the sound words which you have heard from me in faith ... guard the truth that has been entrusted to you by the Holy Spirit who dwells within us" (2 Tim 1:13–14). *Formam habe sanorum verborum; bonum depositum custodi.* When the liturgical rite demands the celebrant's complete submission to its prayers, gestures, and ceremonies, it "swallows him up," like Jonah's fish, and hides him within its spacious confines, so that he disappears into the bright blaze of Christ: "And when they lifted up their eyes, they saw no one but Jesus only" (Mt 17:8).[12] When the celebrant completely submits himself to such a rite, he enters into the *kenosis*, the self-emptying, of Christ; he most of all becomes *alter Christus,* mediating between mutable man and the immutable God. He practices the humility of St. John the Baptist, who said: "*He* must increase, *I* must decrease" (Jn 3:30). Hence the vital importance of recovering the traditional orientation of the priest, who, when the time of sacrifice arrives, should be facing East together with the people he is leading to Christ.[13]

Cardinal Sarah has spoken beautifully of the connection between silence and *ad orientem,* in words that emphasize the unbreakable

---

12. Cf. Mk 9:8. The comparison to Jonah's fish is whimsical, but not beside the point. We know from Our Lord that Jonah is a type of Himself gone into the tomb and resurrected, meeting His disciples on the shores of Galilee (cf. Mt 12:39–41; Jn 21:1). Before Jonah is swallowed up, he is running away from his mission. Once he is overcome by a greater power, he learns to submit and obey, and becomes a prophet whose word effects conversion. There is an exact parallel in the realm of the New Evangelization. As long as churchmen think they will do their work with their own lights and liturgies, their efforts are doomed to failure. Once a priest submits to the great power of the sacred liturgy, he will "learn obedience by the things which he suffered" (Heb 5:8), and will be projected onto the beach of modernity with the humility and zeal of one who has something worthwhile to share, something burning in his heart (cf. Lk 24:32), to convert the poor Ninevites who do not know their left hand from their right hand, or, to give a more up-to-date example, a woman from a man.

13. On the correctness, or better, orthodoxy, of *ad orientem* worship, see Ratzinger, *Spirit of the Liturgy,* 74–84; Uwe Michael Lang, *Turning Towards the Lord* (San Francisco: Ignatius Press, 2004); Gamber, *Reform of the Roman Liturgy,* 77–89, 121–79.

link between external and internal, symbol and reality, liturgical custom and spiritual formation.

> Liturgical silence is a radical and essential disposition; it is a conversion of heart. Now, to be converted, etymologically, is to turn back, to turn toward God. There is no true silence in the liturgy if we are not—with all our heart—turned toward the Lord. We must be converted, turn back to the Lord, in order to look at Him, contemplate His face, and fall at His feet to adore Him. We have an example: Mary Magdalene was able to recognize Jesus on Easter morning because she turned back toward Him: "They have taken away my Lord, and I do not know where they have laid him. *Haec cum dixisset, conversa est retrorsum et videt Jesus stantem.* Saying this, she turned around and saw Jesus standing there" (Jn 20:13–14). How can we enter into this interior disposition except by turning physically, all together, priest and faithful, toward the Lord who comes, toward the East symbolized by the apse where the cross is enthroned? The outward orientation leads us to the interior orientation that it symbolizes. Since apostolic times, Christians have been familiar with this way of praying. It is not a matter of celebrating with one's back to the people or facing them, but toward the East, *ad Dominum,* toward the Lord. This way of doing things promotes silence.[14]

It is the very inflexibility of traditional liturgical forms that gives them their indomitable power to shape us, to change us, to be our fixed reference point, to be the rock on which the anchor of our restless hearts can catch hold. We who are so unstable, so wrapped up in our shifting emotions and poor thoughts, need an unshifting basis of prayer, rich and resonant with the accumulated piety and wisdom of the ages. Only in this way do we come to calmness, arriving at a harbor that mirrors our eternal haven. Only in this way can we put ourselves back together, so to speak, and achieve a wholeness that, left to our own devices, we could never hope to enjoy. The perennial liturgy is a source of sanity and stability for a Church storm-tossed, vexed with heresy, harassed by temptations of compromise with the world, the flesh, and the devil. It is a pearl of great

---

14. "Cardinal Robert Sarah on 'The Strength of Silence' and the Dictatorship of Noise," published at *The Catholic World Report*, October 3, 2016.

price even in the most peaceful of times, but in an age of confusion and wickedness like ours, it is an urgently needed ark of safety, a fortress of truth, a tower of strength, a beacon of light. We may apply to it the words of the Epistle to the Hebrews: "Let us be grateful for receiving a kingdom that cannot be shaken, and thus let us offer to God acceptable worship, with reverence and awe" (Heb 12:28).

We can adapt and apply to the traditional liturgy the words with which the book of Wisdom describes its namesake:

> She is a breath of the power of God, and a pure emanation of the glory of the Almighty; therefore nothing defiled gains entrance into her. For she is a reflection of eternal light, a spotless mirror of the working of God, and an image of his goodness. Though she is but one, she can do all things, and while remaining in herself, she renews all things; in every generation she passes into holy souls and makes them friends of God, and prophets. (Wis 7:25–27)

Liturgy rightly understood is the breath of God's power, an emanation of His glory, giving us a foretaste of that glory and guiding us to the Promised Land. Nothing defiled, disordered, erroneous, heretical, or harmful can gain entrance into the liturgical rites of Catholic tradition, organically built up by the Holy Spirit and preserved from corruption, as was Mary's virginity.[15] The liturgy reflects the One who called Himself the light of the world; it spotlessly mirrors Christ by presenting His mysteries not as empty commemorations but as efficacious signs that unite us immediately and directly to their substantial reality.[16] In this way the earthly liturgy, although limited in time and place, can do all things that Christ Himself did and does, renewing everything else by remaining itself (and by remaining true to itself). The liturgy is an Archimedean

---

15. The finest exposition of the all-important concept of "organic development" is Alcuin Reid's *The Organic Development of the Liturgy*.

16. In §164 et seq. of the Encyclical Letter *Mediator Dei* (November 20, 1947), Pius XII explains how the mysteries of the life of Christ are recounted, reawakened, reapplied throughout the Church's year, and how the liturgy itself beseeches the Lord for a share in the graces obtained and represented by those mysteries.

point: by its fixity, it can move the universe. Through the Holy Sacrifice of the Mass and the Divine Office, the sacraments and sacramentals, eternal and incarnate Wisdom passes into holy souls of every generation and makes them friends of God, and prophets.

The foremost of these holy souls and friends of God is Our Lady. Just as St. John the Baptist was a prophet and more than a prophet (Mt 11:9, Lk 7:26), so, too, Our Lady is more than a participant in the liturgy: in her very person she is a *living liturgy*, the vessel through which Our Lord deigned to enter into space and time, to take on flesh and blood in our midst. She became the bridge between heaven and earth, God and man. She is not a priest but rather the very condition of the possibility of the priesthood—even, in a way, of her own Son's priesthood. Her divine motherhood makes her greater than any ministerial priest, greater than any bishop or pope, and yet totally other than a priest, simply not in the same category as members of the Church's hierarchy. She gives birth to the hierarchy, nurses it, educates it, leads it, wraps her protecting mantle around it. The whole of the Church is a child in the womb of Mary, in the arms of Mary. She is far greater than our structures. She is the very essence and meaning and purpose and goodness of our structures.[17] And women are privileged to bear in their very womanhood a natural likeness to Our Lady which, under the influence of grace, is capable of becoming a supernatural likeness.[18]

This is why clamoring for the involvement or *activity* of women in the sanctuary, whether as priests (which is impossible) or as deaconesses (which is equivocal and confusing, to say the least), or even merely as functionaries in a plethora of minor roles, is not simply a matter of mistaken priorities, but an assault on the metaphysics of God, the logic of the Incarnation, the ethics of our Marian response, and the poetics of the liturgical act. It, too, is a way of

---

17. In the sense that whatever is good, holy, beautiful about these structures is precontained in and exemplified by the Virgin Mary, in the perfections of her body and especially her soul. The Church is, so to speak, a reflection or externalization of the plenitude of Mary's divine virginal motherhood.

18. See Peter Kwasniewski, "Incarnate Realism and the Catholic Priesthood," *OnePeterFive*, July 17, 2015.

saying *Non serviam*: I will not serve the relationship of Father and Son, the descending agency of the *Logos,* the reception of tradition (that is, the *Logos* handed down through space and time), or the natural and supernatural symbolism of the rites.[19] I will not serve the supremacy of Mary and the woman's virginal-maternal role in the order of creation; I will not serve the supremacy of Christ and the man's vicarious role in the order of redemption; I will not serve the very distinction of sexes that makes possible the revelation of God's preferential, passionate love and the irruption into our world of the *miraculum miraculorum,* the Incarnation of the Word.[20]

The eternal contradiction of Satan's attitude is Our Lady's *Fiat*: be it done unto me according to *Thy* word. This *Fiat* takes on a specific profile for each category of Christian.

(1) For the laity, our *Fiat* is to receive, to love, and to live the liturgical forms of our tradition, and not to think that it is a matter of indifference which *logos* we are receiving—one that comprises all ages, or one that derives from modernity.

(1a) For women, the *Fiat* consists in receiving and submitting to the order of the liturgy, which impresses upon us, ever more deeply, the virginal, bridal, and maternal character of the Christian life and of Our Lady in particular. All Christians receive and live this Marian identity, but women are privileged to do so existentially, in a bodily way that makes them living sacraments of Mary's divine maternity—something no male human being can be.[21]

(1b) For men, on the other hand, this *Fiat* includes the possibility that we would be summoned by Our Lord to receive a share in His priestly power and to represent and exercise His priesthood at the altar of sacrifice. In responding to this call, we are not ceasing to be Marian but living out her attitude to the fullest; we are not becoming "agents of change" or "actors" in a modern sense, but rather

19. See Benedict Constable, "Should Women Be Lectors at Mass," *OnePeterFive*, August 12, 2015; idem, "Male-Female Symbolism in Liturgical Roles: Not Bizarre, Just Catholic," *OnePeterFive*, August 13, 2015; Peter Kwasniewski, "Are We God's 'Sons and Daughters'?," *New Liturgical Movement*, February 17, 2014.

20. See Sire, *Phoenix from the Ashes*, 317.

21. Cf. Kwasniewski, "Incarnate Realism and the Catholic Priesthood."

"*patients* of change," ones who will be changed into the image of Christ by ordination and by the discipline of the sacred liturgy. "Thy discipline hath corrected me unto the end: and Thy discipline, the same shall teach me" (Ps 17:36).

(2) The *Fiat* of the clergy and anyone who serves as a liturgical theologian, educator, or minister of any kind is to suffer the liturgy to be itself and to form us, rather than acting upon it and forming it, as if we were still walking around in the apostolic age and had the charisms of the early Church in its embryonic phase, in its pre-Constantinian secrecy,[22] prior to the robust development of public, solemn, formal worship that culminated in the liturgical rites of the Byzantine empire and of the medieval Latin Church. Such perfected liturgical rites are the plenary manifestation of the Word, *incarnatus de Spiritu Sancto,* to which we are bound in filial piety by the very fact of our belonging to the perfect society of the Church, continuously one and visible until the end of time.

(3) The priest, more than anyone else, is called to be not an actor but a transmitter, a transparent communicator of wisdom that is not his own, a borrowed voice of Christ and the Church. As we said before, his entire attitude in ministry and especially at the altar should reflect those words of the Baptist, speaking of Our Lord: "He must increase and I must decrease" (Jn 3:30). Or, in the words of the book of Wisdom, the priest is a breath of God's power, a reflection, a mirror, an image. He is not the reality itself, but participates in it. Exploiting a humble metaphor, Msgr. Ronald Knox compares the good priest to a well-functioning tool utterly in its master's command:

> The philosopher Aristotle, in defining the position of a slave, uses the words, "A slave is a living tool." And that is what a priest is, a living tool of Jesus Christ. He lends his hands to be Christ's hands, his voice to be Christ's voice, his thoughts to be Christ's thoughts;

---

22. The great ecclesiologist Charles Cardinal Journet speaks of privileges uniquely apostolic in his *Church of the Word Incarnate* and its summary *Theology of the Church,* noting that the apostles received and exercised certain powers that no other Christians, including their successor bishops, enjoyed or could ever enjoy.

there is, there should be, nothing of himself in it from first to last, except where the Church graciously permits him to dwell for a moment in silence on his own special intentions, for the good estate of the living and the dead. Those who are not of our religion are puzzled sometimes, or even scandalized, by witnessing the ceremonies of the Mass; it is all, they say, so mechanical. But you see, it *ought* to be mechanical. They are watching, not a man, but a living tool; it turns this way and that, bends, straightens itself, gesticulates, all in obedience to a preconceived order—Christ's order, not ours. The Mass is best said—we Catholics know it—when it is said so that you do not notice how it is said; we do not expect eccentricities from a tool, the tool of Christ.[23]

Because he is a living tool, the priest must avoid at all costs liturgical and extra-liturgical activism, which expresses an attitude of self-absorbed promethean neo-Pelagian domination that is utterly contrary to Marian spirituality. Activism here includes the many forms of liturgical manipulation, exploitation, and narcissism that have marred the face of the Bride of Christ and crippled her work during the past half-century.[24]

(4) For male and female religious, the *Fiat* of Our Lady is the very model of one's entire way of life as a liturgical being who, by God's grace, has chosen to live, as much as possible, for and from the Eucharistic Body of Christ, and, consequently, for those members of the Mystical Body of Christ who are in most need of one's prayers, sacrifices, and works of mercy. Religious are called, above and before all else, to the corporate praise of God in a solemn and splendid way, such that the rest of the Church can catch fire from

---

23. Ronald A. Knox, *The Pastoral Sermons*, ed. Philip Caraman, S.J. (New York: Sheed & Ward, 1960), 342–43.

24. Such activism would also include forms of clericalism that interfere with the laity's zealous fulfillment of their own social, political, and cultural responsibilities. It has often been pointed out (including by John Paul II) that the true vocation of the laity, namely to infuse the Spirit of Christ into the *mores* and laws of the people among whom one dwells, has been eclipsed by the "shortcut" of the clericalization of the laity, whereby their busy-work in the liturgy is taken for a sign of involvement when, in reality, it points to a failure to undertake their God-given tasks outside of the sanctuary and to let the clergy *be* the clergy.

their zeal for the *opus Dei.* Christians who are lukewarm, distracted, even well-intentioned but superficial, are often brought to conversion by the potent witness of a community of monks, nuns, or friars offering up the sacrifice of praise, which makes manifest that God is the alpha and the omega, the first and abiding reality for us and for all human beings. The religious could be described as a person who, having received through no merits of his own the grace of a penetrating awareness of his total dependence on God, has decided to live out this dependence as fully as he can, ordering everything else to this goal, and thereby carrying many others with him. Religious are the ones awake in a world of sleepwalkers. The Church depends especially on them to be generously devoted to the *opus Dei,* alert to the message of liturgical symbols, responsive to the gravitational pull of tradition. In this way, they serve to anchor and orient the rest of the People of God.

To everyone, Our Lady shows us that action proceeds from contemplation and returns to it; that any work we can do for God must be suspended like a bridge between the fixed points of liturgical prayer and personal prayer; that our hectic labor must be oriented to holy leisure, even as this earthly pilgrimage is for the sake of our eternal destiny. The Virgin Mary was not like St. Martha, busy about many things, and complaining that she never got any help. Rather, as St. Luke says, "Mary *kept* all these things, pondering them in her heart" (Lk 2:19; cf. 2:51). For her, what mattered most was the unchanging truth of God and its reflection on the face of Jesus. To this she gently but firmly directed everything else; she was *ad orientem* through and through. In our interior attitude towards liturgy, in our actual practice of worship, and in the ordering of our lives, we should imitate and internalize this theocentric and Christocentric orientation of the Blessed Virgin Mary.

Where do we see this Marian orientation most of all? *Stabat Mater dolorosa, iuxta crucem lacrimosa, dum pendebat Filius.* "Standing beneath the Cross was the sorrowful Mother, weeping, while her Son was hanging there." *Fac ut ardeat cor meum in amando Christum Deum, ut sibi complaceam.* "Inflame my heart with love for Christ-God, that I may be pleasing to Him."

At the Foot of the Cross

On Calvary, we see the inner reality and the archetype of the Holy Sacrifice of the Mass, namely, the bloody, life-giving Passion of the Son of God, by Whose stripes we are healed, by Whose Blood we are cleansed of our sins, by Whose Body, offered up, we are made into a sweet-smelling oblation.[25] St. John devotes two austere verses in his Gospel to the little flock, the congregation gathered at Golgotha:

> Now there stood by the cross of Jesus, his mother, and his mother's sister, Mary of Cleophas, and Mary Magdalen. When Jesus therefore had seen his mother and the disciple standing whom he loved, he saith to his mother: "Woman, behold thy son." After that, he saith to the disciple: "Behold thy mother." And from that hour, the disciple took her to his own. (Jn 19:25–27)

Let us note several things about this scene. First, neither Mary's name nor John's is mentioned, but only "woman" and "the disciple whom he loved." This stresses their anonymity: they are veiled in the presence of the awe-full mystery; they are subsumed into it, they lose themselves in Christ. As St. Paul says: "you are dead; and your life is hid with Christ in God" (Col 3:3).

The account says they are *standing* at the foot of the Cross. Since we are not to read this passage as a "blueprint" for an actual liturgy, one cannot conclude that we ought to be standing throughout Mass (although our Byzantine brethren do stand during the liturgy, but for a different reason—because they are celebrating the resurrection, the *anastasis* or standing up again). Here at Golgotha, standing signifies attentiveness, a giving of oneself completely to the reality present. Mary and John are, to use a wonderful old expression, *assisting at* the Lord's sacrifice. They do so not by speaking or singing or moving around, but by *being present* to Jesus in the depths of their soul. What we see, then, is the "Platonic form" of *participatio actuosa* or active participation: entering into the mystery in a way that is not primarily external or physical, but interior and meta-

---

25. Cf. Is 53:5; Heb 9:22–26, 10:19–22; 1 Pet 1:18–19; Eph 5:2.

physical.[26] This is not to say, of course, that there should be no outward actions, words, and songs. It does show us, however, that the proper stance of those assisting at Mass is one of Marian receptivity and Johannine contemplation, and that the visible and audible signs used in the liturgy, as well as the bodily actions by which we respond to them, should be in service of this Marian-Johannine adoration of the Lamb and hospitality to the Bridegroom. When St. Luke tells us that "Mary kept all these things, pondering them in her heart," he confides to us the very secret of Our Lady's matchless participation in the mysteries of Christ. Indeed, she tells us herself: "My *soul* doth magnify the Lord, and my *spirit* hath rejoiced in God my Savior" (Lk 1:46–47), as if to underline that her praise of God is interior, hidden in the depths of her soul and spirit, and by a kind of overflow bursts forth into the great hymn of the Magnificat.

In a journal of private revelations published with ecclesiastical approval, Our Lord speaks the following words:

> I offered myself to the Father from the altar of My Mother's Sorrowful and Immaculate Heart. She accepted, consenting to bear the full weight of My sacrifice, to be the very place from which My holocaust of love blazed up. She, in turn, offered herself with Me to the Father from the altar of My Sacred Heart. There she immolated herself, becoming one victim with Me for the redemption of the world. Her offering was set ablaze in My holocaust by the descent of the Holy Spirit. Thus, from our two hearts become two altars, there rose the sweet fragrance of one single offering: My oblation upon the altar of her heart, and her oblation upon the

---

26. In other words, the exemplar of the Mass (and of our liturgy in general) is not the Last Supper but the Sacrifice of Christ on the Cross. This is what distinguishes a Catholic understanding of liturgy from a Protestant one. The oft-cited verse "where two or three are gathered in my name, there I am in the midst of them" (Mt 18:20) is, in fact, most perfectly fulfilled on Calvary: Mary the Mother of Jesus, Mary of Cleophas, Mary Magdalen, and John are gathered at the foot of the Cross, and Jesus is there in the midst of them, really, truly, substantially present in the offering of His precious Body and Blood to the Most Holy Trinity for our salvation.

altar of Mine. This, in effect, is what is meant when, using another language, you speak of My Mother as Co-Redemptrix. Our two hearts formed but a single holocaust of love in the Holy Spirit.[27]

This remarkable passage places emphasis on the *unity* of the sacrifice of Christ and His Mother. The account in St. John's Gospel, while it testifies to that unity, also portrays the difference between the principal agent, Christ the Eternal High Priest, and the members of His body, Mary and John. They, too, are offering the unblemished Lamb, but not in the same way in which He is offering it in His very Person, in agony on the gibbet. John is a priest, to be sure, but this one time, on Good Friday, he is assisting "in choir." Mary, too, as we have seen, is greater than any priest, but she does not dare to "compete" with the high-priestly act of her Son. In fact, she would never take upon herself the gift and mystery that Jesus bestowed on His apostles when He made them priests, namely, the power of acting *in persona Christi capitis*, on behalf of Christ the Head of the Church.[28] As *Theotokos* she is greater than that priestly role, yet during her pilgrimage on earth she willingly subordinates herself to it, out of reverence for her Son, whose image is borne by the priest. In the beginning Mary received Jesus directly from the Father, but after the institution of the Most Holy Eucharist, Mary received Jesus from the hands of John, when he gave her holy communion until the time of her Assumption.[29]

The trio of Jesus, Mary, and John at the Cross is the Church's liturgical life in its primordial form and perennial source, and we see in it the *mysterium fidei*, the mystery of sacrifice, charity, handing-over, and continuity, of motherhood and sonship, of unity and diversity, of anticipation, consummation, and perpetuation. Everything that is right about the traditional liturgical praxis of the

27. A Benedictine Monk, *In Sinu Jesu: The Journal of a Priest at Prayer* (Kettering, OH: Angelico Press, 2016), 168.

28. The hierarchical relationship of the priesthood and the laity is comparable to that of husband and wife, which Pius XI compares to the relationship of the head and the heart in the body: see Encyclical Letter *Casti Connubii* (December 31, 1930), §27.

29. There is a parallel to this under the Cross, when she received the lifeless but still divine Body of her Son from St. Joseph of Arimathea.

Church—her "orthodoxy" in its original meaning[30]—may be found exemplified in this icon. Everything that is wrong with contemporary praxis, in its confusing tangle of artificial archaeologisms, novelties, deformations, banalities, and overall dullness or flatness, finds here at the foot of the Cross its bitter but health-giving medicine, the cure of a severe mercy that cuts off our foolish experiments. Our Lord is asking us today to imitate the prodigal son who, having wasted his great inheritance, his patrimony, woke up from his stupor and returned to his father, who re-established him in the family with a lavish sacramental feast.

We can highlight one last aspect of Calvary. There may have been a certain amount of background noise—the rough talk of Roman soldiers casting dice for garments, the occasional jeering of a scribe or a Pharisee—but the impression one gets from reading the Gospel accounts of the Passion is that of an eerie stillness, a pervasive silence that wrapped itself around the mountain like the dark cloud of Sinai. When Jesus speaks, it is a voice cutting through the silence, sounding the deep thoughts of crucified Love, like a cataract of water splitting the rock of hard hearts and saturating the tissue of soft hearts. One is reminded of the atmosphere of a private Low Mass or a Solemn High Mass in the traditional Roman Rite: there is a sovereign stillness in the former, and a majestic authoritative utterance in the latter, that forces one to pay attention: *O vos omnes, qui transitis per viam: attendite et videte*, "O all ye that pass by the way, attend, and see…" (Lam 1:12).

We can be certain that there was not a lot of didactic chatter going on at the foot of the Cross. There is something tremendously disturbing about the Martha-like busyness, the lack of focus and "sonority," and the almost Anaxagorean mixture of roles that characterize the reformed liturgy.[31] As Cardinal Sarah has recently reminded us (echoing many other imploring voices over the years),

---

30. See note 25, page 48.

31. According to the Presocratic philosopher Anaxagoras, nothing is wholly and purely what it is, but everything has a little of everything else mixed in with it. This was how he attempted to explain the observable fact that one substance comes from another: if everything is already *in* everything, anything can come from anything. The liturgical parallel is not hard to see: it is rare to find a modern liturgy in

a Roman Rite liturgy without substantial silence that emerges from *within* its very structure and spirituality is a liturgy that fails to confront us with the mystery of God, fails to integrate us in ourselves as sons of God, and fails to connect us with each other as members of His Mystical Body. Pope Benedict XVI says:

> The word [of God], in fact, can only be spoken and heard in silence, outward and inward. Ours is not an age which fosters recollection; at times one has the impression that people are afraid of detaching themselves, even for a moment, from the mass media. For this reason, it is necessary nowadays that the People of God be educated in the value of silence. Rediscovering the centrality of God's word in the life of the Church also means rediscovering a sense of recollection and inner repose. The great patristic tradition teaches us that the mysteries of Christ all involve silence. Only in silence can the word of God find a home in us, as it did in Mary, woman of the word and, inseparably, woman of silence. Our liturgies must facilitate this attitude of authentic listening: *Verbo crescente, verba deficiunt.*[32]

Any silence and stillness in the modern Roman liturgy would be a welcome change from the non-stop verbiage and busyness; yet there is a problem from which we must not glibly turn aside, namely, that the old liturgy bears silence within itself as it rests at the feet of Christ, like Mary of Bethany, while the new liturgy must accrete silence to itself as a momentary rest from labor, like Martha taking a breather. In the reformed liturgy, silence, when it exists, is usually an awkward pause or caesura introduced at the fault lines of the modules out of which the sequential liturgy is composed. For example, a priest after the homily will just sit there for a while, expecting

---

which anyone is wholly and purely what he or she is supposed to be and nothing else, allowing each role its own integrity. This contradicts *Sacrosanctum Concilium* §28, but few Catholics pay attention to *that* document—least of all progressives who airily invoke it as a blanket justification for their liturgical opinions and practices.

32. Benedict XVI, Post-Synodal Apostolic Exhortation *Verbum Domini* (September 30, 2010), §66. The last phrase may be translated "when the Word of God increases, the words of men fail."

the congregation to soak in his words of wisdom. This is an artificial type of liturgical silence. Real liturgical silence arises when a priest or other minister is performing his ministerial actions silently or *sotto voce,* so that the people can, as it were, hold on to the hem of his garment and join in the action. Fr. James Jackson lays out the difference:

> The silence that the priest maintains here [in setting the veiled chalice on the altar and opening the missal at the start of Mass] and in different places in the sacred liturgy is not an absence of sound. It has no gaps; it is a single great canticle, and the silence acts as an acoustic veil over the whole liturgy to reveal what the liturgy is. The Gregorian Rite has no artificial introduction of silence into the liturgy by the addition of pauses. When silence is at the beck and call of the celebrant, as opposed to the rite, the silence of the priest becomes the whole congregation waiting for him, wondering what is going to happen next. The silence in the Gregorian Rite is given as an integral part of the Mass, determined by the Church through two thousand years of development. And what often seems like silence in our rite is not quite silence; it is rather the priest praying to God in a low voice.[33]

One might call this a "pregnant silence" because it is part of the ritual and filled with its own meaning. The bad kind, in contrast, is somewhat like a stillbirth or a wind egg. Think of it this way: a Buddhist could sit still for a long time, but this would not be Christian silence; and similarly, a priest could sit still for a long time, but this would not be *liturgical* silence. As William Mahrt explains:

> There are dead silences and live silences. Sometimes we are told that there must be silence in the liturgy, and so the priest sits down and nothing happens, and everybody waits for him to stand back up again; that is a dead silence. On the other hand, in a concert of a great piece of sacred music, at the end of the piece there is a hushed silence; no-one dare applaud for several seconds; this is the first instant in which the entire piece has been heard and its full beauty

---

33. James W. Jackson, F.S.S.P., *Nothing Superfluous: An Explanation of the Symbolism of the Rite of St. Gregory the Great* (Lincoln, NE: Fraternity Publications, 2016), 97.

recognized. At that point everyone can say, "Oh, that is what the whole piece looks like, its beauty is awesome." That silence is a very important instant, a communal activity. It is a live silence that is full of meaning, so much so that one might be tempted to despise the person who starts the applause and breaks the silence. Similar silences occur in the liturgy, for example, at the consecration, after communion, and after the gradual and alleluia.[34]

Given that only the traditional liturgy requires the use of the full interlectional chants at High Mass, the silent Canon, and sufficiently thorough ablutions to allow for quiet time after communion, while the modern liturgy is prone to dead silences, we see once again that the restoration of a crucial dimension of liturgy is directly bound up with the recovery of the *usus antiquior*.[35]

I would add that when liturgy is bereft of the "sober inebriation" that arises from the use of Gregorian chant, and, in general, when liturgy is deprived of the *splendor veritatis* of beauty that befits it, we are far less likely to be stirred out of our complacent secularity or pacified in our noisy agitation. Lacking the resources of tradition to engage our senses, imagination, and intellect, we may attend the banquet but miss out consistently on the sweetest and headiest wine, which is tasted only in meditation and contemplation. To those who enjoy these resources of tradition, on the other hand, one may apply the joyful words of the psalmist: "They shall be inebri-

---

34. William P. Mahrt, *The Musical Shape of the Liturgy* (Richmond, VA: Church Music Association of America, 2012), 161. Needless to say, by the "alleluia" he is referring to the authentic melismatic chant found in the old liturgical books, not the peppy "Gospel acclamation" of recent coinage.

35. Of course, the Byzantine tradition does not privilege silence in the same way as the Western tradition has done, but this is one of those deep differences between rites that we need to understand, respect, and preserve. The continuous singing in the Divine Liturgy is one form of worthy doxologizing, and the Roman custom of stretches of silence alternating with chant and polyphony is another form of worthy doxologizing. To think that there should be only one manner of public worship is tantamount to maintaining that there should be only one liturgical rite for all Christians and only one way of celebrating it, an opinion that is superficial in the extreme, not to say impious. Needless to say, there *should* be only the historically developed liturgical rites, not committee-invented ersatz rites; genuine diversity does not include arbitrariness or creativity.

ated with the plenty of Thy house; and Thou shalt make them drink of the torrent of Thy pleasure" (Ps 35:9).

The Wedding at Cana

We all know the story of the wedding feast at Cana—the huge embarrassment about to occur if it becomes known that the wine has run out, the gentle intervention of Our Lady, the provision of copious amounts of the best wine by Our Lord's first public miracle.

We stand to learn a number of things from Cana. Notice the marvelous attentiveness of Mary, her eye for detail, her mindfulness of what is happening around her. "They have no more wine" (Jn 2:3), she says to her Son quite simply, without panic or loquacity. She is completely present to the people, the celebration, the needs of the moment. In this she exemplifies for us that when we are celebrating the mystery of Our Lord's marriage with the Church on the Cross, a mystery made present in the Holy Sacrifice of the Mass, we too must strive to be attentive, mindful, careful, totally present to what we are doing, so that we may give due honor to the Lord and receive from Him an ever-greater understanding of the ceremonies, the gestures and words, the ministers and the things they work with, so that our love of the Bridegroom might be intensified.[36] There is an old saying: *age quod agis,* that is, really *do* what you are doing—give it your whole mind and heart. When we approach the altar, when we assist at Mass, we should bring to it this Marian disposition of total "availability."[37] For ministers in the sanctuary, this obviously means knowing our role as well as we can and focusing on what we are doing *as* we are doing it, in an intelligent and prayerful spirit. For laity in the pews, it means preparing well for Mass, learning more about the liturgy and making an effort to pray it, so that we can assimilate more fully the spiritual riches it contains.

But there is a further lesson at Cana, too, one that is still more

---

36. There are many fine resources we can use. Among the best is Fr. Jackson's book *Nothing Superfluous,* mentioned just above.

37. The philosopher Gabriel Marcel speaks of *disponibilité,* the ready willingness to "dispose of oneself" in service of another.

pertinent to our times. Our Lady notices the problem of the moment: "They have no more wine." She has, one might say, correctly interpreted the signs of the times. The families who planned the wedding, no doubt people of good will with the best of intentions, messed up in their calculations. Their attempt at celebration is rushing towards failure, and only the Lord can save it from disaster. So, too, at the time of the Second Vatican Council, the bishops planned a wedding of Catholicism with modernity, and the liturgical reform devised a new type of "celebration" so as to involve the guests more actively in the drinking and dancing. We may assume plenty of good will, but all the good intentions in the world do not, of themselves, guarantee good wine—the good wine of orthodoxy, which means right worship as well as right doctrine. The conciliar wedding feast, which had been billed as a new Pentecost, quickly ran out of wine in the postconciliar period, to the humiliation and consternation of all, including Pope Paul VI who lamented on June 29, 1972 that "from some fissure the smoke of Satan has entered the temple of God."[38] Vast numbers of guests have long since fled the feast. What, then, is to be done?

First, we must admit that Our Lady's diagnosis is exactly correct for us, too: "They have no more wine." Our calculations, our modernizations, have failed and we desperately need help from a different source than the *aggiornamento* on which we had relied. In spite of the cottage industry of Vatican II triumphalism ("the new springtime," "the new Pentecost," "the great grace bestowed on the Church in the twentieth century," "a sure compass by which to take our bearings," etc.), the ruse is difficult to maintain in the face of doctrinal vaporization, moral libertinism, ossified abuses, yawning indifference, and cultural vacuity. "I know thy works, that thou hast the name of being alive: and thou art dead. Be watchful and strengthen the things that remain, which are ready to die. For I find not thy works full before my God" (Rev 3:1–2).

---

38. A transcript of his words has never been published, but a summary with selective quotations may be found at the Vatican website, including this phrase, which is attributed to Paul VI as a direct statement: "da qualche fessura sia entrato il fumo di Satana nel tempio di Dio."

Second, she says to us, as she said to the servants at Cana: "What-soever he shall say to you, do ye" (Jn 2:5). As with her great *Fiat*, we find in these words a lucid reflection of the spotless mirror that is Mary's soul, she who always does what He says, who always submits to whatever He demands, even when it costs her everything. She knows that her Son can supply the way forward, can provide the new wine that is urgently needed.

And what will the Lord say to His Church today? He will say what He has said to her in every age, with merciful clarity and consis-tency: He will speak nothing other than the very Word of God, in Scripture and Tradition, without any attenuation, diminution, dis-tortion, or extraneous elaboration. This is the wine that is new not because it was made just a few minutes ago but because it flows from the New Adam, the New Song;[39] it is perennially fresh, eter-nally true, delighting the taste of the inward man; it never goes sour, and one never tires of drinking it. Whatsoever he says in Scripture and Tradition, *this* we must do, must believe, internalize, and act upon, without fear of what others will say or think. If the Lord says that marrying someone who is already married is adultery, which can never be allowed, we will accept it without contradiction. If the Lord says that riches are a danger to the soul and that we are not to seek after them, we will embrace His poverty and not promote unbridled capitalism. If the Lord says that all power in heaven and on earth has been given to Him and that we are to make disciples of all nations, we will accept His Kingship over individuals, families, societies, and states, and not dabble with the poison of liberalism and its axiom of the necessary separation of Church and State, which St. Pius X condemned as "a thesis absolutely false, a most pernicious error."[40] Most importantly, because it touches most inti-mately on His very flesh and blood, soul and divinity, we will accept, embrace, and revere His holy mysteries as they have been handed down to us in the liturgical rites of Holy Mother Church—

---

39. St. Clement of Alexandria calls Jesus Christ "the New Song." See *Source Readings in Music History*, ed. Oliver Strunk (New York: Norton, 1950), 63.

40. St. Pius X, Encyclical Letter *Vehementer Nos* (February 11, 1906), to the bish-ops and people of France.

rites organically developed over the centuries under the unfailing guidance of His Holy Spirit.[41] "Jesus Christ is the same yesterday and today and for ever," as it says in the Epistle to the Hebrews (13:8), and He speaks to us the same Word yesterday and today and for ever: the infallible and inerrant word of Scripture, and the unshakeable foundation of apostolic Tradition, expressed through and supported by ecclesiastical traditions that the Church had always venerated until her leaders, caught up in the antinomian spirit of the 1960s, succumbed to the allurements of modernity.[42]

Let us dwell for a moment on this last point, namely, the historically famous veneration of the Church of Rome for its own heritage, the jealousy of Rome for its rites and doctrines, to which we may compare the attitude of Eastern Christians towards the Byzantine Divine Liturgy and the testimony of the Church Fathers. It seems to me that this is simply the ecclesial translation of the innermost spirituality of the Blessed Virgin Mary, who "kept all these things, and pondered them in her heart." Note well how much is packed into that first phrase:

(1) She *kept* all these things, held on to them for dear life, and did not dare to discard them.

(2) She kept *all* these things: she did not sort through them and chuck out what did not suit her, or bothered her, or challenged her, or baffled her, but preserved them all in her heart, in her prayer, in her life. We see this attitude notably in the finding of Jesus in the temple, an occasion on which His Mother seems to express a tender

41. The Lord promised that the Holy Spirit would lead His Church into the fullness of truth. Since the truth of Christ is most of all proclaimed and efficaciously communicated to us in the sacramental rites, there is no area of the Church's life more protected and more guaranteed to be full of truth than her liturgical and sacramental life, *as long as* one is looking at that life as it actually unfolded under the reign of the Holy Spirit, rather than as it was artificially dissected and refashioned by scholars operating by false principles of modern thought and under the false assumptions of the Corruption Theory and the Pastoral Theory (see note 15 on page 41). To *their* work, it is not clear that one may ever attribute the guidance of the Holy Spirit.

42. For an excellent discussion of the different types of tradition and why all of them are important (even if some are more changeable than others), see Chad Ripperger, *Topics on Tradition* (n.p.: Sensus Traditionis Press, 2013), esp. 2–35.

reproach: "Son, why hast thou done so to us? Behold thy father and I have sought thee sorrowing" (Lk 2:48). Yet only a few verses later, we are told that "his mother kept all these words in her heart" (Lk 2:51). Her reaction to the bewildering mystery of her Son is to take it into her soul and cherish it. What a lesson for us, who have been spoiled into thinking that everything should be immediately accessible, free of difficulty, and not demanding of us a long apprenticeship!

(3) She kept all *these* things. In the Judeo-Christian tradition, one does not engage in a generic keeping, a receiving of just anything, it matters not what. Rather, one keeps "*these* things," the deeds of God on behalf of Israel, and the mysteries of Christ on behalf of mankind. It is a specific preservation of what has been concretely given. It is like one's proper name, the name that expresses the irreducible singularity and mystery of the individual person. The Mother of God is named by her parents "Mary," not "the Eternal Feminine" or the "Earth Goddess." Her son is named "Jesus," not "Redeemer" or "Moral Teacher" or "Hero" or "Ideal."[43]

Instead of looking to Mary our Mother and imitating her tenacious "keeping," we have looked too much to modernity, the spirit of which is not merely in tension with but *contrary* to Mary's virtues and her contemplation as the Seat of Wisdom.[44] What she keeps and ponders is ultimately her Son, eternal and incarnate Wisdom, in all the richness of his individuality, the scandal of his particularity. For this reason, Buddhists or Muslims cannot receive and keep as Mary did, and as we ought to do. They ponder things, to be sure, but these things are either errors or half-truths. They are not the deeds of the God of Abraham, Isaac, and Jacob and the mysteries of God Incarnate, Jesus of Nazareth, the Christ of Israel.

What is true for the Blessed Virgin Mary is true for all Catholics:

---

43. Our Lord addresses His Mother as "Woman" from the Cross. However, this is not a generic label meant to replace her personal name, but a symbolic declaration of her role in salvation history, her being the New Eve and the mother of all the living—that is, the woman in whom the mystery of the Church is fully embodied, by whom it is perfectly achieved, and through whom it is perpetually nourished.

44. See William G. White, "Modernity vs. Maternity," *Homiletic & Pastoral Review* 97.10 (July 1997), 61–64.

we have a concrete historical tradition, not a jumble of generalities and platitudes. Our traditional Catholic practices emphasize this fact. Kneeling, while intelligible as a sign in itself, also relates to the humble adoration of the Magi and St. Mary of Bethany anointing the feet of Jesus. *Ad orientem* worship, while intelligible as a cosmic symbol, points to the transcendent God who has revealed Himself to Israel as a thrice-holy consuming fire and as the Orient who breaks in upon the world and will return from the East.

The same combination of universal intelligibility and the "scandal of the particular" is found in the great historic liturgies of East and West. Coming to birth in a particular place, time, and culture, they are highly definite, individualized, unmistakably what they are and nothing else, and over the centuries, they develop a characteristic depth, a sort of "personality," owing to the various influences that act upon them. At the same time, they show a remarkable capacity to be transplanted by missionaries to new places, times, and cultures, where they captivate and shape new peoples for Christ. The very density of their substance contains and conveys the religious signs to which man was created to respond, by the grace of God acting on his natural faculties. In their variety, the traditional Eastern and Western liturgical rites give polyphonic utterance to the unity, holiness, catholicity, and apostolicity of the Church of Christ. Each has its peculiar strengths; no one of them can be mistaken for any other. Once they have solidified, as it were, into their final forms, one does not attempt to mix them: one does not mix up the Byzantine and the Roman, or the Roman, the Ambrosian, and the Mozarabic. Each has to be respected for the concrete tradition it embodies. Those who belong to a certain rite enjoy the privilege and the duty of receiving it, caring for it, preserving it, and passing it on to their descendants. And, although tradition does not derive from us, it does *depend* on us: if clergy and laity do not transmit whole and entire that which they have received, God may allow it to perish in a certain portion of the Church on earth.[45]

As Roman Catholics, we inherit the Roman Rite. This rite is the

45. See Joseph Shaw, "Does Tradition Preserve Us, or We the Tradition?," published at *LMS Chairman,* October 13, 2015.

most ancient of all, going back to a period so early that there was not yet any dispute among Christians about the divinity of the Holy Spirit, which explains the lack of an *epiclesis* in the Roman Canon. It was simply not needed; the entire theology of consecration is different. For the early Christians in Rome, it was enough to ask the Father to do something (in this case, convert the bread and wine into the Body and Blood) because He is pleased with the Son. If the Father grants His paternal blessing, the effect follows irresistibly. It was only later, in response to the Eastern heresy of Macedonianism, that Byzantine Christians thought it desirable to invoke the divine Spirit to bring about the conversion of the gifts. The mid-twentieth century fad of introducing epicletic prayers into Western liturgies—and even worse, of creating new anaphoras where they had never existed before—reflects not only recklessly irresponsible scholarship but a profound betrayal of the apostolic tradition of these liturgies. We are dealing, once again, with an anti-Marian stance: rather than keeping these particular things that the Lord has entrusted to us, we pick and choose, mix and match, invent and discard.

If, therefore, we wish to be like Mary, Catholics of the Roman Rite should receive, keep, and ponder *the Roman Rite* as it has developed organically over time, since it is the embodiment *for us* of the deeds of God and the mysteries of Christ. It is our *liturgical* "scandal of the particular." Just as Jesus was not everyman or no man but *this* male Israelite, born of the house of David in Bethlehem, reared in the village of Nazareth, a mendicant preacher who was put to death as a malefactor by Roman authorities, so too, the Roman Rite is not an open-ended, infinitely malleable structure for liturgical experimentation, but a rite of truly noble simplicity that originated in a tiny area of Italy and grew, slowly but surely, into a magnificent tree bedecked with Gallican ornaments. Benedict XVI hints at this rich identity of the Roman Rite in the opening paragraphs of the Apostolic Letter *Summorum Pontificum*:

> Among the pontiffs who showed that requisite concern, particularly outstanding is the name of St. Gregory the Great, who made every effort to ensure that the new peoples of Europe received both the Catholic faith and the treasures of worship and culture

that had been accumulated by the Romans in preceding centuries. He commanded that the form of the sacred liturgy as celebrated in Rome (concerning both the Sacrifice of Mass and the Divine Office) be conserved. He took great concern to ensure the dissemination of monks and nuns who, following the *Rule* of St. Benedict, together with the announcement of the Gospel illustrated with their lives the wise provision of their *Rule* that "nothing should be placed before the work of God." In this way the sacred liturgy, celebrated according to the Roman use, enriched not only the faith and piety but also the culture of many peoples. It is known, in fact, that the Latin liturgy of the Church in its various forms, in each century of the Christian era, has been a spur to the spiritual life of many saints, has reinforced many peoples in the virtue of religion and fecundated their piety.

It is, in other words, perfectly and absolutely itself and nothing else. Its unique Canon, its ancient lectionary, its cycle of propers and orations, its calendar, all these things make it to be itself and nothing else.

Consequently, the rejection, manipulation, or transmogrification of this rite by Roman Catholics is nothing less than an act of violence against their own identity, a kind of institutional suicide. Since the evolution of liturgical rites is always under the guidance of the Holy Spirit[46] and it cannot be maintained by any faithful Catholic that the Holy Spirit was absent from the Church for the 400 years between the promulgation of the Missal of Pius V and the promulgation of the Missal of Paul VI (much less that He was absent from the development of the liturgy in the period from St. Gregory the Great down to the Council of Trent), it follows that the "wayward

---

46. See Pius XII, *Mediator Dei* §61: "Ancient usage must not be esteemed more suitable and proper, either in its own right or in its significance for later times and new situations, on the simple ground that it carries the savor and aroma of antiquity. The more recent liturgical rites [he is speaking of the Tridentine period] likewise deserve reverence and respect. They, too, owe their inspiration to the Holy Spirit, who assists the Church in every age even to the consummation of the world. They are equally the resources used by the majestic Spouse of Jesus Christ to promote and procure the sanctity of man." From these premises Pius XII goes on to condemn antiquarianism.

and philistine reform"[47] of the liturgy as it took place under Annibale Bugnini, tainted by a combination of antiquarian and modernist principles, rejected the scandal of the particular, disowned the concrete historic tradition of Catholicism, forsook the theology of the Council of Trent,[48] and in all of these ways, offended the Person of Our Lord Jesus Christ, who entrusts Himself to us through the authentic rites and traditions of the universal Church. The meltdown, the hardships, the crises through which the Catholic Church has passed since the Second Vatican Council are divine chastisement for this act of unprecedented hubris against organic continuity with the apostolic rite of Rome. "He hath scattered the proud in the conceit of their heart" (Lk 1:51): this, I believe, would be Our Lady's commentary.

That the vast majority of the over 2,000 prelates who discussed liturgical reform and signed their names to *Sacrosanctum Concilium* had no intention of endorsing a massive liturgical sea change is a fact acknowledged by all who have studied the Second Vatican Council in any detail. They were reassured by the document's explicit statement that "there must be no innovations unless the good of the Church genuinely and certainly requires them; and care must be taken that any new forms adopted should in some way grow organically from forms already existing" (*SC* §23). *Sacrosanctum Concilium* itself exhibits the scheming of Annibale Bugnini and his team in its many loopholes and in the systematic wiping-out of

47. Hugh Ross Williamson, quoting Christopher Sykes, in Joseph Pearce, *Literary Converts: Spiritual Inspiration in an Age of Unbelief* (San Francisco: Ignatius Press, 2000), 351.

48. On this point, the 1969 document of Alfredo Cardinal Ottaviani, Antonio Cardinal Bacci, and a group of Roman theologians has lost none of its incisiveness: *The Ottaviani Intervention: Short Critical Study of the New Order of Mass,* trans. Anthony Cekada (West Chester, OH: Philothea Press, 2010). Even though the flawed first edition of the *General Instruction* was revised, the rite that enshrined the reformers' principles and intentions was left untouched. There is, of course, an abundant literature on the ways in which the new rite fails to respect the canons, anathemas, and pastoral recommendations of Trent and the determinations of other magisterial pronouncements. A good summary may be found in Sire, *Phoenix from the Ashes,* 226–86. Michael Davies' *Cranmer's Godly Order* and *Pope Paul's New Mass* remain classic treatments of the subject.

its internal references to preceding magisterial documents right before the final vote.[49] Like all sins, such deeds are their own punishments and bring still others in their train. That these same prelates only a few years later could accept an upheaval in the entire system of Catholic worship shows the extent to which a heady combination of 1960s revolutionism, ultramontanism, cowardice, groupthink, and wishful thinking can deceive even the elect: "They destroyed the cities, and they filled every goodly field, every man casting his stone: and they stopped up all the springs of waters, and cut down all the trees that bore fruit" (2 Kgs 3:25). Fortunately, Our Lord in His unfailing goodness raised up the minor and major prophets the times demanded, who kept the flame of tradition burning in the midst of the descending darkness.

I spoke earlier of a "marriage between the Church and modernity." Fortunately, every metaphor has its limitations. The Church is not *actually* wedded to modernity; the Church is wedded to Jesus Christ. But in recent decades it would seem that all too many Church leaders have attempted a second marriage, wishing to exchange the sweet yoke of Christ for the harsh burden of intellectual fashion, the ever-elusive "relevance" that leads to supreme irrelevance. For fifty years we have seen an embarrassing infatuation with modernity, an ill-starred romance, and as with all extramarital liaisons, this one, too, must come to an end. In this season of grace, the Lord Jesus is calling His Church on earth to return once more, with humility and repentance, to her first love. He waits patiently for her conversion from the vain pursuit of worldly idols to the stability of sacred Tradition.

---

49. The final draft of *Sacrosanctum Concilium* seen by the Council Fathers contained copious citations of five key documents on sacred music: Pius X's *Tra le sollecitudini* (1903), Pius XI's *Divini Cultus* (1929), Pius XII's *Mediator Dei* (1947), Pius XII's *Musicae sacrae disciplina* (1956), and the Instruction *De musica sacra et sacra liturgia* (1958). However, these citations were removed without explanation from the text on which the Council Fathers were asked to vote. For a full account, including the conciliar document with the original citations restored, see Susan Benofy, "Footnotes for a Hermeneutic of Continuity: *Sacrosanctum Concilium*'s Vanishing Citations," *Adoremus Bulletin* 21.1 (Spring 2015): 8–34, available at https://adoremus.org/bulletin/spring-2015/.

Our Lord ordered the great stone jars of the ages of faith to be filled with tradition. His servants carried out the command—*impleverunt eas usque ad summum,* "they filled them up to the brim" (Jn 2:7)—and He worked His first miracle. The reaction of young Catholics "who have discovered this liturgical form, felt its attraction, and found in it a form of encounter with the Mystery of the Most Holy Eucharist particularly suited to them"[50] is reminiscent of the head steward's at Cana: *Tu autem servasti bonum vinum usque adhuc,* "but thou hast kept the good wine until now" (Jn 2:10). "Wine also in abundance and of the best was presented, as was worthy of a king's magnificence" (Est 1:7). After the poorer wine of the Novus Ordo, we rejoice in the delicious heady draught of the traditional Mass. It comes to the lips of young people today as something fresh, new, and extraordinarily good. For us, too, it is a "beginning of miracles" (Jn 2:11), the sign of the hour of Jesus. We might have attended Mass all our lives without falling in love, without even being aware of what we were doing, but when we meet the heavenly Bridegroom dressed in His royal robes, when we glimpse the High Priest offering His holy oblation in peace, when we behold "the glory of the Lord and the beauty of our God" (Is 35:2), then we are bewildered, fascinated, roused up, enthralled, inflamed. "Thou hast made known to me the ways of life, thou shalt fill me with joy with thy countenance: at thy right hand are delights even to the end" (Ps 15:11). So many of us can relate to Michael Kent's description of his protagonist:

> For him Mass now took precedence over all things; he was absorbed and possessed by it; he could think of nothing else. A day which did not have its origin and center in Mass, was a day lost. More, a life which did not derive its meaning and its reason from the Holy Sacrifice, was equally lost. Here was the beginning and the end of everything, the Life of all life, the Beauty surpassing all beauty, to live without which was death indeed.[51]

50. Benedict XVI, Letter to Bishops *Con grande fiducia.*
51. Michael Kent [pseudonym of Beatrice Bradshaw Brown], *The Mass of Brother Michel* (Milwaukee: Bruce, 1942), 65.

In conclusion, I would like to make a brief remark about the current situation of the Church. It is hardly coincidental that the tremendous moral and doctrinal crisis through which the Church is now passing, where some of her shepherds are calling into question fundamental truths about marriage and the family, is occurring in a body of believers who have been habituated by fifty years of liturgical change into thinking that the most sacred mysteries, the most awesome realities of our Faith, are subject to our control, our desires, our "better ideas," our duty to modernize everything in a vertiginous *aggiornamento.* "You have looked for much, and, lo, it came to little; and when you brought it home, I blew it away" (Hag 1:9). Such attitudes and the reforms that enshrined them have contributed to a loss of basic reverence towards *mysteries received,* such as human life, the existence of two (and only two) complementary sexes, the fruitful love of man and woman, the once-for-all redeeming death of Christ on the Cross, the sacraments of the Church, and time-honored liturgical rites. If we cannot revere our own tradition, which is the result of so many centuries of prayer, devotion, piety, and intelligence operating under the influence of the Holy Spirit, why should we revere *anything* that is said to be a "given"? Natural law stands or falls with divine law, and our apprehension of nature itself stands or falls with our acceptance of the true Christian religion.[52] If we desire the restoration of good morals, we must first restore the virtue of religion, the foremost of moral virtues, by which we offer God fitting worship along the path of tradition. By doing this, we signify our intention to surrender ourselves to Him

---

52. It is true that we have *some* innate apprehension of nature and natural law—without it we could never recognize the truth of divine revelation. It is no less true, however, that our fallen condition occludes our vision and warps our judgment. As St. Thomas says, many important truths accessible to reason will only be discovered by a few of the brightest men, only after a long time, and with an admixture of error (*Summa theologiae* I, q. 1, a. 1; cf. I-II, q. 94, a. 6). God in His love reveals the truths we must know and the law by which we must live. These truths and this law are expressed in and inculcated by the traditional sacred liturgy: *lex orandi, lex credendi, lex vivendi.*

as our first beginning and last end; we abandon the Enlightenment folly of taking ourselves as the point of origin and arrival.[53] Within the safety of the Church's tradition, in the intimate encounter with the glorified Christ who suffered for our sins, we will find again the illumination and the strength to live righteously.

Our Blessed Lady shows us the best way, the true way, the holy way. It begins with "Be it done unto me according to Thy word," culminates in her adoring and co-redemptive silence at the foot of the Cross, lingers lovingly in her life of Eucharistic communion, and finds completion in her glorious Assumption, where she—the very personification of the heavenly Jerusalem and its ineffable liturgy—is taken up by the hand of her Son and led into His eternal wedding feast. Let us follow her with all our hearts, as we walk confidently in the Marian spirit and power of the traditional Latin liturgy.

---

53. In the words of Denis Diderot: "Man is the single term from which one must begin, and to which all must be brought back." Cited in Dena Goodman, *The Republic of Letters: A Cultural History of the French Enlightenment* (Ithaca, NY: Cornell University Press, 1996), 26. Cf. Hull, *Banished Heart,* 218–19.

Cum averterit Dominus captivitatem plebis suae,
exultabit Iacob et laetabitur Israel.

When the Lord shall have turned away the captivity of His people,
Jacob shall rejoice and Israel shall be glad.
<small>PSALM 13:7</small>

4

The New Liturgical Movement: Urgent Care for a Sick Church

I HAVE A PERSONAL LIBRARY chock full of books of liturgical theology and popular devotion from the mid-nineteenth century to the eve of the Second Vatican Council. As I have studied these works over the years, one thing has filled me with growing melancholy: the vast majority of these authors, in their publications before the Council, evinced a deep and tender love of the traditional liturgy of the Church. They knew its every phrase, gesture, and chant, its vessels and vestments, the intricate lines of its rich historical development, the delicacy of its minutiae no less than the grandeur of its broad features. They desperately wanted the faithful to appreciate *just these treasures.* Through indefatigable labors of preaching and publishing, they dedicated their lives to making known the secrets and splendors of the Church's public worship, which had tended to be locked away as the preserve of specialists. Dom Prosper Guéranger's monumental *The Liturgical Year* opened up the treasury of Catholic worship to countless souls—a benefit it still confers. What the Liturgical Movement sought, above all, was this: intelligent, active participation of the faithful *in the traditional liturgy of the Church*—not in some other kind of liturgy.

To put it provocatively, many famous proponents of the Liturgical Movement would be classified as traditionalists today. Were you to take their major writings and quote portions of them chosen more or less at random, without attribution of authorship, probably 90% of readers or more would peg the authors as ultra-conservative or even "rad trad." It is not as if these authors lack innovative or problematic ideas;[1] it is not as if some of them did not go off the deep end in the mid- to late sixties, as did so many priests, monks, sisters, and nuns in the same period. Rather, it is because *we ourselves,* in our liturgical thinking and practice, have deviated so far from Catholic tradition that even the more daring proponents of reform in the mid-twentieth century can nowadays look moderate, restrained, and old-fashioned compared to the voluntaristic chaos in which the local churches find themselves today. Some of the better theologians saw the destruction coming and rued the day. Perhaps the best-known example is that of Fr. Louis Bouyer, who, although he had been an eager and sometimes intoxicated participant in the Liturgical Movement, later diagnosed and bitterly lamented the suicidal trajectory the reform had taken.

Judging from the vast quantity of their publications, most of which are now regrettably forgotten, the pioneers of the Liturgical Movement worked for greater awareness of the *meaning* of the rich tapestry of prayers, rituals, and symbols; for greater congregational singing of the responses and the easier chants of the Ordinary of the Mass (and this really is attainable and worthwhile, as I have seen in decades of experience as a choir director); and for a generally more solemn character for the liturgy, so that there would be an appropriate rhythm of Low Mass and High Mass, reflective of the ebb and flow of the Church's liturgical year, with its feasts and ferias. They wanted the people to be knowingly and lovingly involved in the celebration of the mysteries, not as "detached and silent spectators," to use a phrase from Pius XI,[2] but as engaged participants—engaged, however, in the complex and subtle manner appropriate for human persons: interiorly and exteriorly, in mind, heart, and body, with voice and silence, acting when appropriate, but also, and more fundamentally, receiving, listening, watching, absorbing. *Et si inclinav-*

---

1. Fr. Anthony Cekada speaks at length about some of these problematic ideas in *Work of Human Hands: A Theological Critique of the Mass of Paul VI* (West Chester, OH: Philothea Press, 2010), 13–47. I do not share the author's conclusion regarding the validity of the modern rite of Mass.

2. Pius XI, Apostolic Constitution *Divini Cultus* (December 20, 1928). The pope is not criticizing Low Mass here but stating that the faithful should join in the singing of the parts that pertain to them at High Mass.

eris aurem tuam, excipies doctrinam: et si dilexeris audire, sapiens eris. "If thou wilt incline thy ear, thou shalt receive instruction: and if thou love to hear, thou shalt be wise" (Sir 6:34).

In all of these goals, the pioneers were disappointed, indeed repudiated. Such theologians as Romano Guardini and Louis Bouyer deserve to be considered the fathers not of the superficializing revolution that took place, but rather of groups now dedicated to the liturgical apostolate, like the Priestly Fraternity of Saint Peter or the Institute of Christ the King; and such writers today as Joseph Ratzinger, Alcuin Reid, and Uwe Michael Lang, not Annibale Bugnini, Piero Marini, or Kevin Irwin, merit to be called the legitimate heirs of their theology.

In its late cancer phase, the Liturgical Movement turned into second-rate modern(ist) theology embedded in a prosaic, unimaginative spirituality, with a frightful naiveté about sociology and worship, a lopsided *ressourcement*, and the defects of advocacy scholarship and narrow agendas, such as an archaeologism that does not seek to match the external elements recovered from early Christianity with the cultic mentality and the demanding spirituality underlying them.

Let us consider just this last aspect, as does Catherine Pickstock in her book *After Writing*.[3] Are we trying to make a mockery of ourselves by talking about returning to the practices of the early church? Are we ready to restore solemn penances—the sending out of penitents on Ash Wednesday and their public reconciliation on Maundy Thursday? Shall we revive the severe, humiliating ancient penances that were a regular part of the Church's daily life? Are we ready to begin each Mass with a slow and beautiful procession down the main aisle, accompanied by the chanting of psalms? Are we prepared to heap incense upon the burning cinders, and fill the church with the sound of men's choirs? Are we really willing to follow St. Paul and the whole ancient tradition by forbidding roles to women in public worship? Are we ready to have bishops pronounce, in the

---

3. See Catherine Pickstock, *After Writing: On the Liturgical Consummation of Philosophy* (Oxford: Blackwell, 1998), esp. 169–252.

context of the solemn Sunday Mass, excommunications on stubborn heretics and apostates? This sort of thing was bread and butter to the early Christians. Or are we trying to get back to the simple "house worship" of the very first generation of Christians? How very convenient that we know so little about those first Christians! We can make things up as we go along, supported by highly imaginative hypotheses and reconstructions—reminiscent of artistic renderings of our distant ancestors, hairy broad-browed cavemen, tossing a log on the bonfire—so that unhistorical and revolutionary agendas may be cloaked under an appearance of scholarly authority and pastoral solicitude.

On one occasion a friend and I were talking about whether the laity have a vocation to the mystical life, a question that had been hotly debated in the decades prior to the Council. It is sadly ironic that the *Catechism of the Catholic Church* gave, for the first time, an official positive answer,[4] when never before in the history of the Church has there been so little in her liturgical life to foster asceticism, contemplative prayer, and mystical gifts. The same *Catechism* notes that one's conscience can be properly heard only when a person is "sufficiently present to himself," a "requirement of interiority ... all the more necessary as life often distracts us from any reflection, self-examination or introspection" (n.1779). The *Catechism* describes Sunday as "a time for reflection, silence, cultivation of the mind, and meditation which furthers the growth of the Christian interior life" (n.2186). It describes the prayer of adoration thus: "Adoration is the first attitude of man acknowledging that he is a creature before his Creator. It exalts the greatness of the Lord who made us and the almighty power of the Savior who sets us free from evil. Adoration is homage of the spirit to the 'King of Glory,' respectful silence in the presence of the 'ever greater' God" (n.2628). All of these statements correspond perfectly to the world of the *usus antiquior*, but almost never to that of the *usus recentior*. The old liturgy opened to many serious Catholics a path of asceticism and a path to contemplation. Its beautiful stillness, pregnant silences,

---

4. *CCC*, n. 2014.

nourishing prayers, poignant gestures, and (in those fortunate locales where a musical revival had occurred) its exquisite chant melodies made the regular life of public worship a continual schooling in the prayer of the heart, a repeated call to ever deeper penetration of the mysteries of faith, a recurrent opportunity for exercising the theological virtues, a convivial context for receiving higher graces from God.

All saints agree that the mystical life is founded upon a healthy asceticism. Where is this asceticism present in the new liturgy? Are the Ember Days and Rogation Days celebrated? Is the pre-Lenten season of Septuagesima observed? What of the daily Lenten fast and the multitude of days of abstinence? Why were the *character* of the Lenten collects and postcommunions so radically altered away from the constant theme of detachment from the world, salutary hatred of self, contrition for sins?[5] The changes, which are many and significant, represent a practical repudiation of the fullness of ascetical spirituality, and thus a closing-off of the steep and narrow path of mystical initiation attained at the cost of intense spiritual warfare and discipline. The ancient liturgy is *truly* ancient: it breathes the spirit of the martyrs and confessors, Fathers and Doctors, monks and hermits, mystics and ascetics. "Hath not the Lord made the saints to declare all his wonderful works, which the Lord Almighty hath firmly settled to be established for his glory?" (Sir 42:17).

---

5. See Lauren Pristas, *The Collects of the Roman Missals* (London/New York: Bloomsbury T&T Clark, 2013), 113–58, 217–22. The traditional Roman liturgy relentlessly asks for the grace to keep the Lenten fasts, which it assumes will be our way of asceticism during these forty days, in imitation of Our Lord in the wilderness. By the time the liturgical reform was under way, many Catholics were no longer seriously fasting. What was the solution chosen? Not renewing the effort to teach and preach about fasting, to prompt a rediscovery of this ancient spiritual discipline; rather, age-old prayers were discarded or rewritten to edit out fasting and replace it with vaguer language. In this case, modern man simply redesigned the liturgy to accord with his laziness, instead of humbly submitting to its message of self-discipline. If someone objects: "The Church still encourages fasting; no one is preventing you," I will admit that I am a weak sinner and I need the Church to *require* me to fast. When she demands it, I force my intractable nature to submit. Left free to choose, I am likely to take the easier path. I believe this is true for the vast majority of people.

Where is that spirit today? Which Catholics are coming face to face with it, week after week, day after day?

Pierre Hadot wrote an influential book entitled *Philosophy as a Way of Life,* showing that philosophers of antiquity were more than mere intellectuals; they were striving to be, you might say, saints of the rational life, mystics of *logos,* priests of *sophia.*[6] The traditional Catholic already has his Way of Life: it is the ancient Liturgy, the Church's worship enriched, perfected, solidified over time to serve as a foundation of rock on which to build the interior castle. In this school of endless subtlety and abiding simplicity, he finds an entire way of life which encompasses and transcends the truths and blessings of human or philosophical wisdom. The liturgy gives him at once a broad and clear teaching on holiness and an inexhaustible wealth of new insights, new layers of meaning he may never have noticed before but which are already present in the texts he has always known. The liturgy is where he goes for his identity, purpose, and strength. He does not think of changing the liturgy to conform it to himself; he rather strives to conform himself to the liturgy, to be formed by it and for it, so that Christ Jesus may be formed in him.[7]

This is what the original Liturgical Movement was all about; this is the work the new Liturgical Movement is called to continue.

In the new climate of open and honest discussion of the documents of the Second Vatican Council, we might genuinely wonder about the wisdom of *Sacrosanctum Concilium* §34, and whether it can be said to reflect the best intentions of the original Liturgical Movement: "The rites should be distinguished by a noble simplicity; they should be short, clear, and unencumbered by useless repetitions;

---

6. Pierre Hadot, *Philosophy as a Way of Life: Spiritual Exercises from Socrates to Foucault,* trans. Michael Chase, ed. Arnold Davidson (Malden, MA: Blackwell Publishing, 1995); cf. idem, *Plotinus or The Simplicity of Vision,* trans. Michael Chase, ed. Arnold Davidson (Chicago: University of Chicago Press, 1993).

7. See two notes above for a perfect illustration of the problem.

they should be within the people's powers of comprehension, *and normally should not require much explanation.*"[8]

First, there is no such thing as a *born Christian,* nor a man naturally attuned to symbolism, especially in our age of asymbolic emptiness, when the most elementary religious instincts have been lost or perverted. Everyone needs to *learn* the meaning of symbols and symbolic gestures. Indeed, one of the most important elements of catechesis is Christian mystagogy, that is, initiation into the meaning of all the aspects of Christian worship. Once a layman has learned the meaning of the rituals, gestures, prayers of the ancient rite, he never needs to have them explained again; they remain deeply lodged in the heart, fecundating his spiritual life. Thus, turning the Council's statement on its head, the liturgy in every respect *must* be explained if it is to have and retain any meaning at all. The statement that nothing should need to be explained refutes itself from the very definition of symbol and ritual, which are *interpretive motions towards God* and cannot be absent from worship unless it degenerates completely into no more than an organized social gathering where greetings and handshakes are exchanged. This kind of formal coffee hour would need no explaining; but it is not worship in any sense of the word, much less the renewal of the Sacrifice of Calvary.

To go further, the Council's statement is strange, for the simple reason that *anything* profound requires explanation, inculcation, catechesis—the liturgy above all, as we see in Romano Guardini's or Ronald Knox's masterful sermons on the liturgy, which they

---

8. Emphasis added. I will not here comment on the inanity of the phrase "useless repetition." All of the repetitions found in traditional Eastern and Western liturgical rites make perfectly good sense symbolically and psychologically. Even those that seem to have originated accidentally, such as the "separate" communion of the people with its own Confiteor, prove in retrospect to reinforce some important truth of liturgy—in this case, the essential distinction between the celebrant as *alter Christus* standing in the place of Christ the Head and the other participants as members of Christ's body. The loss of repetition or its arbitrary reduction has greatly marred the poetry and humanity of the liturgy. If anything, it is the *new* Roman liturgy that introduces useless repetitions, be it the tedious reiteration of the responsorial psalm, the laundry list of general intercessions, or aberrations like the Gloria cast as a refrain with verses. (See also the discussion of repetition in Chapters 9 and 11.)

preached to appreciative congregations. To say that the liturgy should somehow be "transparent" in the sense of requiring no prior formation—something quite contrary to the elaborate initiatory practices of the early Church, which prepared her catechumens with such care—is to aim at an *anti-liturgical* goal, a state of affairs that could be achieved only by the virtual abolition of symbolic ritual action.

To go further still, the traditional Roman liturgy is, in a way, *more* transparent, more immediately understandable than its modern substitute, *because* it is more attentive to the majesty and solemnity of the sacrifice and does not attempt to simplify, and thereby cheapen, the content of worship.[9] I once received a letter from a nineteen-year-old layman who, I thought, captured this point rather well. He wrote:

> One of my observations about the liturgical reality has been that, paradoxically, the Extraordinary Form of the Roman Rite is, in a certain way, more clear and understandable than the Ordinary Form. I first began to consider this because the sacred realities being lived out at Mass are, by their very nature, incomprehensible. The only way to even begin to bring a semblance of understanding of these realities to Catholic people is through symbols in the liturgy. So when one begins to *remove* signs and symbols and figurative language, the ability of the liturgy to speak for itself is reduced. . . . In a sense, the Extraordinary Form is clearer because it is less clear, and the Ordinary Form is less clear because it is more transparent.

Although it ignores the short-sighted goal of "meeting the people where they are," the *usus antiquior* is capable of eliciting an immediate response of a far deeper quality. Catholics who attend the ancient liturgy may come away confused as to the details but filled with a sense of mystery and majesty, aware of the sublime nature of true Christian worship. Provided that they understand the rudiments of Catholic doctrine, they have *seen* and *heard* the mystery of the word of God and the Holy Eucharist; they do not need an immediate explanation of every detail. They will grow into the

9. See Chapter 1.

details over time, especially if the priest does his job by judicious explanations in sermons. In any case, "surely understanding the Mass is the business of a lifetime," quipped the poet David Jones.[10] Evelyn Waugh captured the same point:

> The nature of the Mass is so profoundly mysterious that the most acute and holy men are continually discovering further nuances of significance. It is not a peculiarity of the Roman Church that much which happens at the altar is in varying degrees obscure to most of the worshipers. It is in fact the mark of all the historic, apostolic Churches.... I think it highly doubtful whether the average churchgoer either needs or desires to have complete intellectual, verbal comprehension of all that is said. He has come to worship, often dumbly and effectively.[11]

The real crisis of Catholicism at the time of the Council was not located in its mysteries, rituals, or symbols, which are enduring and life-giving, but in the lack of devotion to them on the part of many of the clergy, which begot a lack of desire to lead the faithful into a better understanding of them—and not with a view to "complete comprehension," which is impossible in any case, but for the sake of *worship*. Perhaps the clergy took the mysteries, rituals, and symbols for granted; perhaps some no longer really believed in them, being caught up in a this-worldly faith, practical, humanitarian, and individualistic. The Consilium of Paul VI thought to solve the problem of the collapse of mystagogy by fabricating a symbolically "obvious" ritual that would explain itself, that would stand in no need of lengthy and gradual initiation. It gave us something nearly devoid of metaphysical richness, aesthetic subtlety, psychological depth, and moral urgency. In a sort of inversion of Catholic incarnational spirituality, the Consilium surrendered to the anti-symbolic, anti-sacral carnality of the modern world, where obsession with the flesh—that is, the palpable, immediate, obvious, no-need-to-be-

---

10. Quoted in Pearce, *Literary Converts*, 355.

11. Evelyn Waugh, "The Same Again, Please," published in *The Spectator*, November 23, 1962 (published also in *National Review* on December 4), quoted in Alcuin Reid, ed., *A Bitter Trial: Evelyn Waugh and John Carmel Cardinal Heenan on the Liturgical Changes* (San Francisco: Ignatius Press, 2011), 38–39.

explained environment of daily experience—clouds over the apprehension of invisible spiritual realities.

In the movie *Into Great Silence* there is a scene where a group of monks are talking and one of them mentions that another monastery has dropped a bunch of its practices in order to adapt to the times. An elderly monk says:

> Our entire life, the whole liturgy, and everything ceremonial are symbols. If you abolish the symbols, then you tear down the walls of your own house. When we abolish the signs, we lose our orientation. Instead, we should search for their meaning . . . one should unfold the core of the symbols. . . . The signs are not to be questioned, we are.

That is monastic wisdom, pure and simple. It furnishes us a lesson that may, in fact, be the most important lesson of all in our age of constant change, planned obsolescence, the myth of progress, the seductions of postmodern pluralism. The liturgy, like the divine revelation out of which it emerges and to which it ministers, is our lifeline to God, giving nourishment to our faith, oil to the fire of our charity. If we lose our hold on the sacred symbols that come to us from the cosmos and from revelation, we will indeed lose our orientation to God; we will tear down the walls that surround us, and will lose our faith, our charity, even ourselves. We must not adapt the signs to ourselves, for that will bring about nothing more than an echo chamber, a hall of mirrors that reflects only us. We must rather conform ourselves to the sacred signs, and be molded by them, for they are the finest tools used by the potter's hands.

For this reason, it is a sovereign, non-negotiable, utterly fixed principle that if a certain long-standing practice has (as people will say) "lost its meaning," we do *not* get rid of it—we rediscover its meaning, and perhaps, as our ancestors often did, we even invest it with a new meaning. Under no circumstances do we abolish it. As Fr. Guido Rodheudt says, apropos the "gigantic purge of traditional treasures" in the 1960s:

> Astonishingly, it never occurred to anyone to attempt to encounter what had been forgotten by remembering or to regain the lost understanding, or with the devotion of a child for his grandparents

to have the past recounted anew so as to understand it or to learn to love it, because in the tales told by the elderly we have a guarantee that what once was must never sink into oblivion, because it is vitally necessary for today. Especially when—as with liturgical treasures—it is a question of forms that developed in this way and only in this way, so that they might timelessly unite man with the eternal, regardless of where and how he lives.[12]

In reality, *nothing* "automatically means" this or that: human beings still have to *learn* the language of symbols, just as an infant has to learn how to breastfeed, then crawl, walk, speak words—even if all of this is natural to us and will usually happen in due course. Because we are aesthetic-linguistic creatures, the use and recognition of symbols together with a certain delight in them is natural to us, but the sheer variety, subtlety, and density of symbols, together with supervenient meanings established by convention, require a lengthy education, or, better, initiation. It is for this reason, among others, that so much great literature of the past is becoming increasingly inaccessible to modern young people: they do not have the intellectual equipment, or sometimes the first-hand experiences, required for relating to the elements and connecting them into a coherent whole. They don't "get it"; it doesn't "speak to them."

By the modern logic of cutting out symbols that no longer speak to our contemporaries, one might very well end up with nothing left. "Candles? Oh yes, those were an important source of light to people before electricity. But since we now have electric lightbulbs, candles don't really speak to us anymore. It's just an expensive affectation."

"An altar? Oh yes, that was fine when people still had primitive ideas about bloody sacrifices to angry gods and that kind of thing, but now that we know Jesus just wants a family meal, we should really have a table in the center so people can gather around it and share."

"Incense? Oh yes, people used to imagine prayer rising up like smoke to God in the heavens, but that's a naïve idea that modern

---

12. Guido Rodheudt, "Pastoral Liturgy and the Church's Mission in Parishes—The Dangerous Hermeneutic of a Concept," in Reid, *The Sacred Liturgy*, 273–89, at 279.

astronomy has proved false. God is everywhere and he knows our hearts, so we don't need to burn smelly things to him."

Such argumentation is superficial, since it does not look to the *nature* of the symbols, the way they function as metaphors of fundamental human and cosmic realities. The candle does not merely give light: it burns itself up to give warmth; it flickers responsively to the gentlest motion of air; it pushes away the darkness in its immediate vicinity while leaving the outer darkness; it is comforting to behold and to feel, yet capable of catching other things on fire and burning painfully. Something like this is true of a multitude of religious symbols: the thing out of which the symbol is built may have practical uses, but the burden of its message, a convergence of divine and human interpretation, extends far beyond utility into the highest mysteries of existence. It is not a realm of practical value, but of understanding and loving. Every great symbol is this way, including those that are more distant from our everyday world, that demand a certain interior expansion or journey. Symbols strange, remote, ambivalent, perplexing are often the symbols we need the most, if we are to grow spiritually.

To those who would perpetually adapt the liturgy to modern man, changing it and stripping it down as they go along, Fr. James Jackson makes this rejoinder:

> Does the fact that we no longer see shepherds and flocks every day mean that such images are no longer comprehensible? Is it because no one at our parish has ever met a seraph that the metaphorical power of this messenger no longer speaks to us? Half of all the poetry ever written makes use of images and terms that are not part of daily life. These words and symbols are a part of a biblical and liturgical mother tongue that simply cannot be replaced. It is a language that must be learned, not replaced. Divine realities only gradually yield their full significance. So understanding the liturgy is a lengthy and progressive process of becoming familiar with a particular reality. This is one of many reasons why the liturgy must have a great stability, not just in texts but also in gestures, vestments, and music.[13]

13. Jackson, *Nothing Superfluous*, 2–3.

This "great stability" makes possible a lifelong engagement with the symbols and the mysteries they simultaneously veil and reveal.[14] William Durand, the great 13th-century commentator on the liturgy, says at the start of his magnum opus, the *Rationale Divinorum*:

> Whatever belongs to the liturgical offices, objects, and furnishings of the Church is full of signs of the divine and the sacred mysteries, and each of them overflows with a celestial sweetness when it is encountered by a diligent observer who can extract *honey from rock and oil from the stoniest ground* (Deut 32:13). . . . I, William, bishop of the holy church of Mende, by the indulgence of God alone, knocking at the door, will continue to knock, until the key of David deigns to open it for me (Rev 3:20), so that the *king might bring me into his cellar where he stores his wine* (Song 2:4).[15]

What Durand is saying (and goes on to say at some length) is that he *knows* the liturgy is a treasure trove of mystical meaning, a means of purification, illumination, and communion, and so he will knock continually at the door of the Lord, with all diligence and zeal, until he understands everything he can, turning it to his own advantage and that of the flock he shepherds. *This* is the attitude of true humility, of trust in the ways of Providence, of heartfelt surrender to the sacred liturgy so that it may shape us through and through, unto the image of the New Adam. Durand never dares to blame the Church's liturgy for not being self-explanatory; it is up to us to probe its message through dedicated study and prayer for divine illumination.

This, too, is the reason why a full parish life is required to sustain the liturgy and to initiate generation after generation into this sacred inheritance. The formation of the New Adam is a formation of the whole person, the imagination as well as the intellect, the child as well as the man, the family as well as the individual, from cradle to

---

14. See Chapter 9, "A Perpetual Feast of All Saints."

15. *The* Rationale divinorum officiorum *of William Durand of Mende: A New Translation of the Prologue and Book One,* trans. Timothy M. Thibodeau (New York: Columbia University Press, 2007), 1. This author is also called Durandus, the Latin version of his name.

tomb, before and beyond. As a gem shines more beautifully when placed in a setting of gold or silver, so the traditional Mass is but a part—albeit the most important part—of a whole that surrounds it and endows it with maximal power to form the Christian.

> All the activities of parish life are a preparation for the Holy Sacrifice, or a flowering of it. Because of the sacred nature of the Mass and Holy Eucharist, Catholics require a strong doctrinal and spiritual formation.... Within these [sodalities and confraternities], the faithful have a greater sense of the parish as the locus of their participation in the Mystical Body of Christ.... The parish life in a Fraternity apostolate may be characterized as imbuing Catholic families with a true Catholic identity.... The parish today must also be a bright beacon of light, a sign of contradiction, and a haven for hungry souls in an ever-secularizing world. This mission is carried out first and foremost by the outward expression of its worship of God.[16]

Dom Alcuin Reid has often made a related point: the most curiously neglected passages of *Sacrosanctum Concilium* are those in which the Council Fathers indicate that liturgical reform will be fruitful only if the clergy and the faithful are profoundly immersed in the spirit of the liturgy. Only by a true *formation* in and by the sacred liturgy in all its givenness, objectivity, and splendor can there be authentic Christian renewal and, with it, prudent liturgical reform.

This is what the Liturgical Movement, at its best, was all about; the same marching orders apply to the new Liturgical Movement. We should never forget either our central aim or our primary means—the aim of glorifying the Triune God and saving souls, through the fullest, deepest participation of the faithful in the sacred liturgy. As St. Pius X declared, in words that resound more powerfully than ever:

> Filled as We are with a most ardent desire to see the true Christian spirit flourish in every respect and be preserved by all the faithful, We deem it necessary to provide before anything else for the sanc-

---

16. From a booklet produced by the Priestly Fraternity of Saint Peter for their silver jubilee in 2013.

tity and dignity of the temple, in which the faithful assemble for no other object than that of acquiring this spirit from its foremost and indispensable font, which is the active participation in the most holy mysteries and in the public and solemn prayer of the Church. And it is vain to hope that the blessing of heaven will descend abundantly upon us, when our homage to the Most High, instead of ascending in the odor of sweetness, puts into the hand of the Lord the scourges wherewith of old the Divine Redeemer drove the unworthy profaners from the Temple.[17]

Yet another reason for *Summorum Pontificum*, which has inaugurated the liturgical renewal that the Second Vatican Council attempted but, thanks to the snares of ideology, failed to achieve. Choked by "the cares of the world, and the deceitfulness of riches, and the lusts after other things entering in" (Mk 4:19), the seed of the Liturgical Movement did not bear its promised fruit. Today, wherever the organic liturgy of the Church of Rome still continues on its way, that original seed has been replanted, and fruits are being harvested, thirtyfold, sixtyfold, a hundredfold.

In the liturgy, man is most active, he is most fully acting as man—and he is most receptive, most fully acted upon by God, in order to be divinized. In liturgy, the desire of man to be the master of his fate is actualized in a surprising way: by giving himself to God in the way God has determined, man denies his disordered concupiscence, overcomes his self-destructive autonomy, and draws one step closer to that immortality of bliss for which he longs. All this is truly his work, albeit not exclusively or even primarily his work, for God is the principal agent who brings us into the mystery that infinitely exceeds our created powers, and the gifts He pours into the soul are His alone to bestow and sustain. Although liturgy is the greatest act of man, it is never an act of man *by himself,* but the action of Christ the High Priest, true God and true man, who allows and enables us to participate in His theandric action, His all-sufficient Sacrifice for

17. St. Pius X, Motu proprio *Tra le Sollecitudini* (November 22, 1903).

the salvation of the world. Liturgy is therefore a peculiar kind of action, one in which man is also most *passive,* in the sense of being utterly receptive to the gift God wishes to give him, through the hands of the Church.

If, in league with the radical branch of the Liturgical Movement that populated the Consilium and constructed the modern liturgy, we were to fall into a way of thinking about liturgy as a kind of permanent workshop, an evolving sphere of self-expression, a communal celebration of the people, by the people, for the people, *then* we would truly be guilty of neo-Pelagianism. We would be making ourselves the central agents or actors—activists instead of imitators of the Virgin Mary who received the angel's greeting, gave her consent to the divine initiative, and conceived by the Holy Spirit to bring forth the ultimate gift to mankind: the Son of God, in flesh and blood. The liturgy and its music have and must have this Marian dimension of receptivity, a virginal intention to stay untainted by the profane world and a faithful mothering of the Word-made-flesh.[18]

One important expression of our Marian receptivity is that we receive the liturgy from the Church and her Tradition, we do not create it, and we follow her rubrics and rules, not our own. There *are* norms, rules, standards, because the public worship of the Church does not belong to us, it belongs to her Master, the Lord she worships.[19] In his endlessly insightful *Heresy of Formlessness,* Martin Mosebach defends the much-abused "rubricism" of the tradition:

> Many people regard the rubrics as the most distinctive—and most problematical—feature of the old Missal. . . . Rubricism stands for

18. See the preceding chapter, as well as Chapter 11.

19. Although "duty" has been given a bad name by Immanuel Kant, rightly understood it remains a fundamental reality of Christian life. It is our *duty,* as Catholics, to follow the Church's doctrine and discipline concerning the liturgy. For example, when it comes to sacred music for the Novus Ordo Mass, one may not simply ignore the full teaching of the Second Vatican Council, the *General Instruction of the Roman Missal,* and other documents such as *Sacramentum Caritatis* that allot a prominent place to Gregorian chant in singing the Ordinary and the propers. It is, nevertheless, much easier to do this in the sphere of the *usus antiquior,* where the requirements are so clear and consistent.

a liturgy where all subjectivism, all charismatic enthusiasm, all creative inventiveness has been condemned to silence.... Public prayer, not the prayer of the individual but of the Church's whole Mystical Body, possessed a binding quality that, in an atmosphere of emancipation from all pressure whatsoever, could be felt as a kind of dictatorship. Now, however, after more than a century of the destruction of forms in art, literature, architecture, politics, and religion, too, people are generally beginning to realize that loss of form—almost always—implies loss of content.... Formerly, seminarians learned rubrics so well they could perform them in their sleep. Just as pianists have to practice hard to acquire some technique that is initially a pure torture, but ultimately sounds like free improvisation, experienced celebrants used to move to and fro at the altar with consummate poise; the whole action poured forth as if from a single mold. These celebrants were not hemmed in by armor-plated rubrics, as it were: they floated on them as if on clouds.[20]

Detailed and demanding rubrics ensure that the priest remains a servant—a servant, moreover, of the liturgy as a work of exquisite art that must be rehearsed, internalized, and handled with care. Ryan Topping concludes:

If you no longer see yourself as the servant of a tradition, but as its master, no longer believe that the rubrics veil a mystery, that the soul requires truth to be wrapped in the garment of beauty, then reasonably you are likely to treat the Mass more as a gathering of friends than as a sacrifice of God.[21]

Is this not, alas, precisely what has happened, in spite of the noble witness and teaching of St. Pius X and many of his holy successors? There is such holy sanity in these words of Dom Mark Kirby:

To begin with the liturgy is not to set about tinkering with it; it is to submit to it, as it is. To begin with God is not to engage in a critical analysis of theology; it is to fall prostrate saying, "The Lord he is God, the Lord he is God" (1 Kgs 18:39). To begin with adoration

---

20. *Heresy of Formlessness*, 204, 206.
21. Ryan N.S. Topping, *Rebuilding Catholic Culture: How the* Catechism *Can Shape Our Common Life* (Manchester, NH: Sophia Institute Press, 2012), 77.

is, in the inspired words of the Cherubic Hymn of the Byzantine Divine Liturgy, "to lay aside all earthly cares" in homage to "the King of Kings who comes escorted invisibly by Angelic hosts."[22]

It sounds like an examination of conscience we might pursue: Do we truly *begin* with liturgy as something first, something that preexists us and will continue long after we are gone, rather than something we master, manufacture, produce, shape at will? Do we *submit* to the liturgy, not as we think it should be for "modern man," but as it has come down to us from holy tradition, passing with remarkable resilience and stability through centuries of doubt, dismay, and disaster like a strong ship sailing over the churning waves of a stormy sea? Is our most characteristic action to fall prostrate before the mystery and majesty of God as He deigns to reveal Himself in the ritual words, actions, and signs that He has left among us? Dom Paul Delatte eloquently contrasts the modern reformist mentality with the Catholic stance of faith and grateful acceptance:

> Those who doubt and deny win immediate fame. And the deference refused to tradition, to antiquity, to authority, is given at once and wholly, with infinite thoughtlessness, to the notions of some writer or other, to one of those prophets of the hour who trumpet the vague phrases: progress, evolution, broad-mindedness, and dogmatic awakening. This is intellectual foolery. And it seems to me that good sense and dignity require from us not only an attitude of reserve, but above all a spirit of tranquil resistance and conservatism. Conservation is the very instinct of life, a disposition essential for existence. We shall be truly progressive if we hold fast to this spirit, for there is no progress for a living organism which does not preserve continuity with its past.[23]

Traditionalists might think that such questions need not be put to them, as if they are "covered" by their faithful adherence to traditional forms. This may be an incorrect assumption. We, too, must examine ourselves to see if we are following the full teaching of Holy

---

22. Dom Mark Kirby, O.S.B., "The Supreme Rule of the Council," published at *Vultus Christi*, February 20, 2013.

23. Delatte, *Commentary on the Rule*, 310.

Mother Church in all that pertains to our offering of public worship. For example, in our zeal to set aside a superficial understanding of active participation, are we zealous to embrace St. Pius X's clarion call for the participation of the people in the singing of the Gregorian chants of the Ordinary and the responses that belong to them in a High Mass? Are we careful, as we sift the good results of the Liturgical Movement from the bad, not to throw out the baby with the bathwater? Would St. Pius X, Pius XI, and Ven. Pius XII, among others, recognize us as their children, as the ones who have taken their magisterium to heart and made it shine forth in the world, for the spread of the light of Christ?[24]

The immediate work facing most of us is to offer the sacrifice of praise in either form of the Roman Rite, as they now exist, with as much beauty and solemnity as possible, according to our circumstances, in continuity with the best of our tradition. Surely, in whatever capacity we serve Our Lord, we may consciously strive, in all the ways at our disposal, for the "due solemnity" that befits the celebration of the Church's sacraments and liturgies. Nothing less is worthy of our King to receive, nothing less is fitting for man to give. Assenting to this judgment requires a lofty conception of liturgy and how it is constitutive of man's Christian identity. In Christ, we live and move and have our being; it is no less true, indeed it is rather more true for us pilgrims, that we live and move and have our being in the Eucharistic Christ of the liturgy, which is a moving image of Him and a vehicle through which He comes and goes among us.

---

24. I am aware that certain liturgical novelties and deformations found a place in each of these pontificates: the radical overhaul of the breviary under Pius X, the promotion of dialogue Masses under Pius XI, and the violent "revision" of Holy Week under Pius XII. But these moves were atypical of their general teaching on the liturgy, which gave much practical and speculative wisdom to the Church, a wisdom forgotten today or contradicted in the name of progress.

Every liturgical celebration, because it is an action of Christ the priest and of His Body which is the Church, is a sacred action surpassing all others; no other action of the Church can equal its efficacy by the same title and to the same degree. . . . The liturgy is the summit toward which the activity of the Church is directed; at the same time it is the font from which all her power flows.[25]

The Liturgical Movement prior to the Council lamented the fact that Catholics, generally speaking, did not possess an intimate knowledge of the treasure of their liturgy or cherish a particularly intense desire to live "under the sign" of liturgical seasons and feasts. A combination of clericalism and growing secularization had removed many of the faithful from close contact with the sacred mysteries conducted in the Church, and a rift appeared to yawn between the social mission of Christianity in a needy world and the ritual enactment of age-old, august ceremonies. In spite of a whirl of contrary currents in the aula, the view prevailed at the Second Vatican Council that the liturgy is the *fons et culmen* of the Church, the "font and apex" of the Christian life[26]—a conclusion that would surely have sounded fairly strange back then, but not quite as strange as it does now, when it is well-nigh incomprehensible.

One of the most astonishing things about the Catholic Church today is the almost universal indifference of her members (including, all too often, her clergy) to the sacred liturgy as such. Yes, many parish parking lots are full on Sunday mornings. Many of the laity are "involved" in one ministry or another. Plenty of socializing goes on around the Mass—sometimes, indeed, *within* the Mass, and in the pews before and after Mass. Coffee hours are not unknown across the land. And priests work very hard, often at thankless tasks. But when it comes to being "thoroughly imbued with the spirit and

25. Second Vatican Council, Constitution on the Sacred Liturgy *Sacrosanctum Concilium* (December 4, 1963), §7, §10.
26. Or "source and culmination." See Second Vatican Council, Dogmatic Constitution on the Church *Lumen Gentium* (November 21, 1964), §11.

power of the liturgy"[27] or "living a liturgical life,"[28] the evidence for it is sparse.

Have we not known Catholics who, in spite of their sincere faith, do not seem to "get it" when it comes to the liturgy—people who could not possibly agree with the statement that it is the "source and culmination" of who they are, what they do, why they live, where they are going, and how they will get there? An observation attributed to Cardinal George rings true: "American Catholics are Protestants who go to Mass on Sundays." A nefarious combination of individualism and collectivism prevents many Catholics, regardless of their level of education, from perceiving the loss of the liturgical spirit in the context of the Novus Ordo, the loss of the primacy of the transcendent and of adoration. It impedes them, too, from longing for something more authentically Catholic and reaching out for it even when it is available to them in their own neighborhood or even in their own parish. The individualism makes us wear blinkers and settle for a minimal criterion, namely, "what works for me"; the collectivism encourages a herd mentality that blocks common sense, legitimate critical thinking, and the desire for better things.

In the end, it simply seems that other things are more important to contemporary Catholics than the liturgy. It does not come first and last; it does not take precedence and determine the shape of our days, weeks, years. For such Catholics, Vatican II was wrong about the "font and apex" business, just as far too many might say Paul VI was wrong in *Humanae Vitae,* or John Paul II in *Ordinatio Sacerdotalis.*

How, then, might we describe the predominant view, the one we will find in chancery corridors no less than humble homes? It might be summarized thus: the liturgy is one particular means among many for realizing a personal vision of Christian life. The Christian life is a potpourri or hodgepodge of personally meaningful practices, or, at best, a mosaic of tesserae put together with artistic discretion. The note of modern subjectivism here is unmistakable, and

27. *Sacrosanctum Concilium* §14.
28. See *Sacrosanctum Concilium* §18; §42.

perhaps, also, traces of the scattered, isolated, excessively busy nature of modern life. It can be difficult for people to want to care about something outside the family or outside of work, to stir themselves out of their private world to enter the common and objective world of the liturgy.[29]

It is a great irony of the postconciliar period that the Catholics today who are taking the sacred liturgy *most* seriously—the ones who *are,* quite conscientiously, building their everyday lives on it and around it, following its seasons, frequenting the sacraments and using the sacramentals—are, more often than not, the faithful flocking to the traditional Latin Mass, especially where it is offered as the daily fare of a dedicated chapel or parish. The churches where the "unreformed" Mass is celebrated are exhibiting to the Church at large what the Council meant by "living a liturgical life ... thoroughly imbued with the spirit and power of the liturgy." They are largely the ones buying books like Mary Reed Newland's *We and Our Children: How to Make a Catholic Home* and David Clayton's *The Little Oratory.*

Additional ironies include the fact that there is, in many ways, *more* active participation going on in these communities than is normal throughout the mainstream church,[30] that the magisterium of John Paul II on marriage and family and the importance of sacramental confession is being much more consistently implemented in them, and that, by every standard of Catholic identity and mission,

---

29. I am reminded of the words of Heraclitus (ca. 535–475 BC): "For though all things come into being in accordance with this *logos,* men seem as if they had never met with it, when they meet with words and actions such as I expound. ... As for the rest of mankind, they are unaware of what they are doing after they wake, just as they forget what they did while asleep. Therefore one must follow [the *logos,* namely] that which is common to all. But although the *logos* is universal, the majority live as if they had understanding peculiar to themselves." "To those who are awake, there is one ordered universe common to all, whereas in sleep each man turns away from this world to one of his own" (in Kathleen Freeman, *Ancilla to the Pre-Socratic Philosophers* [Cambridge, MA: Harvard University Press, 1948], 24–25; 30). On the public, objective, and (in a sense) non-emotional nature of the liturgy, see the opening chapter of Romano Guardini's *The Spirit of the Liturgy,* trans. Ada Lane (New York: The Crossroad Publishing Co., n.d.), 17–35.

30. See Chapter 8, "How the *Usus Antiquior* Elicits Superior Participation."

they are rock-solid and energetic. Yet how could this be surprising, if what Vatican II said about the liturgy is actually true, and if that truth is put into practice?

Apart from these enclaves, we are still far from recovering a genuinely Catholic perception and experience of the sacred liturgy as *the foundational, central, and definitive activity of the Christian,* the origin of our identity, the purpose of our existence on earth. This is not to say our identity is exhausted in the liturgy or that we do not need to pursue subordinate goods as well.[31] What it *does* mean is that the beginning of our life in Christ is baptism, the perfecting of our spiritual life occurs in and through sacramental liturgical actions, and that the culmination of our friendship with God in our earthly pilgrimage, as well as our most vital means of staying alive, is communion with the flesh and blood reality of Our Lord. Apart from these, we have no life within us, and we have no life to give to the world. We are Christians insofar as we are sacramental, liturgical, and Eucharistic—and not otherwise. Even our corporal and spiritual works of mercy are Christian only if they are thoroughly steeped in the worship of God and the Spirit of Christ, which we drink in through the liturgy of His Church.

What are the prerequisites for living a truly liturgical life? The liturgy demands *time.* One has to be willing to *give up* something—be it extra time in the office, extra time in recreation with friends, extra down time at home. One has to be, at least to some degree, *at peace*—enough to see a need for prayer and meditation as a work more important than the countless "urgent" items of business or pleasure that clamor for attention. One has to believe profoundly in the words of Jesus: "Seek first the kingdom of God, and His righteousness, and all the rest will be given to you" (Matt 6:33). One has to recognize that the formal, objective, public worship offered to God by the Church is in itself far superior to our private prayers, however indispensable the latter are in their own order.

One reason we are further than ever from developing and practicing these habits is that a shallow, horizontal, and mutable modern liturgy cannot be the foundational, central, and definitive

---

31. As Vatican II points out: see *Sacrosanctum Concilium* §9.

activity of our lives as Catholics. It cannot serve the purpose; it is too exiguous, too amorphous, too human, too insubstantial. P.G. Wodehouse would say: "It fails to grip." Not being either the contemplative reservoir of the Low Mass or the majestic pageant of the High Mass, it comes and goes without seizing hold of our imaginations and our hearts.[32] If we continue to attend it week after week, it is from a sense of duty and a fondness for community. If, like increasing numbers of Catholics, we drift away, it is probably because there was not much to drift away from. Modern Catholics have been given "Doctrine Lite" and "Worship Lite," instead of an all-embracing and all-demanding philosophy of life that aims at total immersion in the Mystery of God. The latter is worth living and dying for. But the former...?

As the world darkens, as governments become more openly and oppressively anti-Catholic, and as too many leaders of the Church continue to bury their heads in the sand (rearranging deck chairs on the Titanic is how I have heard it expressed), there is an ever-intensifying realization that our first and greatest responsibility is *getting our own temple in order*. In the famous slogan of Fr. Zuhls-dorf: "Save the Liturgy, Save the World." That is a task to which every one of us can make a contribution, here and now, in smaller or bigger ways, as the Lord gives us opportunity. The new Liturgical Movement will succeed only if we patiently and persistently move ahead, step by step, determined never to give up until our short-term and long-term goals have been achieved. Of each of us, by God's grace, may the praise of the African deacon St. Celerinus prove true: "He overcame his adversary by the unconquerable might of his own struggle, and opened for others the path to victory."[33]

32. See Chapter 10 on the peculiar perfections of Low Mass and High Mass, and how they are lost in the Novus Ordo's two modalities, the "talkie" and the "Low-High."

33. *The Roman Martyrology*, under February 3.

Another Prayer for the Traditional Movement

O Lord our God,
if Thou dost not build the house,
in vain do its builders labor.
We beseech Thee to inspire with Thy Holy Ghost
all those who labor to build up Thy sacred house,
that Thy people may worship truly and fully,
may worthily receive Thy Holy Sacraments,
and may thus be filled with the abundant grace
obtained through these sacred gifts.
Through Our Lord Jesus Christ, Thy Son,
who liveth and reigneth with Thee
in the unity of the Holy Ghost,
God, for ever and ever.
Amen.

Cum autem venerit ille Spiritus veritatis, docebit vos omnem veritatem.
But when He, the Spirit of truth, is come, He will teach you all truth.
Gospel of John 16:13

5

Different Visions,
Contrary Paths

I N THE EARLY TWENTIETH CENTURY, certain Benedictines and
Jesuits conducted a vigorous debate over the centrality of the
liturgy in the Christian life (and more particularly, in the life of
prayer).[1] Faithful to their age-old emphasis on the *opus Dei,* the
sons of St. Benedict promoted the line of St. Pius X that the sacred
liturgy is the "fount and apex" of the Christian life, the point of
departure for all of the Church's pastoral activity and the goal in
which her entire mission culminates. The communal liturgy of the
Church, ripened over centuries of faith, is the highest expression of
the love and wisdom of the Holy Spirit shared between Jesus Christ
and His immaculate Bride. One might say that the "Spirit of truth"
is at home in the liturgy, which is the most visible and most authoritative manifestation of His invisible presence among us. Perhaps no
one has more perfectly expressed this vision than Dom Paul Delatte
(1848–1937), third abbot of Solesmes:

> All particular liturgies center round, are merged in, and draw their
> strength from, the collective liturgy of that great living organism
> the Church, which is the perfect man and the fullness of Christ.

---

1. Foremost on the Benedictine side were Dom Lambert Beauduin, Dom Maurice Festugière, and Dom Columba Marmion; foremost on the Jesuit side, Jean-
Jacques Navatel and Louis Peeters. Dom Mark Kirby has summarized the debate,
with several quotations, in "The Liturgy: Foremost and Indispensable," published
at *Vultus Christi,* June 21, 2014. Cf. Alcuin Reid, "The Twentieth-Century Liturgical
Movement," in *T&T Clark Companion to Liturgy* (London/New York: Bloomsbury
T&T Clark, 2016), 153–74.

The whole life of the Church expresses and unfolds itself in her liturgy; all the relations of creatures with God here find their principle and their consummation; by the very acts that in the individual as in the whole mass realize union with God, the liturgy pays Him "all honour and glory." In it the Holy Spirit has achieved the concentration, eternalization, and diffusion throughout the whole Body of Christ of the unchangeable fullness of the act of redemption, all the spiritual riches of the Church in the past, in the present, and in eternity.[2]

In contrast, the sons of St. Ignatius, heirs of far-flung missions often undertaken by solitary priests, presented the liturgy as one among many tools useful for personal spiritual growth, with private meditation having a certain pride of place. One seeks and finds the Holy Spirit in the individual practice of the discernment of spirits—done, of course, within the framework of Catholic doctrine and under the guidance of the hierarchy, but still, concentrating on the pursuit of one's own vocation in the world, to which formal public prayer is a useful adjunct, more or less dispensable depending on circumstances. On this view, the "truth" into which the Spirit leads us is less the ontological splendor of truth found in the liturgy and requiring our conformity with it, as it is the propositional truth of dogmatic statements and the existential truth of correspondence between a Christian and his calling.

Illuminating in their frankness, the publications and correspondence associated with this debate disclose the principles underlying each side. Nor can there be any doubt that both views have much to commend them; we cannot say that one or the other is simply mistaken. All the same, there is a trend or tendency in the Jesuit approach, an incipient individualism and subtle subjectivism, that was to bear bitter fruit in the passage of time. Pope Pius XII attempted to adjudicate the dispute in *Mediator Dei* by acknowledging the truths held by both schools while fundamentally siding with the Benedictine framework of his predecessors—a judgment that was to linger in *Sacrosanctum Concilium,* whose general liturgical

2. Delatte, *Commentary on the Rule,* 133.

theology is Benedictine.[3] Hence, we may safely say, as a matter of history, that the armies engaged, the battle was fought, and the Pio-Benedictine vision officially prevailed.

But what about the later history, the post-*Mediator Dei* period from 1948 to 1970, when the Liturgical Movement became radicalized, and reform expanded and accelerated from minor matters to major ones, culminating in the Bugnini liturgy? This period exhibits a strange irony. Apparently, the Benedictines won across the board because everyone during and after the Council—beginning with the Consilium reformers themselves—talks about liturgy as if it is the be-all and end-all of Catholic prayer, at times as if it is the *only* kind of prayer Catholics have. Yet within this assumption, what has triumphed is a "creative," devotional, sentimental, largely subjective notion of liturgy, a utilitarian and custom-designed approach that is utterly contrary to the Benedictine vision of liturgy as objective, formal, stable, and received, an external standard to which we are subject and to which private devotions and personal preferences are to be subordinated.[4]

Speaking of the ripple-down effects of the subjectivism of Kantian philosophy, Fr. Chad Ripperger observes: "We often see this immanentization today: people expect the liturgy to conform to their emotional states rather than conforming themselves to an

---

3. See Dom Mark Kirby, "Until Christ Be Formed in Us," *Vultus Christi*, June 22, 2014. I say that Pius XII *attempted* to adjudicate the dispute" because, in *Mediator Dei*, he inverted the *lex orandi* and the *lex credendi* in such a way as to undermine his own position. (See Christopher Smith, "Liturgical Formation and Catholic Identity," in *Liturgy in the Twenty-First Century*, 260–86; Hull, *Banished Heart*, 48–50.) Moreover, although *Sacrosanctum Concilium* enunciates a Benedictine vision, it immediately dilutes or pollutes it with an activism contrary to contemplative virtue, a utilitarianism contrary to beauty, and a mechanistic philosophy contrary to reverence for living tradition.

4. Even when it comes to our personal prayer, we ought to strive for a maximal harmony with the liturgical feastdays and seasons. It would be strange indeed if our prayer life did not register and resonate with the changing seasons of Advent, Christmas, Epiphany, Septuagesima, Lent, Easter, Ascension, Pentecost, which insert us into the life, death, and resurrection of Christ, and the glorious triumph of His saints. As a blogger insightfully put it not long ago: "We should liturgize devotion as far as we can, rather than devotionalize the liturgy, as happened in the last several centuries when Low Mass became the norm, public practice of devotions

objective cult which in turn conforms itself to God."[5] The searing words of László Dobszay come to mind: "The very fact that the bulk of the clergy protests with intense emotions against this return [to *ad orientem* worship] shows its serious *necessity*; the principal motivation behind the protest is not pastoral care of the faithful, but the psychological distress of the priest."[6] I read an eye-opening interview with a priest, a fairly well-known liturgist, who dismissed the Tridentine Mass as a kind of idolatry because of the impersonal ritualism of it, the exalted cultivation of *form*. Everyone has to be so focused on the *rite* that they become idolaters of it, he opined. Some clergy, accustomed to the ever-changing "meaningfulness" of modern liturgy with its "personal touches" and "accessibility" and "relevance," feel chilled by the objectivity and otherness of formal worship in Latin, and the way its ministers and assistants yield their individuality and idiosyncrasies to the rite. In this way they do not seem to recognize the liturgy as a living icon of Christ through which we touch Him and are touched by Him, at once embracing every age of His Mystical Body and bypassing time in the immediacy of His holy presence.

Like a fantastical beast compounded of two animals, the legacy of the post-conciliar reform fuses a Benedictine insistence on the primacy of liturgy with a Jesuitized re-conception of liturgy as collective private devotion. It is as if new Jesuit wine has been poured into old Benedictine wineskins, causing the one to rupture and the other to run waste. The moment of triumph was the moment of disaster, as the very notion of a rite—a formal ritualized act of common

---

replaced the Office, and some odd feasts crept into the kalendar. . . . Again, let us liturgize our devotion so we do not devotionalize our liturgy." While I have no problem with a quiet and prayerful Low Mass for weekdays, it does seem regrettable that High Mass is not much more common than it is, although as more clergy are ordained for the *usus antiquior,* I believe we will see both the *Missa cantata* and the *Missa solemnis* more and more as a regular feature of Catholic life.

5. Fr. Chad Ripperger, "Conservative vs. Traditional Catholicism," published in the Spring 2001 issue of *Latin Mass* magazine and available at http://www.latin-massmagazine.com/articles/articles_2001_sp_ripperger.html.

6. László Dobszay, *The Restoration and Organic Development of the Roman Rite,* ed. Laurence Paul Hemming (London/New York: T&T Clark, 2010), 93.

worship based on a common orthodox tradition—gave way to a pluralistic, relaxed, malleable, and privatized praxis of variations on a more or less Catholic theme. "Behold, the hour cometh, and it is now come, that you shall be scattered every man to his own, and shall leave me alone" (Jn 16:32). The Consilium's exploitation of *Sacrosanctum Concilium* left us with a volatile mixture that makes genuine reform today much more difficult.

Perhaps the most ironic twist in this complicated debate is the contrast between Pope Francis and his predecessor. Although not a Benedictine by profession, Benedict XVI closely identified throughout his career with the monastic vision of the all-pervasive centrality of the sacred liturgy, where God and man meet most profoundly in praise and in communion, expressing and accomplishing the unity of the Mystical Body of Christ. At his first general audience in April 2005, Ratzinger explained that he had chosen the name Benedict as a homage not only to the Pope of Peace, Benedict XV, but also (and, it would seem, principally) to the Father of Western Monasticism, co-patron of Europe and architect of Christian civilization. With the first Jesuit and overseas pope, on the other hand, we have a pastor who appears to hold those modern Jesuit views that Blessed Columba Marmion and other Benedictines, in the name of fidelity to St. Pius X, so stalwartly resisted in the first half of the twentieth century, and that Ratzinger/Benedict himself patiently opposed in his writings and magisterial acts. We have seen the trajectories of the two schools played out before our very eyes in the magisterium, *ars celebrandi,* and priorities of each pontificate.

It is for this reason that the original Benedictine-Jesuit controversy remains of lively interest and importance for us today, if we would better understand the trials through which the Church is passing in this age.

Permanence and Change in the Liturgy

Until it too went off the rails in the fifties and sixties, the Benedictine school accepted the inherited liturgy as a given, as something willed by God in His Providence, and therefore sought to enhance people's understanding of it, so that this gift would bear fruit in the spiritual lives of the faithful. The Jesuit school was more willing to see the liturgy as a human construct, made up of parts we can change, since we fashioned them to begin with. For the Benedictines, the liturgy had something timeless and immutable about it; its text and ritual were a fertile field for *lectio divina* no less than Sacred Scripture was. For the Jesuits, liturgy was steeped in historical accident, a result of processes of transmission, modification, and legislation, characterized more by change than by stasis. Benedictines desired to lead the thirsty flock to a well that never ceases bubbling with fresh water after so many centuries; Jesuits would rather dismantle and build anew, convinced that nothing was more important than reaching people "where they are at," which, in modern times, translated into drastic simplification and adaptation.

The Benedictine tradition has, more fundamentally, the correct view. It is a fact of history that the liturgy changes over time, it develops, but this it usually does slowly, absorbing surrounding influences, in an organic process. Most often, elements are *added* to the liturgy: it grows, expands, like a plant or animal growing towards maturity. More rarely, it demands pruning, which is typically done carefully and conservatively, out of respect for the growth that has come before. In a strictly biological metaphor, pruning might have to be severe to preserve or promote the health of the plant, but in the case of the Church, we believe as a matter of faith that the growth is broadly governed by the Holy Spirit. One need not attribute every detail to the direct inspiration of God, but one could hardly maintain that the development of the liturgy over a long period of time and in its main features was a corruption.

Just as a living organism reaches a point of maturity after which it no longer grows but preserves itself and reproduces its species, analogously, we can expect the liturgy to develop extensively at first, in its infancy, and then to slow down in its rate of growth as it gradually attains perfection of form, fullness of ritual, text, music, and meaning. Thus, the liturgy will develop more in the first 500 years of the history of the Church than in the next 500, and in the first millennium more than in the second. At least before the middle of the twentieth century, it was taken for granted that the rate of liturgical change had slowed as the inherited forms were of ever-greater coherence and completeness. Change, after a certain point, pertains more to accidental or incidental features, such as the cut of a chasuble or the design of a candlestick, than to what is done or what is said. So much was this the mindset that almost anyone could have preached as Msgr. Ronald Knox did in the mid-fifties:

> Yesterday, today, and forever—cast your mind forward to the last Mass that will ever be said on earth. We find it even more difficult thus to transport ourselves into the future [than into the past]; there will be so many novelties, we feel, that we can form no idea of at present. It goes without saying that the Christian liturgy, already so venerable, is less likely than anything else to be modified by the hand of time.[7]

On the other hand, given that man's nature never changes and Christ's sacrifice never changes—given that man, for whom the liturgy is intended, and Christ, whose worthy praise and sacrifice the liturgy makes present and shares with us, do not vary—one might wonder what exactly *would* develop in the liturgy, and why. For one thing, we cannot say there was something inherently flawed about the simpler apostolic liturgies of the early Church, as if they were defective until they received augmentation and amplification over time. Nevertheless, insofar as it is a human activity, the liturgy does not fall ready-made from heaven but is assembled slowly over the centuries by bishops, monks, and other saints privileged with an experiential savoring of the beauty of God, a living contact with divine glory under sacramental veils. While not reducible to an artifact or construct, public worship is shaped and regulated by men who are cooperating with a divinely implanted instinct for holiness and goodness of form.

The essence of the liturgy was there from the beginning, as the oak tree in the acorn, but the fullness of its expression, the richness of its meaning and beauty, took many centuries to unfold before the eyes of Christian man, until he could behold the tree in all its glory and majesty, and taste the sweetness of its fruits most abundantly. In

---

7. Ronald A. Knox, "First and Last Communions," in *The Window in the Wall: Reflections on the Holy Eucharist* (New York: Sheed & Ward, 1956), 120; also in *The Pastoral Sermons*, 284.

this sense, it was not absolutely necessary that the liturgy develop, but it was supremely fitting that it do so—and the Holy Spirit brooded over this development with bright wings, as He led the Church into the fullness of truth (cf. Jn 16:13). The Lord told His disciples: "Truly, truly, I say to you, he who believes in me will also do the works that I do; and greater works than these will he do, because I go to the Father" (Jn 14:12).

Because development comes from the saints *and* slows down over time as the public liturgy of the Church matures into a determinate set of prayers and practices that express the mysteries of the Faith with ever-greater fullness and beauty, it can never be legitimate for the Church to change her liturgy in a radical manner. For to do so would necessarily imply a negative judgment on the "greater works" of which Jesus speaks, a kind of blasphemy against the Holy Spirit by implying that it was not in Christ's name but rather Beelzebub's that the Catholic Church promulgated her liturgy throughout the centuries.[8] Thus, although development is natural and good, a certain *kind* of change—namely, one characterized by sharp discontinuity—would necessarily be bad, a corruption or deviation rather than the flowering of an organic reality.

An essay I once read argued that man's existential identity as pilgrim or *viator* is the reason why the liturgy must change in each generation. The writer, from the Reform of the Reform school, was attempting to explain how there could be room for something as drastically different as the Novus Ordo, while simultaneously upholding the value of keeping the *usus antiquior* available, as stipulated by *Summorum Pontificum.* The proposed solution involved asserting that some modern people needed a more modern liturgy, while others did not and could do fine with the more ancient one.

But the fact that man is a pilgrim is irrelevant to whether the liturgy, as such, should change. After all, man as man never changes; he is always this kind of being, with certain powers in need of certain objects for their perfection. A liturgy imbued with divine and human strength will *permanently suit* this pilgrim being. Nor does his Savior change, or the Sacrifice by which his salvation was (and

---

8. Cf. Pius XII, *Mediator Dei* § 50, § 59, § 61.

is) accomplished. A different kind of liturgy, were it fashioned, would only suit a different kind of being. To have permission to undertake a radical liturgical alteration, there would have to be not merely a substantial change in man—a thing which happens all the time, whenever conception or death occurs—but also an *essential* change, the emergence of a new species, together with the arrival of a new Savior and a new Sacrifice. There is, after all, a Christology latent in every act of worship, in any ritual, utterance, or music.

Liturgy, indeed, is a transitory action, but its origin, meaning, and finality are unchanging. It is a temporal event with a permanent nature, in that respect much like man himself, who comes into being and changes throughout his life and yet always lives by the same immortal soul, which endows him with a singular and everlasting identity. An *individual's* spiritual development takes place within and by means of an *unchanging* liturgy, which acts as a fulcrum for his elevation, a center for his revolutions, a focus for his shifting sight.

Selective Antiquarianism and the Denial of Continuity

The liturgical reformers of the 1960s and 1970s claimed that their decisions were motivated by a desire to recover elements of Christian antiquity and the worship of the "early Church." Hugh Ross Williamson put his finger on the essential absurdity of this position:

> The return to the "primitive" is based on the curious theory of history, sometimes referred to as "Hunt the Acorn." That is to say, when you see a mighty oak you do not joy in its strength and luxuriant development. You start to search for an acorn compatible with that from which it grew and say: "This is what it *ought* to be like."[9]

If one were a collector of acorns, it would make sense to ignore the tree and hunt for the seeds from which it sprang. But in the teaching of Jesus, the kingdom of God—which is made present in our world above all in the sacred liturgy—is not meant to stop at the

---

9. Cited in Pearce, *Literary Converts*, 353.

stage of a seed: "To what is the kingdom of God like, and whereunto shall I resemble it? It is like to a grain of mustard seed, which a man took and cast into his garden, and it grew and became a great tree, and the birds of the air lodged in the branches thereof" (Lk 13:18). When the Lord took the seed, the Idea, from His divine mind and cast it into the garden of the Church, it grew under His beneficent care until it became so great a tree that every nation on the face of the earth could lodge in its widespread branches, which are the many rites and usages of East and West. This fullness of growth is the seed explicated, actualized; it is the seed's *telos* or goal. It may be that a little pruning is needed now and again; one does not, however, attempt to reduce the mature plant to a seed. In his potent critique of the "anti-liturgical heresy," Guéranger notes how heretics always combine idealistic antiquarianism with febrile innovation:

> Without exception, all the sectarians commence with the vindication of the rights of antiquity. They would cut Christianity off from all that the errors and passions of man have mixed in, from whatever is "false" and "unworthy of God." They want nothing but the primitive, and they pretend to go back to the cradle of Christian institutions. To this end, they prune, they efface, they cut away; everything falls under their blows, and while one is waiting to see the original purity of the divine cult reappear, one finds himself encumbered with new formulas dating only from the night before, and which are incontestably human, since the one who created them is still alive.... Their affectation for preaching antiquity succeeded only in cutting them off from the entire past.[10]

Beyond this general critique of the antiquarian mentality, however, we may point to a number of particular problems with it.

First, there is a simple problem: we know relatively little about worship in the apostolic period, and what we know is full of contra-

---

10. Dom Prosper Guéranger, *Institutions liturgiques,* 2nd ed. (Paris: Société genérale de Librairie catholique, 1878), vol. I, pt. 1, ch. 14, n. 4. The translation is adapted from the one provided at http://catholicapologetics.info/modernproble ms/newmass/antigy.htm.

dictory or at least conflicting indications.[11] Scripture gives us some precious insights, but rich detail on liturgical praxis comes much later on, when a significant amount of development had already taken place.

Second, the very fact that significant development *occurred*, and occurred with the approval of the leaders and people of the Church, should be enough to convince us that liturgy, too, is part of that "fullness of truth" into which Jesus promises we will be led by the working of the Holy Spirit (cf. Jn 16:13). Hence, both as plenitude and as truth, it is *impossible* to maintain that the organic development of the liturgy through the centuries results in a corruption from which we must retreat by returning to a prior era or stage of our worship, or that this development reaches a point where it has alienated the people and can no longer speak to them truthfully and effectively of the mysteries of Christ.[12]

Third, the particular ways in which the liturgy grew in reverence, solemnity, and symbolism are no less in God's Providence than the original institution of the Most Holy Eucharist at the Last Supper. Hence, it is *prima facie* illegitimate to suggest that stripping away developments (called "accretions" by the scholars) is a path back to a liturgy that is somehow more perfectly what the Lord intended.

11. See Paul F. Bradshaw, *The Search for the Origins of Christian Worship: Sources and Methods for the Study of Early Liturgy,* 2nd ed. (New York: Oxford University Press, 2002).

12. Absolutely to be included in this claim is the preservation of the Latin language in the West, which is *not* an impediment to the fruitful participation of the people, as we shall argue further along in this book, and as large numbers of Catholics have experienced for themselves. On the other hand, the attempt to apply this argument to the Novus Ordo—that is, to claim that we are not permitted to view it as a corruption that should be abandoned in favor of a healthier stage of the rite—fails because this liturgy is *not* organically developed from the historic Roman Rite but is a committee fabrication from bits and pieces of the Western heritage, with novel material mixed in (e.g., only 17% of the orations from the preconciliar *Missale Romanum* were incorporated unchanged into the Missal of Paul VI: see Cekada, *Work of Human Hands,* 244). Since it is not a development guided by the Holy Spirit, it need not be accepted as the true inheritor of the title of Roman Rite; rather, it is a corruption from which the Church needs to be rescued, much as the liturgical reformers mistakenly believed they were rescuing the People of God from the Dark Age of Counter-Reformation Tridentine Catholicism.

This colossal begging of the question proved to be a fertile source of hundreds of more or less inventive Protestant paraliturgies, each an attempt at reproducing the Lord's Supper in a biblically faithful or at least biblically unobjectionable manner. No one denies that a gentle pruning or careful reorganization of certain aspects of the Church's liturgy has been necessary from time to time, but it is no less certain that the structure, ritual, major prayers, and chants have been left intact out of a humble spirit of reverence for what has been handed down, that is, *traditio.*

We can see the dissembling of the liturgical reformers in the *selectivity* of the ancient elements they retrieved, while ignoring elements they happened not to agree with. If the reformers had sincerely wished to make the liturgy more like what they might have viewed as its "high period," they would, for instance, have re-introduced majestic processions and have preserved or re-established the custom of preaching and chanting from an elevated, ornamented ambo.

If one wishes the "common people" to participate actively in the liturgy, then one will respect the most elementary facts of human psychology: a slowly processing line of beautifully vested ministers gracefully approaching the altar, to the accompaniment of the mighty sound of the pipe organ or the heavenly melody of chant, engages the senses and the soul with a deeper and more lasting effect than an ill-clad priest shyly stepping out of the sacristy door and beginning Mass at a toothpick lectern (as I often saw happen in Europe). Here is the acid test: if any element or aspect of the liturgy does not convey to a young child that this activity is different and special, then it has, at some level, *failed.* The bowing priest reciting the Confiteor, the acolyte swinging a censer, the subdeacon, deacon, and priest hierarchically aligned during solemn Mass, the awesome stillness of the Roman Canon—all of these things speak directly to the heart, even to the heart of a little child who sits still and watches.

Along these lines, historian Henry Sire contrasts the richness of Catholic life centered on a noble liturgy with the barrenness of modernized Catholicism:

> For all the attacks of the pedants, the traditional Catholic liturgy, with its attendant devotions, made up a whole of potent beauty

and imaginative persuasion, which bound souls to the Faith as no rationalist invention does. In its place, the new Mass has set an experience of soul-destroying secularity at the heart of every Catholic's ordinary experience of his faith. The phrase soul-destroying is no exaggeration, for the clearest achievement of the new liturgy has been to drive away millions of the faithful. The old liturgy was a nourisher of souls, the new is a starver of them. And those lost have been especially the young, not least through the versions of the liturgy specially devised for them. It was the old Mass, pointing to a higher world, that captured the imaginations of children and held them for life. The Church in the past kept its faithful because it offered them unmistakably the things that make for conviction: moral truth, clear doctrine, and a beautiful and authentic liturgy.[13]

Organic: Endangered

In conversations on the liturgy, the word "organic" is used to describe the kind of change agreed to be legitimate, necessary, and good, and to distinguish it from the violence of artificial alteration on the basis of ideology. But have we reflected sufficiently on what is meant by "organic"?[14]

It will not, I think, be controversial to claim that there has been an increasing loss of any sense of the organic. The scientific, mechanistic mentality not only produced the age in which we live, but now shapes our way of interpreting the world. We rarely have to wait for fruit out of season; we live in enclosed, controlled environments, from the little boxes on wheels in which we are transported, out of contact with the elements, to the stationary boxes we inhabit and work in. For most of us, everything is instant and prepared for our immediate consumption—food, entertainment, and even knowledge (not wisdom, but "brain content"). Even human relationships become subject to the same expectations. Very few people have had to wait for two or three months before they can harvest something from their farm to take to their table and eat. Many do not prepare

13. Sire, *Phoenix from the Ashes*, 377.
14. For further reflections, see Reid, *Organic Development*, 303–11.

their own food, let alone provide the direct means to heat their homes or water or food, nor do they drink clean water that they themselves had to lift and carry from an outside source. The things that really sustain us are far removed from our regular experience.

In short, we do not have to wait for things to grow; change based on perceived wants or needs is expected to be instantaneous or nearly so.[15] The main metaphor we use to describe ourselves and our work is that of the machine that "runs" rather than the living thing that grows. What is the contrast between the organic and the mechanical? One "takes" time and the other "makes" or saves time. But time is just a constant, is it not? How we use it affects our perception and appreciation of it, or our irritation and frustration with it. The farmer is not impatient with the wheat for taking its time, because he knows it must do so and cannot be rushed. The business-man is perhaps impatient with the train because it is a few minutes late and he is "running behind." Time is (at least in part) in our perception, and a long time or a short time is entirely relative. Important, complex, personal, beautiful, or mysterious things should and often must take considerable time, and they will never save us time. Only a fool would think that we can find shortcuts. Or rather, when we make the shortcuts, we find that we have bypassed the experience.

Organic matter is never preserved unchanged. We attempt to preserve things that are dying or in danger of disintegrating. But organic things have a cycle all their own, living things have a cycle programmed into their very DNA—a component lacking in machines. Part of the organic development is the death of the plant itself, and, over its lifetime, the death of portions of it seasonally.

15. I am convinced that the urge of popes and committees to tinker with the liturgy, altering this, adding that, and suppressing the next, which has been a constant feature of Catholic life for over a century now and has left us with a veritable library of missals and breviaries, is the result not of faults in the liturgy but of the influence of a Baconian-Cartesian mechanistic mentality, which, having become omnipresent in society, finally came to roost within the halls of the Vatican. The idea that growth should be gradual and slow, and that a certain "irrationality" and "inefficiency" is part of God's plan, is grievously irksome to moderns, who are impatient to get on with the business of improvements.

The fig tree has to produce fruit to ensure the continuation of figs in the world. When the plant is diseased, injured, or past its prime, it will not bear fruit but put its energy into the leaves and stalks. The expert vinedresser prunes, sometimes severely, in order that the vine may continue to produce good, healthy, abundant fruit. An inexperienced or careless gardener, in contrast, may cut the plant back to where its very survival is doubtful. It takes a great deal of patience and care to bring the plant back to life from its seemingly dead state and build it up so that it can once again produce fruit. For many people, however, when something appears dead or broken, it is tossed out. We just get a new one, an improved version.

The early liturgical reformers such as Romano Guardini and Josef Jungmann were asking how one might prune the vine of the glorious and ancient Roman liturgy so as make it healthier and more vibrant, renewing in it the capacity to transmit life and sustain vigorous growth and production. Did they arrive at prudent ways to do that? And even if they did, were they not elbowed out of the way by the careless, impatient gardeners who began to cut away until there was little left but the stump? And then the inept gardener did little to tend the plant, adding on a prosthesis instead of living grafts. Indeed, it is quite as if the gardener had decided to become a mechanical engineer, replacing the plants with machines that, externally, performed similar tasks: they unfolded pretty blooms at certain times of year, they released perfumes, they slowly rotated as the sun rotated, they registered temperature and hydration.

But they were not alive. And the bees knew it. They never came to visit these artificial flowers that could offer them no pollen.

The Humility of Tradition

As I read an article on the twenty-fifth anniversary of the Priestly Fraternity of St. Peter, I was struck by a quotation from Father Bisig, the founder of the Fraternity and its first superior general:

> The Priestly Fraternity of St. Peter serves the faithful by retaining Latin liturgical traditions, the Church's source of continuity. This is done, not out of nostalgia or a reactionary disposition, but out

of humility. At the same time, we are called to live joyfully under the paternal authority of the successor of Saint Peter. This is done out of humility as well.[16]

There is profound wisdom in this statement. First, Fr. Bisig notes the plain but so often forgotten fact that the Latin liturgical tradition embodied in the *usus antiquior,* not to mention a host of related devotions and customs, is "the Church's source of continuity." The mission of worship and sanctification entrusted by Our Lord Jesus Christ to His Church on earth was faithfully carried out over centuries, even millennia, through the very forms we now call "traditional." These are the handiwork of the living Spirit of Christ, the repository of His wisdom and power, the participation of His majesty and beauty, and they will for all eternity be, in God's eyes, the way in which the Catholic Church carried out her one and only mission of salvation.

Hence, any liturgy whatsoever celebrated by the Church today *rests upon* and *has its meaning from* the liturgical tradition that preceded it. To adapt an analogy from the Epistle to the Romans, just as the Gentiles are like a wild olive branch grafted onto the olive tree of Israel, so too, the Novus Ordo is like a branch grafted into the age-old Roman tree. If that strong tree had not existed and did not exist, and if its sap were not still and always capable of nourishing the tree, neither could any new branch live and bear fruit. To change metaphors, the work of the Fraternity and other societies and communities dedicated to preserving the Latin liturgical traditions is like that of master gardeners who care for the oldest, most exquisitely beautiful, most precious trees in the orchard of the Lord. As apple and tomato growers know, heirloom varieties give the tastiest fruit.

Fr. Bisig goes on to say that the Fraternity pursues its mission not from nostalgia or a reactionary disposition, but "out of humility." Often traditionalists are accused of being arrogant, of looking down their noses on Catholics who are not holy enough or enlightened enough to prefer the traditional liturgy to the modern one. No doubt such attitudes can be found. But it has been my experience in

16. In *Religious Life: The Magazine of the Institute on Religious Life,* vol. 37, n.5 (September–October 2013).

many different communities and countries that the deepest motivation of a traditionalist is the humility of desiring to *receive* the wonderfully rich tradition of the Church with gratitude, appreciation, docility, and love—the humility to want to be shaped by what the ages of faith and the saints have passed down to us. This stands in stark contrast to the pride of wanting to shape what we do to match ourselves and our age, as if *we* were the measure of all things. Is the sacred liturgy the clay and we the potter? Should it not be the other way around? It is disturbing that so many liturgists and pastors in the last half-century thought they were such expert judges of their (and our) spiritual needs that they could massively alter the centuries-old ways of worshiping bequeathed to us by the Church of our ancestors. *Confusi sunt sapientes, perterriti, et capti sunt: verbum enim Domini proiecerunt, et sapientia nulla est in eis.* "The wise men are confounded, they are dismayed, and taken: for they have cast away the word of the Lord, and there is no wisdom in them" (Jer 8:9). Anyone who can feel easy in his mind about liquidating or tearing up vast swaths of orchards, farmlands, homesteads, in favor of sleek and efficient modern structures and methods, is the one truly lacking in humility, wisdom, mercy, humanity. Evelyn Waugh, who, having died in 1966, was spared the imposition of the Novus Ordo, registered his protest in 1962 at the arrogance of the up and coming clergy of his day:

> I lately heard the sermon of an enthusiastic, newly ordained priest who spoke, perhaps with conscious allusion to Mr. Macmillan's unhappy phrase about Africa, of a "great wind" that was to blow through us, sweeping away the irrelevant accretions of centuries and revealing the Mass in its pristine, apostolic simplicity; and as I considered his congregation, closely packed parishioners of a small country town, of whom I regard myself as a typical member, I thought how little his aspirations corresponded with ours.[17]

Some time ago, *Rorate Caeli* described the careful researches of an expert in the quondam papal liturgy of Rome as a "sorrowful"

---

17. Waugh, "The Same Again, Please," 34.

task because nearly everything he was documenting, "the slow ceremonial growth of twenty centuries," had been cast off:

> The little quirks naturally added and eliminated in such a development were cut off and burned. What generations of popes, bishops, priests, monks carefully pruned and watered was cut by misinformed "liturgists" filled with utmost ahistorical arrogance and anachronistic condescension, who cut off the roots instead.

Where, one cannot avoid asking, is our ability to receive gently, gratefully, humbly, as did the Blessed Virgin Mary? Why must we be the masters and possessors of liturgy? How will we imitate Jesus Christ who said and did nothing but what His Father gave Him to say and do, if we insist on determining what we shall say and doing what pleases us, rather than submitting to the yoke of tradition and the burden of our historical identity, the scandal of the particular?

There is a great humility in preserving what Our Lord, *through* His Church, has given us, yes; but there is also a great humility in submitting to what Our Lord, *in* His Church, has established over us. The love of the Latin liturgical traditions can never, in principle, be opposed to communion with and rightful obedience to the Sovereign Pontiff, the successor of Saint Peter, just as the Pope can never abrogate a longstanding liturgical rite, which is "sacred and great" for all generations.[18] I say "in principle," because history shows us moments of tension *in fact,* and we are living in one such moment right now; but difficulties of season, circumstance, or temperament never touch the essential duties and obligations of both pastor and people. Put differently, the relationship between fidelity to tradition and obedience to authority may be serene and joyful at one time, perplexing and troubled at another, but it is an unbreakable relationship that stands at the center of Catholic identity. If a Catholic gives up either element, in that act he betrays the unity of the Church.

Fr. Bisig, then, has said three very important things, the importance of which I hope and pray will become ever more apparent to

---

18. Benedict XVI, Letter to Bishops *Con grande fiducia.*

Catholics as time goes on, in whatever way, or from whatever source, they come into contact with these truths.

First, preserving the liturgical tradition benefits *all* the faithful, because it keeps alive and active in our midst the source of the continuity of the new with the old, the offspring with the parent, the extrapolation with the origin. Whenever, wherever, and however the new liturgy benefits from the presence of its predecessor, this will be an efficacious sign that it is not, in fact, altogether opposed to it, which would render it illicit. If, on the other hand, the reformed liturgy were to be viewed and celebrated as totally *other,* as a kind of contradiction of the Roman Rite prior to 1969, this would be an infallible sign that something seriously wrong had occurred—a sign of material heresy and incipient schism, regardless of who its proponent may be.

Second, we retain the Roman liturgical tradition out of humility and not out of pride—the humility of loving what has been given to us, not the pride of rejecting what is new or rejecting the authority that can give us new things as well as old, but never the new without the old. For the new without the old is formless and void.

Third, we remain obedient to the legitimate authority of the successor of Saint Peter, again in a spirit of humility. For humility recognizes that there would not be a Church, and we could not receive her treasures, were there not a visible body with a visible head—and this, in spite of any personal tensions or doctrinal difficulties there have been and will be. It is not for nothing, after all, that the emblem of the Fraternity is the keys of Saint Peter with tears falling over them. That is an emblem to which all of us, in this valley of tears, can relate.

Sedebit populus meus in pulchritudine pacis,
et in tabernaculis fiduciae, et in requie opulenta.

My people shall sit in the beauty of peace,
and in the tabernacles of confidence, and in wealthy rest.

Isaiah 32:18

6

Formed in the Spirit and Power of the Liturgy: Reflections on *Summorum Pontificum*

I DISTINCTLY REMEMBER the day of July 7, 2007.

Over the course of the preceding year, there had been a number of amicable but highly tentative discussions about the extent to which the traditional Latin Mass should find a place in the life of the newly established college where I worked, which was to open its doors to students in August 2007. At that time, the Gregorian Rite was the preserve of a vibrant minority of Catholics gratefully receiving the ministrations of Ecclesia Dei communities, along with the occasional Lone Ranger priest who had managed to secure episcopal permission or who had been tapped to provide this service for a group of the faithful. Adherence to the old Mass was slowly growing, but the movement dwelt in the margins, in the shadows.

For our college as for so many communities, the appearance of *Summorum Pontificum* changed the whole conversation, forcefully and yet peacefully. There was no longer any question of whether the old Mass would be welcome at our school; it was a foregone conclusion for those who wished to be obedient to the Magisterium, as we did. Rather, we began working out a practical plan for making it available.

For Catholics loyal to the Church's Tradition, this *motu proprio* meant the end of a sort of Thirty Years' War of outrageously mis-

135

matched armies. It was a surprising triumph for the faithful who had insisted that the ancient liturgy, the Mass of the saints, has and will always have an important place in the Church's life, and who begged to be able to worship God as so many generations had done before. Pope Benedict XVI established equal canonical rights for the two "forms" of the Roman Rite. He did not say they were altogether equal in every way; he noted that the *usus recentior* is more prevalent, while the *usus antiquior* "must be given due honor for its venerable and ancient usage." Nevertheless, for the immediate peace of the Church, what matters most is that, canonically speaking, they are *equal*. After Pope Benedict, the traditional form can never be seen as the ugly duckling, the unwanted stepchild, the nutty aunt of the family, or a radioactive material to be encased in lead. It is part of the living heritage of every Roman Catholic priest, every Roman Catholic believer.

In the United States alone, the growth of the traditional Latin Mass is impressive indeed: from about 20 Sunday Masses in 1988, to 220 in 2006, to somewhere in the vicinity of 500 today. The religious communities that either serve the faithful in active ministry or utilize the old liturgical books in their contemplative life have prospered and grown. As some of their literature has playfully said, the only vocations crisis facing them is the lack of space in which to house their candidates and the lack of money with which to provide for their training. This contrasts painfully with the situation in the mainstream Church, too many of whose leaders are still wandering in the desert of modernity, wondering what happened to the once-filled churches and seminaries, and thinking that "more of the same" has got to be the solution. In reality, it is time for something completely different—something altogether different from the postconciliar *modus operandi*. Something so different ... it is, thankfully, the same as that which the Roman Church has always had for all her centuries, with the natural growth and flux of an organic reality.

The former prefect of the Congregation for Divine Worship and the Discipline of the Sacraments, Antonio Cardinal Cañizares Llovera, made just this point in a preface he contributed in 2013 to a book by Fr. Alberto Soria Jiménez, O.S.B.:

Also to be noted is Benedict XVI's concern to emphasize that the Church does not discard her past: by declaring that the Missal of 1962 "was never juridically abrogated," he made manifest the coherence that the Church wishes to maintain. In effect, she cannot allow herself to disregard, forget, or renounce the treasures and rich heritage of the tradition of the Roman Rite, because the historical heritage of the liturgy of the Church cannot be abandoned, nor can everything be established *ex novo* without the amputation of fundamental parts of the same Church.... But the *motu proprio* also produced a phenomenon that is for many astonishing and is a true "sign of the times": the interest that the Extraordinary Form of the Roman Rite elicits, in particular among the young who never lived it as an ordinary form, [an interest] that manifests a thirst for "languages" that are not "more of the same" and that call us towards new and, for many pastors, unforeseen horizons. The opening-up of the liturgical wealth of the Church to all the faithful has made possible the discovery of all the treasures of this patrimony for those who had not known them—among whom this liturgical form is stirring up, more than ever, numerous priestly and religious vocations throughout the world, willing to give their lives to the service of evangelization.[1]

The New Evangelization will stand or fall on the strength of authentic liturgical renewal, and this renewal will stand or fall depending on whether or not it is rooted in the traditional Latin Mass as an immense good in itself and as a constant point of reference for the modern form, until such time as the modern form can be either thoroughly revised or phased out into oblivion.

It may be conceded that the *motu proprio* and its accompanying letter are not perfect. Even taking *Universae Ecclesiae* into account, some thorny theoretical and practical difficulties remain. For example, if the explicit requirement in canon law that seminarians be well instructed in Latin is routinely ignored, how much hope is there that, on the basis of a papal commendation, they will be taught the traditional Mass, Office, and sacramental rites as a component of their comprehensive training in the Roman Rite? If priests are ordained to celebrate a certain rite, and the Roman Rite

---

1. Translation courtesy of *Rorate Caeli*, July 16, 2014.

currently consists of two forms, how can deacons be said to be qualified for priestly ordination if they are incapable of celebrating half (so to speak) of their rite—and this, the older and fuller half? And will a mere legislative framework adequately defend the rights of priests and the faithful when little or no effort is made to *enforce* the Church's standing law or to protect clergy from misguided superiors? Disciplinary actions of incredible harshness against traditional religious communities and individual priests continue to make headlines. We are far, alas, from the peaceful resolution Pope Benedict wished and worked for; in fact, it would be no exaggeration to say that the Pope's impassioned invitation to his brother bishops has been culpably rejected by many:

> Let us generously open our hearts and make room for everything that the Faith itself allows. . . . What earlier generations held as sacred, remains sacred and great for us too, and it cannot be all of a sudden entirely forbidden or even considered harmful. It behooves all of us to preserve the riches which have developed in the Church's faith and prayer, and to give them their proper place.[2]

In spite of this mixed reception and internecine strife, we still have abundant cause for rejoicing in all that the Lord has done through his servant Benedict and through this courageous incentive to the modern Counter-Reformation. For there can be no doubt that *Summorum Pontificum* has reshaped the liturgical landscape profoundly and permanently.

The most important thing right now is for priests everywhere to live confidently according to what Pope Benedict established as their canonical right—that is, to celebrate the *usus antiquior* for the glory of God in communion with His saints, for their own priestly benefit, and for the spiritual nourishment of their flocks. And to do this means learning the old Mass if they have not already done so— a challenging task, but by no means insurmountable. I have known and worked with several priests who started from scratch and who, having achieved their goal, feel privileged and blessed to be able to offer this venerable rite of the Mass. Instructional resources and

---

2. Benedict XVI, Letter to Bishops *Con grande fiducia*, July 7, 2007.

workshops are abundantly available. Priests, men of God, shepherds ordained for the altar and the flock: take courage, be stouthearted! Respond generously to this great invitation, this movement of grace sweeping through the Church.

A decade has passed since the promulgation of the great *motu proprio* of Pope Benedict XVI, already included in the most recent edition of Denzinger[3] and destined to be seen as one of the most important papal interventions of the modern period. Wherever the *motu proprio* has been received with obedience and put into practice by faithful sons of the Church, the fruits have been marvelous, well-nigh miraculous. Through learning and celebrating the *usus antiquior*, the priesthood of countless priests has been renewed, deepened, focused, enriched, re-connected with the fundamental spirituality of the Roman Catholic Church. This legislative act has provided a timely remedy for the demoralization of the clergy, the desacralization of the liturgy, and the deracination of the Christian people. Thus for its ambitiousness.

The same period has brought to light ambiguities and tensions in the *motu proprio* that future generations will have to resolve. For example, how exactly can one have two forms of the very same rite, when historically, and logically, there ought to be only one? If the shift to a reformed liturgy did not create a break within the Roman tradition, how then could it have been possible later on to establish, on equal canonical footing, two versions of the same rite? They are said to be two "uses" of the same rite, and yet there is far less difference between the Dominican, Carmelite, and old Roman uses (to take a few examples) than there is between the old Roman and the new Roman. The *motu proprio* did not attempt to solve these difficulties, but took a pragmatic approach, content to abide with perplexity. Thus for its modesty.

We must return, again and again, to certainties. *Summorum Pontificum* obliges Catholics to do the following:

3. *Enchiridion Symbolorum* (43rd ed.), n. 5109.

1. Acknowledge that the *usus recentior* or "Ordinary Form" is valid and licit;

2. Acknowledge that the *usus antiquior* or "Extraordinary Form" is valid and licit;

3. Accept that Catholics should be free to worship the Lord by participating *either* in the one form *or* in the other form. Neither of the forms *need* be present in *each* parish or chapel, but, except in special cases, both will be readily available to the faithful who seek to worship with the one or the other.

This is the bottom line of *Summorum Pontificum* as a practical document. If there are many Novus Ordo Masses but no traditional Latin Masses within a reasonably conceived geographical sphere, then one or more clergy are failing to meet the spiritual needs and rights of the faithful in their care. They may not necessarily *want* to meet those needs and rights, but meet them they must, if they are to be good stewards of the mysteries, loyal sons of the Church, and true shepherds of the flock. The account they must give of their lives before the Eternal Judge will include an accounting on this point, too.

Pope Benedict XVI speaks of the Novus Ordo Missae as the "ordinary expression of the *lex orandi*" (Art. 1) and says, in the letter to the bishops, that "the new Missal will certainly remain the ordinary form of the Roman Rite, not only on account of the juridical norms, but also because of the actual situation of the communities of the faithful." Curiously, some people take Pope Benedict XVI's language to be *prescriptive* when it is obviously *descriptive*. He is describing a state of affairs, not prescribing how things ought to be.[4] How they *ought* to be is up to the Holy Spirit and the Catholic faithful; it is not the stroke of a papal pen that will determine whether or not Catholics make the *usus antiquior* their liturgical norm. The *motu proprio* unquestionably smoothed the path by which an increasing number of Catholics are *in fact* taking the *usus antiquior* as their normative liturgy, but it neither established nor disestablished anything. It noted that Catholics would, in the majority of cases, be attending

---

4. I shall come back to this point below.

the Novus Ordo, but it also pointed out that the old rite had never been abrogated and should be available to all who seek it. This established the necessary foundation for a potentially limitless expansion of the *usus antiquior,* to the point that it could become once again the norm that it had been for four centuries (and, in essence, for a millennium longer than that).

By its own internal logic, the *motu proprio* could not have been saying that the Novus Ordo must remain the norm; rather, it is the norm currently, and yet there is no *inherent* reason why it must remain so for any particular parish, diocese, religious community, or even the universal Church. This is why we are seeing dedicated parishes created for it, and religious communities adopting it and flourishing under its beneficent influence. At a time when religious practice in the West is precipitously declining, we see the springing up of oases of faith, including thriving Catholic families, wherever the traditional liturgy is securely in place.

In the prudential order, Benedict XVI needed to reassure the faithful that no one will be forced to switch over from the modern form to the traditional form. But he made it likewise clear that if the clergy or the faithful should wish to embrace the *usus antiquior,* they are free to do so, without molestation. They have to accept that the Missal of Paul VI is valid. They do *not* have to take it as normative for their own public worship—otherwise parishes and religious communities that exclusively employ the *usus antiquior* would not be able to exist. There is no minimum requirement as to the number of Novus Ordo Masses clerics or laity have to attend per year. They do not have to believe it is the better or best form of the Roman Rite. They are perfectly free to prefer the older form of the Mass, or of the Divine Office, sacramental rites, and blessings. They may use the older form exclusively (provided they are fulfilling their Mass attendance obligations as Catholics); they are free to think it a superior liturgical rite, as far as the qualities proper to liturgy are concerned; they may believe that churchmen, even at the top tiers, made a tremendous mistake in pushing it aside. Such is the radical freedom for tradition that Pope Benedict XVI injected into the life of the Church.

There is nothing in the Church's law, whether canon law or *Summorum Pontificum,* that requires of a Catholic anything more than the three points stated above. Hence, if anyone starts to demand *more* of a Catholic, or concedes him *less,* they are acting in their own person, and not on behalf of the Church; they are speaking of themselves and not of God (cf. Jn 8:44); they are acting as vigilantes who have given themselves the job of policing and protecting the mainstream Church from the "dangers" and "errors" and "bad attitudes" of tradition-loving Catholics. It is hard to see how such threatening behavior can possibly be reconciled with the rights of the faithful, observance of canon law, respect for ecclesiastical tradition, or, ultimately, fraternal charity.

Whatever its ambiguities or limitations, *Summorum Pontificum* remains the ultimate challenge to the modernist and progressivist tendency to treat traditionally-minded Catholics as if they were so much rubbish waiting to be picked up, carried off, and buried in the landfill, along with their missals, chasubles, copes, birettas, maniples, aspergiliums, and other popish paraphernalia. Traditional Catholics do not deserve the ostracism, the contempt, or the double standard to which they are so frequently subjected. Liberal and conservative Catholics who do not recognize and repent of this spiritual problem in their own lives will have sins to answer for, even as traditional Catholics may sin by reacting to provocations and persecutions with disproportionate anger, excessive sadness, or despair.[5]

Pope Benedict XVI desired to be a peacemaker and to encourage precisely those behaviors of generosity that would eventually heal the rifts, even as they paved the way to the restoration of liturgical tradition. It remains a scandal that so many professedly "good Cath-

---

5. Despair would include the attitude of discouragement that I have heard attributed to some Catholics who have grown weary of asking, over and over again, for the old Mass, without tangible result. For reasons we will never fully understand in this life, God in His Providence tests some people more than others. When He allows frustrating obstructions and delays, it is in order to call us to more intense prayer and action. A community that has met with no success in implementing the *motu proprio* should pray novenas, sign up for holy hours, get monks and nuns praying for them, invite clergy from outside, organize an Una Voce chapter, and relentlessly set up meetings and write letters to any and all relevant parties, never letting up until the provisions of *Summorum Pontificum* are acknowledged and realized.

olics," clergy included, continue to ignore the legal demands of *Summorum Pontificum* and the real spiritual needs of many faithful children of the Church in every land. Those of us who are on the receiving end of bad treatment need to redouble our prayers, penances, and forgiveness, while we continue seeking to actualize the enormous promise of the *motu proprio* in our midst.

On Friday, October 26, 2007, only six weeks after *Summorum Pontificum* had become the law of the Church, the founder of the *New Liturgical Movement* weblog, Shawn Tribe, published some perceptive remarks about the meaning of the terms "ordinary" and "extraordinary" as found in the *motu proprio*.[6] I remember thinking at the time that he was getting too worried about the possible misunderstanding of this pair of terms, but years of experience have convinced me that he was right. I have encountered more than one person who argued along these lines: "Benedict XVI was saying that this form of the liturgy is out of the ordinary—and should remain that way."

While "Extraordinary Form" has become a common way to refer to the traditional Latin Mass (and one can understand why: it has the advantage of brevity and an easy symmetry with "Ordinary Form," particularly when one abbreviates them as "EF" and "OF"), nevertheless, the phrase can be misleading, because it is an *extrinsic* description, based on the current liturgical situation, in which one form has *de facto* prominence over the other: the ordinary is that which is more commonplace, and the extra-ordinary that which is relatively uncommon. But if we put ourselves in mind of a parish run by the Fraternity of St. Peter, the Institute of Christ the King, or another such society of apostolic life, the opposite situation obtains: the "Extraordinary Form" is the *ordinary* liturgy for the people— indeed, the only one, for all intents and purposes.

Mr. Tribe drew our attention to a point of vital importance that

6. Shawn Tribe, "'Ordinary' and 'Extraordinary': A Discussion about Interpretive Keys to Their Meaning," published at *New Liturgical Movement*, October 26, 2007.

deserves to be brought forward as soon as a conversation starts to hinge or fixate on the OF/EF terminology—namely, that Benedict XVI in *Summorum Pontificum* and its explanatory letter to the world's bishops makes use of other expressions as well: the Missal of St. Pius V,[7] "the Missal of Blessed John XXIII" (in fact, he uses this phrase more often than any other[8]), "the old Missal," "the ancient Latin liturgical tradition," and the *"usus antiquior."* The clarifying instruction *Universae Ecclesiae* of 2011 speaks of "the older liturgical tradition" and frequently calls it the *"usus antiquior"* or "older use."[9] There is no evidence that Pope Benedict was legally and officially giving a single name to the traditional Latin Mass any more than he was doing the same for the modern Roman Rite. The official documents of the Church use multiple names for them, and for good reason: each name conveys something important that the other names do not convey. The unofficial names also add to the portrait: Gregorian Rite, Tridentine Rite, classical Roman Rite, and so forth.

A failure to recognize the diversity and purpose of Pope Benedict's nomenclature can lead to a situation where the "extraordinary" of "EF" is used to fend off ordinary Catholics who desire, or desire more regularly, that which Benedict XVI asked the clergy to offer generously. "No," responds the nay-sayer, "the Church says this Mass is out of the ordinary—rare, marginal, exceptional, not the norm for us." If the nay-sayer went on to suggest that the "E" in "Extraordinary Form of Mass" meant somewhat the same as the "E" in "extraordinary minister of Holy Communion," one could disprove the claim by pointing to the fact that there are whole communities, and even a Personal Apostolic Administration (quasi-diocese) in Campos, Brazil, that are permitted to celebrate exclusively the Extraordinary Form, while there is not a single church in

---

7. In Art. 1: "the Roman Missal promulgated by St. Pius V and reissued by Bl. John XXIII."

8. Pope Benedict XVI defines the older form of the Mass in reference to John XXIII eight times in the motu proprio and once in the accompanying letter. In contrast, he uses the expression "extraordinary form" only three times in the *motu proprio* and twice in the accompanying letter.

9. See Pontifical Commission Ecclesia Dei, Instruction *Universae Ecclesiae*, §5, §8a, and §15.

the world where extraordinary ministers of Holy Communion are legally allowed to be the *ordinary* ministers of Holy Communion, for the simple reason that it is metaphysically impossible for them to become so without first changing their state in life (or, for many, their sex, *quod absit*). In any case, an argument based on the concept of "extraordinary ministers of Holy Communion" would be specious and disingenuous in the extreme. After all, where are Extraordinary Form Masses multiplied (in accordance with *Summorum Pontificum*) in the same way extraordinary ministers of Holy Communion are multiplied (contrary to a host of Vatican documents)? In reality, the "extraordinary" in one phrase means one thing while the "extraordinary" of the other phrase means another; we call this an equivocal (or more precisely, an analogous) use of language, the existence of which should not be a stunning revelation for those acquainted with either poetry or theology.

I knew a priest who took the "extraordinary" of "EF" in a restrictive sense, as if it meant "that which should remain marginal or rare," but the logic of *Summorum Pontificum* and the wide range of permissions the Vatican has granted since approximately 1988 shows that the "extraordinary" here has a descriptive rather than a prescriptive force. It is declarative, not imperative. In contrast, the restrictive sense *is* employed in the phrase "extraordinary ministers of Holy Communion," which came into being solely for emergency situations.[10] Since there are already whole parishes, religious orders, and even a diocese that exclusively employ the "Extraordinary Form" of the Roman Rite, the "extraordinary" here cannot mean rarely or exceptionally permitted, but simply that, socially and institutionally speaking, it is out of the ordinary. Put differently, "Ordinary Form" and "Extraordinary Form" are sociological or demo-graphic terms: they state what the global pastoral situation

---

10. Many years ago I published a conspectus of all pertinent magisterial statements on extraordinary ministers of Holy Communion between the years 1969 and 1997, when the last major Vatican statement was issued. The article may be found at https://www.ewtn.com/library/Liturgy/EXTRMIN.HTM. The Congregation for Divine Worship subsequently clarified that the expression "extraordinary minister of the Eucharist" is never to be employed, since the *only* minister of the Eucharist is the bishop or the priest. See *Redemptionis Sacramentum,* §§155–56.

is, but do not prescribe how it *should* be, or imply a judgment on which form should be more normal in a particular community.[11]

The comparison I like to use is this: driving the wrong way down a one-way street is certainly extraordinary and can be justified only by an emergency, but driving to work taking the scenic country road rather than the speedy interstate is also extra-ordinary in that most people do not do it, but it is completely legal and, in fact, more beautiful. And some people may choose to drive exclusively on the country roads. Perhaps, like Mary of Bethany, they have chosen the better part.

Summorum Pontificum is a fine example of papal diplomacy. It assumes that the Ordinary Form is the norm for the vast majority of Catholic communities, and that, for now at least, it must remain in currency, while the Extraordinary Form is gradually added back to the life of the Church. Thus, it seems to me that, given standing liturgical law, the pastor of a parish could *not*, solely on his own authority, declare that his parish will, from a certain point onwards, be exclusively Extraordinary Form. On the other hand, it seems equally clear from the *motu proprio* that if there is a stable *coetus fidelium* capable of supporting an *usus antiquior* parish (particularly if there is an empty church or a church in danger of closure), the local bishop could not reasonably say: "Sorry, this is not the normal liturgy of our diocese and you can't have it." The fact that the *usus recentior* is, so to speak, the default setting does not mean it *must* be the default for every Roman Catholic believer or community of believers. As mentioned before, we know this cannot be so

11. When Benedict XVI cites "juridical norms" as indicative of the status of the Ordinary Form—"Already from these concrete presuppositions, it is clearly seen that the new Missal will certainly remain the Ordinary Form of the Roman Rite, not only on account of the juridical norms, but also because of the actual situation of the communities of the faithful" (Letter to Bishops *Con grande fiducia*)—he is referring to the fact that Paul VI instituted the new Roman Missal for the universal church, in such a way that he and others understood this act of institution as a replacement of the former Roman Missal. Accordingly, if a new church is built and a priest is assigned to it, the default is that he will celebrate the Ordinary Form. However, this is a far cry from saying that the Ordinary Form is "what believers *ought* to be following," and that they may follow the Extraordinary Form "by way of exception."

because of parishes and religious houses that exclusively celebrate the *usus antiquior,* with the Church's permission.

Let us consider some of the implications of all of this for postconciliar Church policy. Under Pope Paul VI, it was thought by most Catholics that the whole liturgical life of the Church had been overhauled, in such a way that the old was definitively retired and the new authoritatively imposed. Gone, defunct, inoperative, impermissible, was anything for which a new equivalent had been created. But this strong line had already started to wane under the Polish pope, and it was permanently retired by the Bavarian. Today, the traditional Roman calendar (as of 1962), the old *Martyrology,* the old Divine Office (including the Office of Prime), the rite of tonsure, the minor orders, the subdiaconate, the sacramental rites and blessings of the *Rituale Romanum,* the *Pontificale*—all of this is back in use, deemed fully legitimate;[12] according to Pope Benedict XVI, none of it was ever abrogated or abolished. This is all the more welcome in that serious problems in all of the reformed ceremonies and their official books have been identified and thoroughly critiqued over the past forty years.

Consequently, all of this heritage can be taken up again by a community and become *normative* for that community. For Catholics who belong to a Fraternity of St. Peter parish, Epiphany is *not* the Sunday after New Year's, but January 6 (as it had always been, prior to recent decades); Ascension is *not* on the Sunday after Ascension, but takes place forty days after the Resurrection (as had always been the case)—and this, *regardless* of the Ordinary Form's Ordo; the feast of St. Thomas Aquinas is March 7, not January 28; and so forth. The *real* calendar for these *usus antiquior*-attending Catholics is the 1962 calendar; they are not, as it were, pretending or playacting. There is, at this time in the Church's life, a unique coexistence of two forms of the Roman Rite, each with its own structure of

12. Albeit with some restrictions, most notably this one: "Only [or At least] in Institutes of Consecrated Life and Societies of Apostolic Life subject to the Pontifical Commission Ecclesia Dei, and in these where the use of the liturgical books of the *forma extraordinaria* is maintained, is it allowed to use the *Pontificale Romanum* of the year 1962 for conferring major and minor Orders" (*Universae Ecclesiae* §31).

Mass and Office, feasts and ferias, sacraments and sacramentals—and therefore *it cannot be said that one of these forms is normative in an unqualified sense for all Roman Catholics.* The Novus Ordo may be the norm for most Catholics, but it is not obligatory and it is certainly not in itself superior, as if the new is always to be preferred whenever there is a choice of forms. Such views would contradict the equality of the forms and the now-widespread existence of exclusively Vetus Ordo communities, both parochial and religious.

When Benedict XVI in his Letter to Bishops of July 7, 2007 speaks about "the actual situation of the communities of the faithful" and their "degree of liturgical formation," he is admitting that the nature of a given community *has* to be taken into account when determining the proportion of the Ordinary to the Extraordinary Form. There is, in other words, no "one size fits all" pattern that could be superimposed on every group of Catholics. Some communities will not enjoy the privilege of having the *usus antiquior,* while others may employ it exclusively. The Church permits both extremes and every permutation in between—although *Universae Ecclesiae* does imply that every Catholic should be exposed to the older liturgical form when it says, apropos *Summorum Pontificum,* that "the Letter has the aim of bestowing[13] on *all* of the faithful the Roman Liturgy in the *usus antiquior,* considered as a precious treasure to be preserved."

We can perform a simple thought experiment. The number of traditionalist priests ordained each year in France is steadily rising and the total number of diocesan clergy is falling precipitously. Years down the line, it is almost certain that the former will outnumber the latter.[14] What will the bishops do? Close more and more churches, or bite the bullet and entrust them to priests who celebrate only, or primarily, the *usus antiquior?* If country parishes over time

---

13. This is from §8a. The Latin original says: *omnibus largire fidelibus*—the *usus antiquior* should be "bestowed on all the faithful," not merely "offered" to them, as the official translation at the Vatican website has it. The difference is significant. The official translation is misleading at times, as is the case with many Vatican documents. The Latin Mass Society of England and Wales has prepared a more literal translation.

14. See "Traditional Priests in France until 2050," published at *Centurio,* July 6, 2014.

went in the *usus antiquior* direction simply out of necessity, would there not eventually be a tipping point when the two forms were, let us say, 50/50 in their representation? And if that is surely conceivable, why not a century in which the *usus antiquior* becomes the norm and the *usus recentior* a permitted alternative? Whatever shift takes place, we can be sure that a day will come when the terminology of "ordinary" and "extraordinary" will seem quaintly old-fashioned.

Back on that fateful day of March 7, 1965, when Pope Paul VI celebrated the first mostly-Italian Mass at the parish of Ognissanti in Rome, he said in his homily: "Today's new way of prayer, of celebrating the Holy Mass, is extraordinary." Less than five years later, Montini's "extraordinary" vernacular Mass had become altogether ordinary, in spite of centuries of tradition and the clear teaching of Pius XII's *Mediator Dei,* John XXIII's *Veterum Sapientia,* and the Second Vatican Council. Half a century later, we are witnesses to a striking reversal happening at the grassroots level. For an increasing number of Catholics, the "extraordinary" Latin Mass is becoming altogether ordinary once again, in a development that can only be called natural, normal, and healthy, with plenty of youthful momentum.

If one reads a lot of Catholic literature from the late sixties and throughout the seventies and eighties, one encounters a peculiar smugness in the authors, a self-satisfaction at the success of what they could easily have dubbed their own "Glorious Revolution." They believe that they have sung a new Church into being, "just like that," built on the ruins of centuries of fortress-mentality Counter-Reformation Catholicism, now safely leveled to the dust.

But as the years roll on, and especially after the unexpected advent of Benedict XVI, a new note begins to be sounded in the magazines, journals, and newspapers of the regnant party—a note of anxiety about the increasingly undeniable fact that there is now an *alternative* to the prevailing paradigm. There is, surprisingly, competition in the open market. Suddenly one hears the former partisans of diversity and experimentation thunderously condemning the presence of the Other, because it simply does not *belong*. Alterity is all fine and good until it is really *significant* alterity. Then it has to be melted down and poured into the popsicle tray of institutional uniformity. The promoters of diversity suddenly sound like those who support a "free market" as long as it favors big government and big corporations.

Wherever it springs up, the traditional Roman Rite attracts God-thirsting souls, and Catholic culture starts to spring up again alongside of it, or rather, within it and from it. Yet in many places, this new opening to grace is not tolerated by the establishment. The fallacy of a *petitio principii* rears its head: "Because people aren't interested, and no one will come, therefore we won't make it available." This is the desperate maneuver of one who is afraid of something— afraid, perhaps, that what was sacred and great for past generations of Catholics might be found to be sacred and great by Catholics today who never knew it before.

One would think churchmen would and should do *anything* that promised to win souls for Christ, including the strange experiment of Tradition. *Salus animarum suprema lex.*[15] When an institution is bleeding its members, when a local church is facing a catastrophic collapse in sacramental practice, one would expect its leaders to attempt even desperate and unlikely expedients, such as the revival of traditional Catholic practice. The passage of time has taught us, alas, that there are some, including far too many high-ranking clerics, who would rather lose Catholics than give up the *aggiornamento*. An empty church is at least a church with no Latin Mass, and empty pews will at least have no large homeschooling families that study Latin, wear veils, and give the Church vocations. Potential disaster averted.

A sign of contradiction and a thorn in the side: this is the vocation of the traditionalist in the Church of today. Maybe someday it will be different, and the traditionalist can once more *be* the Catholic, without an uncomfortable distinctiveness, without the duty of criticism and opposition. After all, for long stretches of Church his-

---

15. "The salvation of souls is the highest law": the fundamental principle of all Church law.

tory, every believing Catholic was *ipso facto* a traditionalist. There was not a perilous choice between being a Catholic in obvious communion with all of one's forebears and being a Catholic who is aggiornamentoed and avant-garde.

Summorum Pontificum has been insightfully described as the single greatest proof—and guarantee—of the hermeneutic of continuity. Perhaps it may prove, in the long run, to be the only incontrovertible evidence of continuity. How do we know that the Church of today is the same as the Church of yesterday and of every age? Because she celebrates the same liturgy, one characterized by slow development under the influence of the Holy Spirit. This is the very badge and banner of Catholicity.

In her magnificent book *Cistercian Europe: Architecture of Contemplation,* Terryl Kinder describes how medieval Cistercian architecture, seemingly simple and humble, is actually extremely subtle in its relationship to the cosmos and particularly the light of the sun:

> What there is in a Cistercian abbey—and in abundance—is the presence and the play of light. It is sunlight that animates the buildings by day, outlining every protuberance and recession, giving full value to architectural detail. When trying to understand light in an abbey, the role of silence needs to be underlined, for speaking draws attention away from visual subtleties. In order to experience fully the movement of light and shadow in a Cistercian church, one needs to be present throughout the day from morning until evening, in winter and in summer, at dawn, when it is raining, and in the reflected light of snow. The evolving luminous effect is most apparent when one is sitting in the same stall, the very slowness of the moving light providing a perfect backdrop to contemplative life. Then the subtlety of the architecture and its detail may gradually reveal itself to those who have grown aware and can see it.[16]

16. Terryl N. Kinder, *Cistercian Europe: Architecture of Contemplation* (Grand Rapids: William B. Eerdmans; Kalamazoo: Cistercian Publications, 2000), 385–86.

In other words, you have to live patiently and attentively with this architecture before it reveals its secrets to you, and once you have learned its language, you are ushered into a world of spiritual symbolism that echoes and amplifies the longings and thoughts of your own prayer. One has to be a humble apprentice, an assiduous observer. Anything truly great takes time and effort to master, or, if it is not the sort of thing that can be mastered, to appreciate and assimilate.

This example from the world of medieval architecture reminds me of the striking words Benedict XVI addressed to bishops in the letter accompanying *Summorum Pontificum*:

> The fear was expressed in discussions about the awaited *motu proprio*, that the possibility of a wider use of the 1962 Missal would lead to disarray or even divisions within parish communities. This fear also strikes me as quite unfounded. The use of the old Missal presupposes a certain degree of liturgical formation and some knowledge of the Latin language; neither of these is found very often.

In noting how a "certain degree of liturgical formation" and "some knowledge of Latin" are required for the *usus antiquior,* Pope Benedict voiced a polite but stinging critique of the paucity and superficiality of liturgical formation found among many Catholics today as well as the pathetic and scandalous lack of Latin among the clergy, contrary to the express requirements of canon law.[17] It is as if he said: "You need not fear a sudden disarray in the Church, since the use of the classical Roman Rite, which presupposes the very things that the original Liturgical Movement and then Vatican II called for—namely, sound liturgical formation and the retention of Latin—are hardly to be found nowadays. Things are so bad that the old Mass, with its very great goods, will not immediately be able to spring back to life and take over."

Can we not see this as an implicit critique of the Novus Ordo, which, according to its architects' express intentions, was meant to require little in the way of formation? It was designed to be self-

17. See *Codex Iuris Canonici* (1983), can. 249.

explanatory, an "instant liturgy" like the instant coffees and dehydrated foods popularized in the Space Age. After all, in one of the most embarrassing sentences ever consigned to the text of an ecumenical council, we read: "The rites ... should be within the people's powers of comprehension, and normally should not require much explanation."[18] Never mind the fact that the people's powers of comprehension have to be *deliberately formed and informed* in order for the language of the liturgy to make sense, and never mind the fact that the mysteries into which we are thrown are permanently and unfathomably mysterious, comprehensible and explicable only to a certain point, beyond which they dazzle and humble the human mind with their unapproachable light. As Benedict XVI frequently said in his homilies, man is not naturally Christian; we are not born redeemed; we must be born anew in water and the Holy Spirit, we must receive instruction and then nurture our faith all our lives. Part of this process of *becoming Christian* is learning assiduously the vocabulary of the sacred, the language of the supernatural, the symbolism of the liturgy.

It is true, as Guardini reminds us, that many of the signs and gestures used by the Church have their origin in the order of creation, which speaks (or can speak) to man at the level of nature. For example, proceeding to a place and bowing to it or kissing it seems to be the kind of gesture that any human being will interpret as a sign of reverence for something special. Lifting a precious object high into the air towards the heavens is another such sign, this time of offering. However, there is fairly little that is specifically *Christian* about these natural gestures, and that is why the liturgy has much work to do to flesh out the theological meaning of natural signs. Moreover, there are *revealed* signs whose meaning cannot be gleaned without the benefit of exegesis. Making the sign of the Cross or burning incense before the Blessed Sacrament is not intelligible apart from catechesis. For both of these reasons, the exegesis that the liturgy itself already is will have a double function: to aid the accurate apprehension of the content of the mysteries and to

---

18. *Sacrosanctum Concilium* §34; for further discussion, see Chapter 4, 94–103.

guarantee their superintelligibility, to protect their very mysteriousness. Hence, a liturgy that is more dense in symbols has the power not only to lead one more deeply into the doctrine of the Faith but also to humble and dazzle the intelligence.

Three conclusions suggest themselves. (1) Taken in its totality, the Christian liturgy is not and can never be within the sphere of the people's powers of comprehension in the absence of "formation in the spirit and power of the liturgy."[19] (2) Normally, and especially for the modern man who spends his life deracinated from nature and culture, the liturgy *will* require much explanation. (3) Lastly, the worst place to explain liturgy is *within* the liturgy, even though the attempt to do so has been the trend for the past fifty years.

The original Liturgical Movement desired a serious formation for the clergy and the faithful so that they could yield themselves intelligently and willingly to the profound riches of the rites handed down to us, preserving intact their ultimately impenetrable mysteriousness that was the secret of their magnetism for devout souls. The Consilium decided instead on a horizontalized and transparent meeting format in which business is conducted in a linear fashion, "no congregant left behind," with no residue of unintelligibility, no need for outside effort or inward suffering, and no submission to cultural forms that transcend our age as God transcends the entire created order—Latin being, perhaps, the most notable symbol of such a cultural form.

To the objection that Latin could not be considered "transcendent" when it was a language in common use, there are two responses. First, the liturgy in every age has featured something that transcended its age: the very core of the liturgy is an unanticipated irruption of the divine into the world that never ceases to provoke wonder in a soul awake, and the remaining layers of the liturgy formed around this, as a pearl forms around a grain of sand. Second, as Christine Mohrmann and Uwe Michael Lang (among others) have discussed at length, liturgical Latin is a formal, hieratic, high-register language that could never have been mistaken for the

---

19. As *Sacrosanctum Concilium* §14 recognizes.

familiar or "vulgar" tongue of the marketplace, even by a native speaker.[20] Thus, although some cultural forms incorporated into the liturgy, in their origin Hebrew, Greek, Roman, Gallican, etc., may be more or less strange to a given congregation at a given time, the entire *ensemble* of elements is strange, wondrous, in that this totality belongs to none of us, comes from outside of us, goes beyond us, and, as a result, draws us beyond ourselves. The Novus Ordo's ruthless reduction of this kind of strangeness is one of the reasons it is so ill-equipped to rescue "modern man" from the grip of secularism, materialism, and nihilism, and so powerless to compete against more superficially attractive religious and pseudo-religious cults. The heart of man is raw hunger for love, and modernity is a starvation diet that leads either to lethargy or passionate revolt.

> There are some who by nature are able to subsist on a meager diet of dried plums, and be content; there are others in whom this hunger for love is so deep and fierce that they must feast at a banquet, or fall into madness and vice. For such as these dried plums will never suffice; and if so be they are sworn to stay their hunger with the love of heaven alone, it is they above all who most need the gift of God.[21]

It is not difficult to see a certain pattern among those who discover the traditional Latin Mass and begin attending it regularly. As a Catholic becomes more educated in both the Roman liturgy and the spiritual life, he finds the Novus Ordo less satisfactory. One notices more and more its thin rationalism, its openings for egoism, its heavy-handed didacticism, its lack of tranquility, its surprising distance from the interior world of great spiritual masters such as St. Benedict, St. Bonaventure, St. Gertrude, Thomas à Kempis, St. John of the Cross, St. John Vianney. The classical Roman liturgy expresses to perfection the great themes of these spiritual masters,

---

20. See Uwe Michael Lang, *The Voice of the Church at Prayer: Reflections on Liturgy and Language* (San Francisco: Ignatius Press, 2012); Christine Mohrmann, *Liturgical Latin: Its Origins and Character* (Washington, DC: Catholic University of America Press, 1957).

21. Kent, *Brother Michel*, 158.

with a beauty, clarity, and forcefulness that is refreshing, invigorating, and habit-forming. It seems as if young people in particular, when serious about their faith, are quick to recognize the strengths of the old and the weaknesses of the new.[22]

Whether one knows it or not, seeking to be formed "in the spirit and power of the liturgy" is, *ipso facto,* becoming suited for the traditional Latin Mass, prepared to benefit from the feast it spreads before us. To become more prayerful, more accustomed to meditation, is to be in motion towards the *usus antiquior*—at least in the best of circumstances, when this trajectory can be peacefully completed. Tragically, as with storm-tossed ships too far from shore to find a safe harbor, many Catholics do not discover their own liturgical heritage because it is simply not readily available to them. They will do what they can with the poverty of prayer forms they are offered, but it will be like poor children who cannot flourish on a scanty diet, or who can do so only by a special divine favor outside of the ordinary course of things.

Let us return to the lines quoted above from Pope Benedict XVI's letter to bishops of July 7, 2007. Having quoted them, a certain commentator went on to say:

> The extraordinary form is difficult in the way that anything that's rewarding but exacting is difficult, like classical music when what we know is mainly popular music. At Mass in the ordinary form, we experience it as something that projects itself from the sanctuary into the pews: it meets us halfway. At Mass in the extraordinary form, "Introibo ad altare Dei," I will go to the altar of God. In the United States, a number of Catholics higher than anyone might have predicted from a survey of Catholics worldwide prefer to do the harder thing.[23]

The classical liturgy begins, in a sense, with the inner man and

22. Catholics involved in Juventutem chapters, Fraternity parishes, or Institute oratories will know from experience the phenomenon I am describing. As a teacher, I get to see this regularly. One of my college students wrote in an essay: "We do not immerse ourselves in the [Novus Ordo] Mass as much. It is more rushed and there is less concern with what every movement and every item means."

23. Nicholas Frankovich, "It's Extraordinary," published at the *First Things* weblog, September 26, 2013.

works from there to the outer man. This is why it is a harder, more demanding way, a more deeply transformative way—one that is, for that very reason, more full of joy, and more productive of fierce devotion. This liturgy, stable and strong, demands that we be formed and educated by it, for without that schooling we cannot make progress to the higher grades. It prompts the development of new faculties of seeing and hearing; it requires an exodus from our surroundings of pop culture and intellectual fashion; it calls us to a strange land, like Abram being summoned from Ur to Canaan.

Latin is the intuitive symbol of this stripping of oneself and donning a new garment, a formality fit for standing in the presence of the Lord. When Latin was *de facto* abolished, a potent sign of the changeless transcendence of God, of human nature, and of the activity of worship was lost, with immensely damaging consequences. Change and accommodation, seen as goods in themselves, took the place of stability and identity. As Michael Baker observes:

> Latin is not a dead language; it is fixed language. You can't fiddle with it. Vernacular languages are in flux and their mutability detracts from the liturgy's fixity. The vernacular also provides a vehicle for the priest who likes to hear the sound of his own voice. Adoption of the vernacular opened the door for serial abuses and the name of those abuses is "legion." The liturgy is a formalised ritual of worship. It is not meant to be marked by personal input.[24]

Baker's point echoes the words the psalmist puts on the lips of sinners: *Linguam nostram magnificabimus; labia nostra a nobis sunt. Quis noster dominus est?* "We will magnify our tongue; our lips are our own. Who is Lord over us?" (Ps 11:5). We will magnify our vernacular tongues, for they belong to us, we are their masters; how dare a fixed ancient language lord it over us? Yet it is precisely our humble submission to this rule of language, which embodies the rule of faith and the authority of mystery, that allows us to magnify the Lord rather than ourselves. Dom Guéranger poignantly

24. Michael Baker, "It's the Council That's the Problem," published at *Super Flumina*, June 22, 2016.

describes how and why the Protestants settled on the vernacular as a weapon of de-catholicization:

> Since the liturgical reform [of the sixteenth-century] had for one of its principal aims the abolition of actions and formulas of mystical signification, it follows necessarily that its authors had to vindicate the use of the vernacular in divine worship. This is one of the points of greatest importance in the eyes of sectarians. Cult is no secret matter, they say; the people must understand what they sing. Hatred for the Latin language is inborn in the hearts of all the enemies of Rome. They recognize it as the bond among Catholics throughout the world, the arsenal of orthodoxy against all the subtleties of the sectarian spirit, the most powerful weapon of the papacy.
>
> The spirit of rebellion which drives them to confide the universal prayer to the idiom of each people, of each province, of each century, has, moreover, produced its fruits, and the reformed themselves constantly perceive that the Catholic people, in spite of their Latin prayers, relish better and accomplish with more zeal the duties of the cult than do most of the Protestant people. At every hour of the day, divine worship takes place in Catholic churches. The faithful Catholic who assists leaves his mother tongue at the door. Apart from the sermons, he hears nothing but mysterious words which, even so, are not heard in the most solemn moment of the Canon of the Mass. Nevertheless, this mystery charms him in such a way that he is not jealous of the lot of the Protestant, even though the ear of the latter does not hear a single sound without perceiving its meaning. . . .
>
> We must admit it is a master blow of Protestantism to have declared war on the sacred language. If it should ever succeed in destroying it, it would be well on the way to victory. Exposed to profane gaze, like a virgin who has been violated, from that moment on the liturgy has lost much of its sacred character, and very soon people find that it is not worthwhile putting aside one's work or pleasure in order to go and listen to what is being said in the way one speaks in the marketplace.[25]

25. Guéranger, *Institutions liturgiques,* vol. I, pt. 1, ch. 14, n. 8; translation adapted from the one provided at http://catholicapologetics.info/modernproblems/newmass/antigy.htm.

The reader may be wondering about the Eastern sphere, where there was never a single language in which liturgy was celebrated. This is true; surely it was possible for divine Providence to allow many languages in the formal worship of the Church. The vernacular Byzantine liturgy leads the ego to *kenosis* through clearly differentiated and fully predetermined roles and spaces for different actors in the liturgy, the waves of repetitious prayer, and the chanting of age-old modal melodies. Divine Providence guided the Western sphere of the Church in a different manner that makes all the difference *for Roman Catholics.* With the rarest of exceptions, *all* liturgies in what we call the "Latin Church" were conducted in Latin for over 1,500 years, regardless of their diversity in many other respects. The language necessarily acquired a unique status and function due to its long, stable, and intimate bond not only with the Church's solemn public worship but also with the articulation of her doctrine, the codification of her discipline, and the development of her high culture, especially in sacred music. Latin came to be more than a means of communication: it became a sign of putting on the mind of Christ in the communion of the one Church. It expresses more than the freight of its words; it expresses the *traditio* or handing down of the words, as determinate and worthy of reverence. As we know from linguistics, language is not merely an indifferent medium for thought but is the matter that enters into hylomorphic composition with the conceptual form. Latin thus has a constitutive and essential relationship with the Western rites: it is not only a vehicle for the transmission of symbols but is itself a primary symbol, the royal clothing of the King in this part of His cosmic domain.[26]

Perhaps surprisingly, it was none other than two twentieth-century popes, Pius XI and John XXIII, who put a definitive seal of magisterial approval on this understanding of the intrinsic role of

---

26. The same thing may be said of Gregorian chant: it is not an indifferent musical vehicle, but *the Latin rite as music.* This is why it always holds chief place in the liturgy, even after the development of musical masterpieces in a variety of styles. (This principle applies, *mutatis mutandis*, to the various Western rites and uses and the bodies of proper plainchant belonging to them, e.g., the Ambrosian rite and the Dominican "rite.")

Latin in the Roman Catholic Church.[27] It is no exaggeration to say that due to the abandonment of Latin and the mad rush to vernacularize everything, the Latin Church is in a state of rebellion against its cultural fatherland, its linguistic self-identity. It is in a state of spiritual schizophrenia. This progressive de-Latinization is the outward sign of an inner self-hatred or self-loathing of historical Catholicism, an existential disease and corruption eating away the healthy tissue of the body like a malignant tumor. This tumor is not incurable, however; it requires but the wisdom and courage to leave off building the tower of Babel and to return to the traditional Latin liturgy, with its pure doctrine and refreshing savor.

Quotidian speech and "personal input" is not the light which enlighteneth every man that cometh into this world (cf. Jn 1:9). "What there is in a Cistercian abbey—and in abundance—is the presence and the play of light." This, indeed, is what we find in the traditional Latin Mass and throughout the Roman liturgy as a whole: the presence and play of a divine light that illuminates man's total condition, as a sinner redeemed in Christ, destined for immortality and fighting the battle of good against evil, in the midst of truths that never change and lies that pull us away into the superficial and the ephemeral. It is this irresistible presence and liberating play of light, worlds removed from the anthropocentric spontaneity and creativity exalted by modernity, that we have discovered in the Mass of Ages and everything that goes with it. With a shock of joy, we have embraced that gift, or rather, yielded ourselves to it, with all the fervor of young love, foretaste of eternal blessedness.

Liberals hate *Summorum Pontificum* because they understand perfectly well that the revival of the old liturgy constitutes a challenge to key principles behind the liturgical reform and to nearly all of its practical outcomes, which, in turn, represents a challenge to the entire program of modernization attributed (fairly or unfairly) to

27. See Pius XI, Apostolic Letter *Officiorum Omnium* (August 1, 1922); John XXIII, Apostolic Constitution *Veterum Sapientia* (February 22, 1962).

the Second Vatican Council. It is not so much a "turning back of the clock" as a destruction of the clock, that is, the peculiarly modern Western assumption that our practices have to be periodically changed—or perhaps even perpetually changing—lest they become stagnant and meaningless. In reality, it is too much change that brings meaninglessness; it is having no perennial source that leads to stagnation and dryness.

Imagine this scenario: you have a community, half of which attends a feisty charismatic Novus Ordo and the other half a whispered Latin Low Mass. Both celebrations are permitted by the Church. The charismatics are probably going to be thinking: "We're the ones who are really open to the working of the Holy Spirit, and we show it in the way we praise God with hands and voices. Those Catholics who just kneel quietly at a Latin Mass while the priest does everything—they're sure missing out!" The Latin Mass-goers are probably going to be thinking: "This is the way that countless men and women were sanctified for centuries; this is an intimate encounter with Our Lord in His Passion and in the mystery of the Eucharist. Here I have a vivid sense of the Presence of God, and it keeps me going throughout the day or the week. It's so sad to think of how the charismatics are stuck at the level of their emotions and don't reach this deeper experience!"

Neither way of thinking is completely correct; each verges on caricature. A charismatic may enter into the Holy Sacrifice and the silent glory of the Eucharistic Lord; a traditionalist may sing the Gloria vigorously and fervently beseech the Holy Spirit. But, *humanly* speaking, do we not see that these groups, having made choices that tend in opposite directions, stand in judgment over one another? Is it possible for the one group *not* to think that what they are doing is better than what the other group is doing—so much better that, in an ideal world, the other group would not exist? No, it is not possible; for otherwise they would not be doing what they think is better. This is why a "chant-crazed Latin-loving charismatic guitarist/vocalist" is about as rare as a functional democracy.

In much the same way, the majestic cathedrals of the Age of Faith stand in judgment over the sterile modernist churches of Corbusier and his imitators; the great paintings and sculptures that cover the

Christian world stand in judgment over cubist hulks and felt banners; the soaring melodies of Gregorian chant and the mystic har-
monies of polyphony stand in judgment over the worldly sentimentalism of contemporary church music; vestments of silk bro-
cade and lace albs stand in judgment over polyester drapes and vel-
cro-albs; ornate bejewelled gold chalices and patens stand in
judgment over clumsy faux-Franciscan cups and plates. It is not
possible for such things merely to "co-exist," let alone to comple-
ment one another. They are antagonists in a duel for the face of the
Church and the soul of the people. A church *looks* like this or that;
the people *are* this or that. We are dealing not with the Catholic
"both-and" but with the metaphysical "either/or."

Let us take an example: kneeling to receive communion on the
tongue from a properly ordained minister. A traditional Roman
Catholic thinks that this way of receiving, which developed naturally out of reverence for the Blessed Sacrament and achieved total
stability for centuries of devotional life, is superior *in every way* to
the practices introduced in recent decades. With full consistency,
then, a traditional Catholic will also think that the modern practice
of receiving communion in the hand, standing, from lay ministers,
is a bad thing, that it had a bad origin and has bad consequences. In
such matters, it is simply not possible—I repeat, not possible—for
everyone to smile and agree that everything and everyone is wonderful, wonderful, wonderful.[28]

Pope Benedict XVI arranged that the Novus Ordo and the *usus
antiquior* should co-exist in order that "mutual enrichment" might

28. I am of course aware that Eastern Christians receive the Lord standing.
However, first of all, this was their long-standing custom, as kneeling was ours, and
as they ought to keep their custom, we ought to keep ours. Second and more
importantly, outside of a concentration camp, they would not expect lay people to
administer Holy Communion. Third, the layman never handles the sacred vessels,
for the handling of which the priest's hands have been anointed. Fourth, the layman receives tilting his head back like a baby bird, with a cloth beneath his chin,
and the priest standing above him, as is fitting to his hierarchical position. All in all,
the traditional Eastern practice and the contemporary Western practice have practically nothing in common.

occur—presumably a sort of cross-pollination of the one by the other. If one looks at Ratzinger's papal example and reads his works, and if one looks to such figures as Cardinal Ranjith, Cardinal Cañizares, Cardinal Burke, and now Cardinal Sarah, it seems that 90% of the enrichment will go in one direction, namely, from the *usus antiquior* to the Novus Ordo, since the former possesses great riches of which the latter stands in desperate need. It is like St. Martin of Tours cutting off a piece of his ample cloak to cover a naked shivering beggar. As for the 10% where the older form could learn from the younger one, we may safely say it concerns just the sort of things that *would* have happened slowly, were it not for the bungling of a certain committee.

All this being the case, the result is plain: as long as the Novus Ordo and the *usus antiquior* co-exist, they are a standing challenge to one another, and they could not *not* be. If the Novus Ordo world does not assimilate the lessons that the *usus antiquior* can teach it, we are on a straight road to liturgical Armageddon. Either the philosophy of *Summorum Pontificum* will bridge the enormous abyss between the two forms by bringing the modern Roman Rite into a more obvious harmony with the preceding liturgical heritage, *or* we will see over time a dramatic intensification of our internecine conflicts. Having two supposedly equal forms of the same rite is a recipe for radical instability *unless* there can be a genuine and profound rapprochement between these forms. And we can be certain this will never happen by the older form becoming hip, trendy, and modish, swapping Gregorian for guitars. It will happen instead when the modern form relinquishes its counterfactual claim to be "just what the doctor ordered."

As with everyone else who ponders such questions, I have no idea what the long-term results will look like. Will there still be a Novus Ordo or an *usus antiquior* a century hence? Will there be an energy-efficient hybrid? If mutual enrichment actually occurs, will we see one or the other form fall away as dead weight, so that the sanity of a common worship may be restored to the Roman Church? God alone knows.

Meanwhile, it is our task to appreciate and live by the immense riches of our liturgical heritage and to share them with others while we await better, happier, more peaceful days. Like the joy of the Lord, this treasure is one that no man on earth can take away from us, because it belongs to Christ and His Church as a permanent endowment.

In the Dogmatic Constitution on the Church of the Second Vatican Council, *Lumen Gentium,* there are two paragraphs we might profitably revisit in light of *Summorum Pontificum* and the difficulties many have faced as they work to see it widely and generously observed. The first paragraph concerns bishops:

> For it is the duty of all bishops to promote and to safeguard the unity of faith and *the discipline common to the whole Church,* to instruct the faithful to love for the whole Mystical Body of Christ, especially for its poor and sorrowing members and for those who are suffering persecution for justice's sake (cf. Mt 5:10), and finally *to promote every activity that is of interest to the whole Church,* especially that the Faith may take increase and the light of full truth appear to all men.[29]

As *Summorum Pontificum* and its later clarification *Universae Ecclesiae* explain, the canonical discipline of the Catholic Church recognizes the traditional Latin Mass as never abrogated, equal in legal status to the Novus Ordo, permissible everywhere to any priest who is capable of celebrating it—and a treasure to be made available to the laity whether they request it or not, but obviously and especially if they do request it. This is "the discipline common to the whole Church," whether an individual bishop may like it or not, and it is his *duty* to promote and to safeguard the law established in the *motu proprio.* Moreover, as these and other documents indicate, the movement to recover the more ancient liturgical use of the Roman Rite as part of our Catholic life today is precisely "an activity that is of interest to the whole Church," as being ordered to effecting a reconciliation at the heart of the Church. The bishop therefore has

---

29. *Lumen Gentium* §23, emphases added.

a duty to *promote* this activity, and he may not ignore, downplay, undermine, or feebly attend to it.

The counterpart to this teaching is given further along in a passage that speaks about the goods the laity have the *right* to receive from their shepherds, and how lay people should handle situations where their rights or legitimate needs are not being met:

> The laity have the right, as do all Christians, to receive in abundance from their spiritual shepherds the spiritual goods of the Church, especially the assistance of the word of God and of the sacraments. They should openly reveal to them their needs and desires with that freedom and confidence which is fitting for children of God and brothers in Christ. By reason of the knowledge, competence, or outstanding ability in which they may be strong, they have the ability, and at times even the obligation, to express their opinion on those things which concern the good of the Church.[30]

Notice the strong language here: the laity have the right to receive *in abundance* the Church's spiritual goods, especially the assistance of the word of God and of the sacraments. When we take this together with the legislation in *Summorum Pontificum* that permits not only the more ancient form of the Holy Sacrifice of the Mass but also the traditional rites of the sacraments, we can see that the laity may justly claim from their shepherds the provision of that abundant assistance. To this is added the freedom and the obligation, in accordance with the dignity of the baptized Christian, of making known one's "needs and desires" and one's "opinion on those things which concern the good of the Church."

Duties and rights are correlative. The faithful have a right to receive abundant spiritual nourishment, particularly in the form of the Mass and the sacraments, and both John Paul II and Benedict XVI clarified repeatedly that this right extends to the nourishment that Catholics receive from the *usus antiquior* of the Mass and other traditional sacramental rites. For their part, the bishops have a duty to uphold universal ecclesiastical discipline (which includes *Sum-*

---

30. *Lumen Gentium* §37.

morum Pontificum and *Universae Ecclesiae*) and to provide generously for the spiritual health of their flocks by meeting their needs
fair and square. And how is a bishop to know which needs are legitimate and which are fraudulent? By taking seriously the inherent
dignity of Catholic tradition and by paying heed to the law of the
Church that exists to protect and promote it, for the salvation of
souls. Again: *Salus animarum suprema lex.*

It all comes back to the *motu proprio*: are we willing or unwilling
to embrace it? "He that hath an ear, let him hear what the Spirit
saith to the churches" (Rev 2:7).

A Layman's Prayer before Mass

Though my body may not stand before Thy altar,
let my soul stand there.
Though I may not offer Thee the Host and Chalice,
let me offer Thee myself instead.
Though by my word I may not change the bread and wine
into Thy Most Precious Body and Blood,
by my love and obedience
let me be transformed into Thee.
And though I may not drink at the altar
of the Chalice of Thy Blood,
grant that I may drink It truly,
in whatever form Thou hast prepared It for me.

(Michael Kent, *The Mass of Brother Michel*)

167

Propter verba labiorum tuorum ego custodivi via duras.
For the sake of the words of thy lips, I have kept hard ways.
PSALM 16:4

7

Laying Our Foundation on Solid Rock

T HE GERMAN NOVELIST Martin Mosebach, who has also become well known for his eloquent and outspoken defense of the traditional Latin Mass, articulates a particular problem that many in the Church today face—namely, the problem of a certain self-consciousness and critical spirit invading our prayer life as Catholics. Here is how he puts it:

> Perhaps the greatest damage done by Pope Paul VI's reform of the Mass (and by the ongoing process that has outstripped it), the greatest spiritual deficit, is this: we are now positively *obliged* to talk about the liturgy. Even those who want to preserve the liturgy or pray in the spirit of the liturgy, and even those who make great sacrifices to remain faithful to it—all have lost something priceless, namely, the innocence that accepts it as something God-given, something that comes down to man as a gift from heaven. Those of us who are defenders of the great and sacred liturgy, the classical Roman liturgy, have all become—whether in a small way or a big way—liturgical experts. In order to counter the arguments of the reform, which was padded with technical, archaeological, and historical scholarship, we had to delve into questions of worship and liturgy—something that is utterly foreign to the religious man. We have let ourselves be led into a kind of scholastic and juridical way of considering the liturgy. What is absolutely indispensable for genuine liturgy? When are the celebrant's whims tolerable, and when do they become unacceptable? We have got used to accepting liturgy on the basis of the minimum requirements, whereas the criteria ought to be maximal. And finally, we have started to *evaluate* liturgy—a monstrous act! We sit in the pews

and ask ourselves, was that Holy Mass, or wasn't it? I go to church to see God and come away like a theatre critic.[1]

This, then, is what we might call "Mosebach's Paradox": the more circumstances compel me to become an armchair expert in the nature, structure, rubrics, and history of the sacred liturgy, the more inclined I am to become a spectator and critic when I assist at Mass. Traditionalists face this problem in acute form. Many of them know quite a bit about the riches, beauties, and subtleties of the liturgy as well as the vandalism, carelessness, and sacrilege that have been visited upon it, so they are more sensitive than most Catholics to the slightest abuse, aberration, or vacuum of meaning.

Can we get past Mosebach's Paradox, or are we doomed—because of the tragic decision to rend asunder the Roman liturgical tradition—to be critics forever? Can we break through to a childlike apprenticeship to the sacred liturgy, giving ourselves totally to it without second-guessing or analyzing, comparing and contrasting? Can we be like St. Thérèse, following the little way of confidence and love?

Even amidst the worst internal crisis the Church has ever suffered, I believe that this is something we *can* do, but only by laying our foundation on solid rock—the traditional liturgy itself. A wholehearted immersion in the Mass of the saints, making it our personal point of reference, will help us shake off the dismay, agitation, and feeling of schizophrenia that so often result from bouncing back and forth between different forms of Mass, with the different worldviews, priorities, expectations, and habits they embody or encourage. In the spirit of St. Benedict, we need to make the best effort we can to achieve *stabilitas loci*, stability of place, by binding ourselves to one rite, one calendar, one community, one chapel or parish, one traditional Catholic way of life that is fully integrated and fully integrating.

There is a peacefulness and naturalness that comes from knowing what one is going to get or what one is supposed to do. For a layman, there is nothing more consoling and conducive to prayer than

---

1. *Heresy of Formlessness*, 25–26.

showing up at a traditional Latin Mass and being able to rely on the sameness of everything that will happen, from start to finish—everything for the glory of God and the sanctification of the people, even in the humblest conditions. There is nothing more liberating and lovely for me as a cantor and choirmaster than to show up on a Sunday morning and know, without a moment's doubt or hesitation, exactly which chants the schola must sing, because it is laid down for us and, in most cases, has not changed for centuries. It all just *works*, everything comes together with a blessed inevitability, and one can surrender to the Mass, to prayer, to the Lord. It is a recipe for sanity and sanctity in a world that is characterized by escalating insanity and unholiness.

Having traveled a fair amount in my lifetime, I have had two very different kinds of experiences as a Roman Catholic looking for a Mass to attend. The first can be described as the "oh my goodness, what kind of a church have I managed to get myself into!" experience: being obliged to take the nearest Sunday Mass on hand, one is usually distressed or grieved beyond measure by the hootenanny one is forced to endure. The other kind of experience is the opposite: the blessing of finding a church where the traditional Latin Mass is celebrated. One steps in, and the atmosphere is devout. A bell rings, the priest comes to the altar and commences his prayers. Perhaps there is chanting, too, or just the pregnant silence of many Catholics praying side by side, focused on the one thing necessary. Suddenly it does not matter where one is on the face of the earth; deep down and all around, it is the same, even as Jesus Christ is the same yesterday, today, and forever. Yes, there are minor regional variations in pronunciation or ceremonial, but the overwhelming *sameness* of the Holy Sacrifice of the Mass emerges, dominates, and descends like a balm on all who are present.

It seems to me that here lies a way to begin overcoming Mosebach's Paradox. If we can do it, if the conditions of our life allow for it, we ought to make a decisive break with pluralism, excessive variety, options galore, speaking out of both sides of our mouths, juggling with both hands, and give ourselves simply, completely, and bravely to the traditional worship of the Catholic Church. Over time, with God's help, we will stop being theater critics. We can regain something of our lost innocence. We can indeed look for the maximum, because we know that we are touching the seamless garment of Christ, handed down to us over the course of nineteen centuries, lovingly embellished by each passing generation. The traditional Mass is, in truth, a gift from Heaven—one that we could never deserve, and one that will never pass away as long as the world endures. It is time now for us to yield ourselves to it and to know a peace that surpasseth understanding.

Doing violence to one's family heritage is always bad, it can never be good. No less is this true of the Church, the Family of God, on her pilgrimage through history. Casting away precious gifts from the inheritance of the saints, removing or watering down the means of sanctification passed down to us, is always bad, it can never be good. It bespeaks a loss of gratitude, a confusion of priorities, and an unchaste mingling with the spirit of the age, which is always opposed to the spirit of the Gospel.

Making it harder for Christians to sanctify time, to understand secular time in relation to sacred time, is always bad, it can never be good. Hence, the abolition of the millennium-old "Sundays after Pentecost," by which most of the year was tied back explicitly to the great mystery of the outpouring of the Holy Spirit upon all flesh, and its replacement by "Sundays of Ordinary Time," was simply a mistake, a deviation; it could never have been good. To have abolished the beautiful season after Epiphany, when we bathe in the afterglow of the Word-made-flesh, and the ancient season of Septuagesima, which helped Christians prepare for the rigors of Lent, were and are contrary to the good of the faithful.

To have contradicted, manipulated, or exaggerated the directives of *Sacrosanctum Concilium* in order to carry out a liturgical revolution that was neither debated nor desired by the Council Fathers was destined to be cursed by the just God, for such mendacity and violence cannot be blessed.

Once modernism invaded the sanctuary and permeated the liturgy, its victory was won. There was no need for explicit theological modernism at this point; it had triumphed by invading the nerve center of the religion and spreading its poison from there throughout the Church on earth. The battle against Modernism, in spite of the promising military exploits of St. Pius X, has been lost, as regards the "new Church" that emerged after Vatican II. The only portion of the Church that is still fighting Modernism are the traditional enclaves that cherish and celebrate the Mass of our forefathers, the Mass of Trent, the Mass of the Roman Church back to St. Gregory the Great and before. This Mass, with all the sacramental rites surrounding it, perfectly enshrines and expresses the Catholic Faith in its full integrity, beauty, and incarnational transcendence. In its absence, that integrity is broken apart, that beauty is forgotten or denigrated, that incarnational transcendence is suffocated by the gnostic secularism of modernity.

What the baptized have a right to, and what our children deserve for the good of their souls, is the liturgy as the Church herself gives it to us. Neither the Constitution on the Sacred Liturgy nor the Novus Ordo Missae as promulgated by Pope Paul VI mandated or even so much as mentioned:

- the priest facing the people;

- the habitual use of laity to distribute the sacred species;

- the reception of holy communion on the hand and in a standing posture;

- the involvement of women and girls in the sanctuary as substitutes for acolytes;

- the abolition of the Latin language;

- the substitution of pop-style songs for the chanted Ordinary of the Mass and of vernacular hymns for the chanted propers of the Mass.

Most of these practices are post-conciliar innovations or novelties that fly in the face of Catholic tradition. All, without exception, are notorious embodiments of what Pope Benedict XVI has called the "hermeneutic of rupture and discontinuity," whereby Catholic doctrine, life, and worship have been divorced from longstanding (and, in some cases, even apostolic) Catholic tradition.

As a result, habitual attendance at such Masses is not a liturgical formation but more truly a liturgical *deformation* that disposes Christians to a false understanding of the Faith. I am speaking here in regard to the *Ordinary Form*; the praxis of the typical Western parish is a deformation even of *that* form of the Roman Rite, which—as the work of Gamber, Ratzinger, Dobszay, Mosebach, Pristas, and others has exhaustively shown—is *itself* a deformation of the Roman Rite in what is now called its Extraordinary Form. In other words, those who attend the typical parish Mass are experiencing a *doubly deformed liturgy*: the celebration is deviant from its own rubrics and available elements of continuity, and in addition to that, it is an objective deviation from the traditional Roman liturgy. How is a well-formed and well-nourished Catholic supposed to emerge from this chaos of liturgical novelty and obscuration? There is no Christ without tradition. There is no Church without tradition. There is no liturgy without tradition.

Mosebach has aptly spoken of the "hemorrhaging" of the Western church. I shall speak here as a parent to whom immortal souls have been entrusted. To the extent that our children are miseducated by an already deformed liturgy celebrated in a deformed manner, we are contributing to the *perpetuation of the problem,* not to its providential solution, which consists either in returning wholeheartedly to the tradition or, at very least, celebrating the Ordinary Form as reverently, solemnly, and beautifully as possible. Practically, this will often be a question of the "lesser evil." Most of us are not fortunate enough to be living near a parish or chapel staffed by the Fraternity of St. Peter, the Institute of Christ the King, or some other such society, so the question will be: Which liturgy, within reasonable distance from where I live, is *most in accord* with Catholic Tradition? Where is the Ordinary Form celebrated with the fewest departures from the established norms? Where is its overall Gestalt most Catholic in spirit?

Now, an objection could be raised to this line of argument. Is it not important for children to experience a parish, to become acquainted with its families, to socialize after Mass, and so forth? Do they not need to have that "horizontal" experience of the People of God in their locale? All things being equal, this would be true, and in optimal conditions it is true. But we are living in a crisis situation where the very *meaning and identity* of Catholic faith and life are at stake. The social good is a good indeed, but it pales in comparison to the good of divine worship, which more nearly touches on the infinite divine good itself. We are *more* obliged to cultivate faith, hope, and charity towards the Blessed Sacrament and the Blessed Trinity than we are to cultivate neighborly relationships, and when the latter stands in tension with the former, the former must be preferred. The proper formation of mind and heart by the power and sanctity of the Church's liturgy is more urgent, more profound, and more lasting than the social formation that may occur among parishioners at the local Novus Ordo parish. Naturally, if one can find a traditional parish or chapel that *also* meets the family's social needs (and this, fortunately, is becoming a little easier as time goes on and the effects of *Summorum Pontificum* continue to spread), one should thank the Lord for lavish mercies to poor sinners.

Pope Benedict XVI was fond of quoting the famous line of St. Benedict: "Let *nothing* be put before the *opus Dei*," that is, the worship of God. This principle is true for all Christians, not only for monks and nuns. When we parents do as we are supposed to do in this regard, the Lord will add the rest: "Seek ye first the kingdom of God and His righteousness, and all these things will be added unto you" (Mt 6:33).

Sacred Scripture says: "In much wisdom is much vexation, and he who increases knowledge increases sorrow" (Eccles 1:18). The more a devout Catholic studies the history, theology, and spirituality of the Roman liturgy, the more he or she tends to become deeply discontented with the current state of affairs; and if this student has been fortunate enough to experience the traditional Latin Mass, Divine Office, sacramental rites, blessings, processions, and so forth, sharp melancholy and intense indignation are bound to ensue. How could it be otherwise? One comes to see the vast, rich treasures that were squandered; one comes to see the shallow, brittle academic novelties that were set up in their place. One sees how it is a replay of Esau trading his birthright for a mess of pottage (or a pot of message), except that this time, it was, grievously, Jacob who did the trading. The Novus Ordo becomes, in a sense, largely spoiled for those who, making an earnest inquiry into the history of the Roman Rite, acquire a keen awareness of the imaginative archaeologisms and audacious innovations introduced by the Consilium in the 1960s.[2]

For example, knowing how *and why* the new "preparation of the gifts" was put together and the old Offertory abolished makes it all the more distracting, even distressing, to hear in person those quasi-Jewish prayers of blessing, which are a complete fabrication and aberration in the Roman Rite (or really, in any classical rite).[3] Or knowing how and why the venerable Roman Canon, most ancient of anaphoras, was criticized, nearly cancelled out, and, although retained, eventually marginalized by other manufactured anaphoras that have zero place in the Roman liturgical tradition is enough to make one shudder every time the shorty-sporty Eucha-

2. I do not deny that similarly dark business took place in the 1950s revision of Holy Week, as documented in a number of places, such as Don Stefano Carusi's "The Reform of Holy Week in the Years 1951–1956," trans. Fr. Charles W. Johnson, published at *Rorate Caeli* on July 25, 2010, and Gregory DiPippo's "Compendium of the 1955 Holy Week Revisions of Pius XII," published in multiple parts at *New Liturgical Movement*. Nevertheless, even this revision cannot compare with what was done across the board to the entire order of Mass, lections, calendar, Divine Office, *Rituale, Pontificale,* etc. in the 1960s. The Pian reform was the foundational act of violence that, by laying hands on the most solemn part of the liturgical year, made the remainder of the desecration *a fortiori* possible.

3. See Cekada, *Work of Human Hands,* 286–88. As Bishop Athanasius Schneider has said: "The third wound is the new Offertory prayers. They are an entirely new creation and had never been used in the Church. They do less to express the mystery of the sacrifice of the Cross than that of a banquet; thus they recall the prayers of the Jewish Sabbath meal. In the more than thousand-year tradition of the Church in both East and West, the Offertory prayers have always been expressly oriented to the mystery of the sacrifice of the Cross (see, e.g., Paul Tirot, *Histoire des prières d'offertoire dans la liturgie romaine du VIIème au XVIème siècle* [Rome, 1985]). There is no doubt that such an absolutely new creation contradicts the clear formulation of Vatican II that states: 'Innovationes ne fiant . . . novae formae ex formis iam exstantibus organice crescant' (*Sacrosanctum Concilium,* 23)" (from the lecture "The Extraordinary Form and the New Evangelization").

ristic Prayer II is selected.[4] It is not easy to go back through those church doors, time after time, fully aware of the spectacle of rupture and discontinuity playing out before one's eyes and ears in so many texts and gestures—or more often, in so many screaming *absences* of text and gesture.

How easy, how fruitful, how consoling it would be if one could simply attend the traditional Latin Mass and peacefully drink in its secrets, its wealth of prayer, its pure and holy adoration! Yet we are still far from a situation in which it is possible for most Catholics to attend the *usus antiquior* on a regular basis.

My role as a choir and schola director has obliged me to continue to provide music regularly for both the *usus antiquior* and the *usus recentior.* With the former, the work is pure joy: I can yield myself to the flow of the liturgy, for which so much of the music is pre-determined, and find great consolation in the fixed ceremonies and prayers, so full of ageless Christian meaning. With the Novus Ordo, things are much more difficult, whether it be navigating the many possible realizations of liturgy that may occur depending on the celebrant, or simply finding my bearings in the midst of an awkwardly modular, relentlessly verbose, ceremonially-challenged prayer service.

At times I can find "pegs" in the new liturgy to hang on to, which enable me to enter into liturgical prayer without too much critical reflection. If, for example, Mass is celebrated in such a way that the preparation of the gifts is done silently while the Offertory antiphon is being sung, I am able to forget about the *faux* ritual, since my attention is being drawn to the chant, which is truly an element of continuity in the rite. Cloaked in this way, the silent Offertory begins

---

4. Eucharistic Prayer II is an example of both "the exaggerated and senseless antiquarianism" and the "search for novelty" condemned by Pope Pius XII in *Mediator Dei* (§8; §§59–64): cobbled together from bits of Hippolytus thought—mistakenly, as it turns out—to be an early Christian anaphora, given a last desperate edit at a Roman restaurant the night before its due date, and nevertheless so inadequate in conveying the theology of the Mass as a true and proper sacrifice that its content was found unobjectionable by Protestant consultants. The learned and judicious Fr. Hunwicke has written more than once on the groundless innovation of multiple anaphoras in the Roman Rite.

to look like the real thing; there is a welcome appearance of continuity with the Roman tradition, even if the substance of it is still lacking. In general, Gregorian chants being sung, times of silence, people kneeling for communion, and, above all, the priest facing *ad orientem* are substantial helps to me in maintaining an interior calm and a focus on the Lord. One ceases to be the theater critic (to recall Mosebach's mordant phrase) and becomes the simple believer. But when these traditional elements are mostly or altogether absent, as they too often are, what hits me in the face is the massive fact of discontinuity, together with my knowledge of the dubious and, at times, modernist *reasons* for that discontinuity.

One is hit with a left hook and a right hook—an immediate, aesthetic, intuitive reaction, and an intellectual, spiritual, reflective reaction, both negative. One *feels* it to be wrong in the moment; one *knows* it to be wrong in principle. And that makes the time at church poorly spent: one can become frustrated and annoyed, one can (at times legitimately) judge that one does not have the right dispositions for receiving Holy Communion. Is it not true for a large number of the faithful, larger than officialdom would ever admit, that the Ordinary Form as typically celebrated puts a serious, almost fatal cap on our genuine "active participation"? Far from helping us along on the road to perfection, attracting us with its inner mystery and outward beauty, such a Mass is an event we just try to get through as quickly and painlessly as possible, hoping we will not think too much about anything we are seeing or hearing, and perhaps making a promise to ourselves as we leave that we will not loudly complain about it all the way home or over the pancakes. How ironic, that a rite so drastically overhauled and reworked with a view to "reaching the people at last" and soliciting their hearty involvement has, in reality, soured and repelled so many of the faithful over the decades! It has even made distasteful the very *concept* of active participation, in spite of the great value of this venerable principle properly understood.[5]

---

5. See Chapter 8. How often do we find traditionally-minded Catholics resolved *not* to sing the Ordinary chants at Mass or *not* to speak certain prayers like *Domine, non sum dignus,* simply because any such involvement reminds them of the coercive

With all this spiritual trouble that my decades of studying the liturgy have brought, do I ever find myself wishing that I did not know the various things I now know? If I could turn back the clock to a time when I naïvely thought the reformed Mass was perfectly fine and had merely suffered from random incidental abuses, would I *prefer* a state of ignorance, in order to have an easier time worshiping in this impoverished zone, this region of dissimilitude?

No, in all honesty, I cannot say that. My spiritual life would never have grown as it did, nor my grasp of sacred theology, had it not been for the beauty, reverence, and profundity of the traditional liturgy that I discovered as a young man, fell in love with, and now long for ceaselessly. I would not today be a Benedictine oblate praying the Divine Office, which is a source of tremendous vitality, light, and consolation to me. My situation is far from optimal, due to the irregular availability of the traditional liturgy in my community, but I do not regret bearing the cross of knowledge, which has opened to me a whole world of wonders to which I would otherwise be blind. It is a flowering cross, and I imagine the same is true for many who love traditional ways.

Sometimes people ask me why it makes such a difference whether one attends the Novus Ordo or the *usus antiquior.* "Are they not essentially the same—the Holy Sacrifice of the Mass? Don't you get Jesus at either?"

Usually the one asking this common question does not really grasp how great the difference is between the forms, and how much they actually *form* us, how much they express and shape the very content our faith. The liturgy is an ethical-aesthetic event, not a supernatural slot-machine for receiving a sacrament. How we worship is itself a definite exercise of faith, hope, and charity, one that prepares us well or ill for union with the object of these virtues. Liturgy is an icon of Christ and, in a way, an icon of man approaching

psychology of the Novus Ordo? Among the many evils that may be laid to its charge, we may thank the reformed liturgy for undermining over half a century of patient papal encouragement of communal chant and the numerous initiatives around the world, such as Ward Method schoolrooms, that were bringing such a beautiful form of participation back to ordinary Catholics.

Christ. Our very self-understanding and our orientation to God, our assimilation of His mysteries, is determined by the rite. One reaches the mystery *through* the liturgy; the mystery is proportioned to the mind and heart by the texts, actions, music, silence. In a sense, the mystery is *given shape* by the liturgy, even as it gives shape to the worshiper. Hence, *pace* conservatives, it is not as simple as "overlooking" the human instruments to allow the divine agent to work; that would be like saying a husband could overlook his wife because she is, after all, a secondary cause, while God is the real primary cause. No child will be conceived that way, nor any marriage problem solved!

It is far more like the relationship between the meaning of a play, the words of it, and the way the words are presented—or even better, between a piece of music and its performance. The music has its real existence *in* the performance, and one accesses it *through* the performance. Just as the music has no real existence apart from the performance, neither has the liturgy some objective or generic essence by which we are perfected, in abstraction from the subjective and specific experience of liturgy here and now, in this or that form. We are perfected by the thing as it actually exists and functions, not by its technical validity or licitness. Attending the Ordinary Form is, in most cases, like listening to amateurs acting out a Shakespeare play bowdlerized by Victorians, or listening to a string quartet playing badly out of tune and time.

The reduction of liturgy to validity and licitness is truly one of the most subtle and pernicious reductionisms of the modern age, since it has long prevented urgently necessary conversations about the mystical-ascetical ascent to God through the contemplative dimension of the liturgy, with its companion goods of fidelity to tradition and cultural excellence. *This* is the conversation that we must have, precisely for the sake of encountering the real Christ, the just and merciful Pantokrator, and for the preaching of Him to our contemporaries—including our own children. A traditional Catholic is one who stalwartly resists all reductionism and minimalism as sins against the glory of God and the salvation of His people. With the humility of one who knows himself to be unworthy but with the intense desire of one who is poor and needy, he begs for the riches of the Church's tradition, the banquet of the king's sons. He is asking for bread, eggs, and fish, not stones, serpents, and scorpions (cf. Lk 11:11–12). May the shepherds who stand in for Christ, and who must therefore answer Him at the dread judgment, make true in our day the prophet's promise: "I will fill the soul of the priests with fatness: and my people shall be filled with my good things, saith the Lord" (Jer 31:14).

Let us, then, not run away from painful knowledge and vexing wisdom, if bearing this burden will motivate us all the more to seek out the good things of the Lord and fill our souls with them. No one can desire to receive them more ardently than Our Lord desires to give them to us, and, although He allows delays, obstacles, and setbacks to test our earnest resolve, no one, ultimately, can annihilate the gifts He has bestowed on His Church. They remain in His fiery Heart and generous hand, and He will never cease to give them to His beloved Bride, the Church.

That the Lord may be counted on to provide does not excuse us from doing what is in our power to be deserving of His providence. It is His very generosity that demands of us a corresponding activity by which we strive to be worthy of His gifts. I shall expand on this point with an image. It feels easier to walk downhill than uphill, but it is harder on the knees. It feels harder to climb uphill, but the beautiful view at the top is always worth the effort. As hikers often experience, you will be walking along a narrow trail, perhaps in the midst of crowded trees, thinking the small thoughts that go with one step after another. You turn a bend, and suddenly the whole world opens up in a breathtaking vista that almost makes you feel dizzy, as if the beauty might subvert your muscles. That beauty was put there by God, not by you, and yet it took your effort to reach it. We make the trails, we walk on them, but the beauty is from above; it was there before we existed and it will long outlast our mortality. Human effort was the indispensable condition for the sight of this beauty.

The same is true of the liturgical tradition: it is God's immense gift to us, it comes before us and goes beyond us, we did not generate it and we cannot, of ourselves, guarantee it. It is a gift given to us in trust; it is *not* our possession to dispose of, like a piece of clothing, a book, or a vehicle we own. Its intrinsic worth as well as the identity of the giver obliges us to work hard to preserve it, to know it intimately, to live it as fully as we can; in short, to be *worthy* of it. What we absolutely must *not* do is to think that it would be better to create an alternative, easier, more controllable "tradition" and attempt to rejoice in it. That would be like planting a giant flat screen at the end of the trail and looking at a filmed sunset.

The notion that we should strive to make ourselves *worthy* of our liturgical tradition is one that is, I am afraid, quite unfamiliar today, because of decades-long bad habits induced by reformers, revisers, translators, and other committee members who placed themselves over and above the tradition as its superiors, its judges, its improvers, its improvisers. This is not and cannot be the attitude of one who, conscious of his own limitations and of the narrowness of any age, people, or culture, gratefully and humbly receives a noble inheritance, rejoices in its prayer-saturated beauty and stability, and delivers it integrally to his successors—perhaps embellished with additional signs of reverence and devotion, if he has been prompted to originate them.

A Catholic who is aware of himself, who senses the smallness of his vision and the greatness of the tradition that precedes and carries him, is, in fact, *relieved* that he does not have to make things up as he goes along; he need not second-guess the river along which he floats. He lets himself be the ready instrument of a far greater actor, the mouth through which the same word continues to sound, the hand or foot that executes the head's bidding:

> This beauty which fell on his ears, which enveloped and possessed him, which humbled him with its austere and stately measures, was too great to have its source in him. Arising elsewhere, it flowed through him; he had no part in it, except to lend, to give, himself. His voice? Perhaps; but Another sang.[6]

6. Kent, *Brother Michel*, 299–300.

As an instrument, a voice, a servant, he does not fear messing up that which was whole and safe and salvific before he even came to be and which will continue long after he is gone. He simply strives to order His life according to the gift of tradition, so that he may be ever more pleasing to its divine author, ever more apt to receive from Him the grace of further insights into it and deeper affection for it. The prayers of such a one are truly humble and destined to be heard, because he is grateful for what the Lord has granted and industrious in making use of it, instead of second-guessing Him and looking askance at His decrees.

No matter how much emphasis we place on divine initiative and generosity, there *is* something important, something indispensable, that the individual—the bishop, the priest, the deacon, the religious, the layman—must contribute in order that the tradition will not die out or shrivel up. True, he does not have to *invent* the tradition, but neither can he ignore it or treat it lightly. He must embrace it or else it will cease to exist.[7] In the end, the recipient must actually, energetically *receive*. Receptivity is no passivity, much less inertia, but the most vital activity of the creature in relation to God in His eternal mystery and to all that is supernatural.

In a famous interview published in *The Latin Mass* magazine, Alice von Hildebrand addressed this issue head on. When asked: "There are those critics of the ancient Latin Mass who point out that the crisis in the Church developed at a time when the Mass was offered throughout the world. Why should we then think its revival is intrinsic to the solution?," she replied:

> The devil hates the ancient Mass. He hates it because it is the most perfect reformulation of all the teachings of the Church. It was my husband who gave me this insight about the Mass. The problem that ushered in the present crisis was not the traditional Mass. The problem was that priests who offered it had already lost the sense of the supernatural and the transcendent. They rushed through the prayers, they mumbled and didn't enunciate them. That is a sign that they had brought to the Mass their growing secularism.

7. See the superb article of Joseph Shaw, "Does Tradition preserve us, or we the Tradition?," published at *LMS Chairman*, October 13, 2015.

The ancient Mass does not abide irreverence, and that was why so many priests were just as happy to see it go.[8]

The law of entropy states that any system left to itself, without new energy added to it from outside, will lose order, will devolve or unwind. The tendency of the material world, taken as a closed system, is towards unraveling. If order cannot somehow be re-introduced, decay is unavoidable.

In the little universe of the liturgy, that necessary principle of order is reverence for texts, music, rubrics, and decorum handed down in the life of the faithful and sustained by Church authority properly exercised. These things—the reverence, the handing down, the sustaining—can be contributed only by living human beings who correspond with the grace of the Holy Spirit. As long as they are supplied, the liturgy thrives and continues along its way, undiminished, introducing new energy from outside, from the inexhaustible Heart of Jesus. Without these things, however, the liturgy as an *opus hominis* is doomed to disintegration. The man who lets himself become unreceptive or, worse, hardens his heart against the gift, becomes unworthy. The loss of a wealthy inheritance is just punishment for the failure to value one's family name, one's spiritual aristocracy.

Liturgical decadence, deviation, and disorder are, like the natural tendency of entropy, a downhill walk for fallen man. Left to himself, left without the guidance of the tradition willed by the Holy Spirit and the example of many saints who have shown us how to walk the often grueling uphill path of fidelity, fallen man will make liturgy conform to his own whims and wants, his own programs and purposes—something easier, and more damaging. It is the uphill climb, prepared for by self-discipline, that leads to the magnificent vista, the glimpse of a vast and humbling beauty that can only come from the mind of the Creator. "Hate not laborious works, nor husbandry ordained by the Most High. Number not thyself among the multitude of the disorderly" (Sir 7:16–17).

A story will illustrate this point. As part of my work I lead a Gre-

---

8. "Present at the Demolition: An Interview with Dr. Alice von Hildebrand," *The Latin Mass,* Summer 2001, accessed at http://www.latinmassmagazine.com/art icles/articles_2001_su_hildebran.html, January 11, 2017.

gorian schola consisting of men enrolled in the college. For six years running, the schola has sung the traditional office of Tenebrae for Maundy Thursday; this past year we added the office for Holy Saturday as well. It has been wonderful to see the growth from year to year: the schola boasted twice as many members in 2017 as in 2012, and the congregation was about four times as large. The singing has improved as we become habituated to the psalm tones and texts, and the faithful in the pews, who have all the psalms in booklets, voluntarily sing along just a bit better each year.

For me, this prompts a couple of heartening reflections. The first is simply that our Holy Mother Church gives us so many beautiful resources for entering into the mystery of Our Lord Jesus Christ—if only we would use them! Yes, it takes time and effort and planning, as a two-and-a-half hour service of Latin chant is not something one can do at the drop of a hat. But it is worth it in the end. The people are edified, their hearts immersed in the darkness of the Passion, which the office of Tenebrae probes and evokes without sentimentality or haste. The singers themselves feel that the Lord has worked in and through them. The inherent sacredness and sanctifying power of these services draw in the faithful who are seeking for ways to observe the Triduum with great devotion. In short: we do not need to invent new things; we need to rediscover old things that have always worked and will always work, wherever men and women are hungering for God.

The second reflection is that the best and deepest things take time to assimilate, to understand, to perfect. When it comes to liturgy in particular, we have to fight tooth and nail against the modern spirit of immediate gratification and quick results. When we first did the office of Tenebrae, we could barely chant the music, let alone follow the texts. The people stumbled over the psalms. It was not exactly elegant. But we did it anyhow because we saw it as a mountain worth climbing, no matter how many bruises along the way. The next year it was a little easier; one felt oriented and clued in. The year after, the psalm tones came more naturally and the responsories felt like old acquaintances. A year later, more fellows were volunteering to sing the nine readings. The fifth year, for the first time, I was not worrying about the music and found myself drawn deeply into the meaning of the psalms and readings. It took me five years to get to that point. It is like a treasure chest containing exquisite treasure but locked with formidable locks: you work at it patiently because you know that the yield is worthwhile.

Nothing valuable comes cheaply. Many people, maybe even most people, value a challenge that corresponds to their dignity, calls upon all their powers, rewards their efforts. This truth is brought out vividly by the contrast between Tridentine and non-Tridentine altar serving. The former is much more demanding, takes an investment of time, requires precision, thoughtfulness, and obedience to commands—but the boys and young men go in for that, thrive on it. If we pay attention to the way human beings are made and what calls forth their greatest potential, we will see anew the wisdom of the Church in placing at our disposal such hard-won treasures.

There is a scene in the remarkable (and far too little known) novel *The Mass of Brother Michel* where the titular character reflects on the difficult climb from earthly love to the love of God. How well these words apply, *mutatis mutandis,* to the traditional liturgy!

> While it is true beyond question that this love of heaven rewards and satisfies the heart, filling it with riches of joy and beauty and delight as no love of earth can ever do, it is likewise true that this love may not be enjoyed without cost: for so God has ordered it. But the cost, far from tempting us to part with it, convinces us rather of its exalted worth. A man will permit trash to be stolen from him without a struggle, but a treasure beyond price he will defend with his life. And if he must fight to keep it, and is wounded in the encounter, he regards his hurts as of little moment, provided only he has beaten off the thief, and preserved his treasure from harm. So it is with this heavenly treasure, this gift of love, which God has given us: how little would we esteem it, if to keep it cost us nothing! Because of the cost, we know that it is not our virtue, but His gift; because of the cost, we are reminded into how hideous a state we should fall, did He withdraw it from us; because of the cost, we are on our knees daily, beseeching Him for grace to preserve and defend it to the end; because of the cost, we value it and cherish it the more.[9]

9. Kent, *Brother Michel,* 158–59.

After a lapse of over twenty years, I re-read—this time aloud with my children—*The History of Rasselas, Prince of Abissinia,* by Samuel Johnson. If Johnson's style is delightfully and pompously old-fashioned, the moral he puts forward is timeless. Rasselas is a young prince trapped inside a kingdom from which all evil and suffering have been banished. He has all the pleasures and comforts life can provide, yet he is miserable, discontented, because he is deprived of the single greatest need of human nature: the longing for something beyond, something unknown, unexpected, grand, that makes sense of everything else and without which nothing has any meaning. At one point early on Rasselas cries out: "Give me something to desire."

Quare tristis es, anima mea, et quare conturbas me?

Reading this outcry, I was struck by how well it conveys the fundamental problem with the reformed liturgy and the entire culture that surrounds and sustains it. The new liturgy was so obviously designed with the goal of total accessibility that it leaves nothing to long for, to discover, to stumble upon by surprise, to puzzle over, to be mystified about. It has no residue of unintelligibility, no multi-layered super-intelligibility. What you see and hear is what you get; the participant is, as it were, satisfied in every way, with the "evil" of incomprehension and the "suffering" of iconic-architectural-liturgical exclusion set aside. In the revised rites there is no freedom, anonymity, spaciousness, or fascination. Everything is planned out as a tête-à-tête over the table. One is paralyzed with overdetermination; one cannot mentally breathe or sigh; reflection, repentance, adoration, interior surrender are well-nigh impossible to achieve. The pleasures and comforts of active participation are present in abundance—yet we suffer a chilling boredom, a terrible sense of want. We are lacking the one thing necessary for liturgy as such: the sense and the reality of *mystery.* We, too, cry out: "Give me something to *desire.*"

Laudamus te. Benedicimus te. Adoramus te. Glorificamus te.

In the traditional liturgies of Eastern and Western Christianity, this unnameable, indomitable, attractively terrifying mystery is always present. It is both willing and unwilling to be called by all the names we can muster from creation and history. It is both found and not found in silence and solemnity. Always on the periphery, on the edge, barely glimpsed but never caught, embraced but escaping our grasp. When we immerse ourselves in such a liturgy, we are satisfied and unsatisfied, we find something we are looking for and leave hungering, thirsting for more. We never "get to the bottom of it." Boredom is not even on the table: something too strange, too superhuman, is happening. We are obviously in the presence of . . . a Presence that is sovereignly indifferent to our petty wishes and whims, preferences and prejudices. We are simply *in the Presence*. A challenge is put to us, a gauntlet thrown down: Will you dare? Will you dare to desire more, keep desiring more and more? Will you go far, far beyond your comfort zone? "I am almost afraid to begin a journey of which I cannot perceive an end," says Nekayah, the sister of Rasselas, when they are escaping the kingdom of "tasteless tranquility."

Accendat in nobis Dominus ignem sui amoris,
et flammam aeternae caritatis.

In this escape there is a great risk for us, that we will be scared off—put off by the deafening silence, turned off by the uncomfortable solemnity, which could care less about whether we are "getting it." We are so much *not* the point that we can think ourselves superfluous; we can squirm at the thought of our intensifying smallness and of the greatness, the objectivity, the imperial dominion of the Lord. But our eyes adjust to the supernatural gloaming, our ears are tuned anew, our mind falls into peace at last and our heart knows, for the first time, a longing that cannot be assuaged. We begin to feel how refreshing it is not to be pandered to, talked down to with dumbed-down language or gestures—how liberating it is *not* to be the one focused on and constantly "invited" (that is, cajoled) to say, think, feel, do, x, y, and z. We begin to see how it is all focused on Him: *DEO gratias*. In this experience of raw exposure before the silent All-Seeing, there is great promise for us: the possibility that we will be carried off by the startling realization of our nothingness and neediness, wherein God has placed an immensity of desire to which only He, the Infinite, can respond. "Give me something to *desire*."

Suscipe sancta Trinitas hanc oblationem.

The Catholic Church will never be able to flourish in spiritual health until there is restored in her a liturgy of desire, infinitude, inaccessibility; a liturgy of receptive participation and active asceticism; a liturgy utterly free from the vanity of human chitchat, committee jargon, and slavish pandering to modernity; a liturgy that, like pure white light, is loftily indifferent to the subjective kaleidoscope of emotion and sentimentality. This is the liturgy that will draw and produce the "man of desires" (Dan 9:23, 10:11, 10:19). Without it, desuetude, decay, and death will be our lot. Man is made by God for God, for divinity, for transcendence, for mystery, and if he cannot find these in the Church, he will despairingly search for substitutes in a host of false religions and evanescent ecstasies.

Laudans invocabo Dominum, et ab inimicis meis salvus ero.

May the Lord deliver us from evils that are all the worse for their camouflage of good, and bring us to the painful yearning for the living God that is expressed with such fiery vehemence and humbling disinterestedness in the rites and doctrines of tradition. *Desiderio desideravi hoc pascha manducare vobiscum*: "With desire have I desired to eat this pasch with you" (Lk 22:15).

Et vidimus gloriam ejus, gloriam quasi
Unigeniti a Patre, plenum gratiae et veritatis.

Effundam super domum David et super habitatores Hierusalem
spiritum gratiae et precum: et aspicient ad me quem confixerunt.

I will pour out upon the house of David and the inhabitants of
Jerusalem the spirit of grace and prayers: and they shall look
upon Me, whom they have pierced.

ZECHARIAH 12:10

8

How the *Usus Antiquior* Elicits Superior Participation

HOW MANY TIMES do lovers of the classical Roman Rite hear the objection: "The new Mass is better than the old because it allows for more active participation on the part of the faithful," or "The old Mass just had to be reformed eventually, because the priest was the only one doing anything, and the people were all mute spectators." My aim in this chapter is to refute such claims and to demonstrate that, if anything, the opposite is true.

Active Participation

People who sit down and study *Sacrosanctum Concilium* are often struck by how much of this document is unknown, ignored, or contradicted by contemporary Catholic practice. The most notorious victim of journalistic simplification has been the notion of "active participation" or *participatio actuosa*. The word *actuosa* means fully or totally engaged in activity, like a dancer or an actor who is putting everything into the dancing or the acting; it might be considered "super-active."[1] But what is the notion of activity here? It is actualizing one's full potential, entering into possession of a good rather than having an unrealized capacity for it. In contemporary English, "active" often means simply the contrary of passive or receptive, yet from a Christian perspective, these are by no means contrary. In imi-

---

1. Forcellini's authoritative lexicon says that *actuosus* "properly is one who is totally engaged in the act or motion of the body ... such as an actor and a dancer, who for this reason are called *actuosi*."

tation of the Blessed Virgin Mary, I can be *actively receptive* to the Word of God;[2] I can be fully actualizing my ability to be acted upon at Mass by the chants, prayers, and ceremonies, without my doing much of anything that would be styled "active" in contemporary English. As John Paul II explained in an address to American bishops:

> Active participation certainly means that, in gesture, word, song and service, all the members of the community take part in an act of worship, which is anything but inert or passive. Yet active participation does not preclude the active passivity of silence, stillness and listening: indeed, it demands it. Worshippers are not passive, for instance, when listening to the readings or the homily, or following the prayers of the celebrant, and the chants and music of the liturgy. These are experiences of silence and stillness, but they are in their own way profoundly active. In a culture which neither favors nor fosters meditative quiet, the art of interior listening is learned only with difficulty. Here we see how the liturgy, though it must always be properly inculturated, must also be counter-cultural.[3]

Dom Alcuin Reid succinctly explains the Council's intention:

> The Council called for *participatio actuosa,* which is primarily our internal connection with the liturgical action—with what Jesus Christ is doing in his Church in the liturgical rites. This participation is about where my mind and heart are. Our external actions in the liturgy serve and facilitate this. But *participatio actuosa* is not first and foremost external activity, or performing a particular liturgical ministry. That, unfortunately, has been a common misconception of the Council's desire.[4]

In everyday speech, the word "active" tends to connote activism, in the sense in which the Americanists excoriated by Leo XIII in *Testem Benevolentiae* exalted the "active" virtues of secular engagement over what they called "passive" virtues, such as contempla-

---

2. See Chapter 3.

3. John Paul II, *Address to the Bishops of Washington, Oregon, Idaho, Montana, and Alaska* §4.

4. "The Liturgy, Fifty Years after *Sacrosanctum Concilium,*" published at *The Catholic World Report,* December 4, 2013.

tion.[5] In the liturgical sphere, "active" has been wielded like a sickle to cut down various modes of receptivity, the alert absorption of listening, the silence conducive to meditation.[6]

What we need to recover, therefore, is that deeper sense of engagement that begins and ends with interior activity—faith leading to contemplation, contemplation feeding the flame of charity—for which the *usus antiquior* is so well suited. As Aristotle showed long ago, the most divine of human activities, and the one in which the essence of happiness consists, is contemplation.[7]

Since *Sacrosanctum Concilium* establishes that participation is first and foremost interior and then is further expressed and solidified through external actions such as singing responses and adopting postures, it is clear that the Council Fathers did not intend to use *actuosa* to mean "hyperactive." They intended to underline what Pope Pius XI had already said decades earlier, namely, that the faithful should not be inert spectators at Mass, but should enter into it with mind, heart, and body. Archbishop Salvatore Cordileone offers the following gloss:

> Perhaps a better word to express this teaching of the Council ("actuosa" in the original Latin) is "engaged": we are present to the liturgical action, allowing it to seep down into the depths of our consciousness. Thus, in speaking of the "restoration" of the sacred liturgy, the Council fathers articulated their vision of restoring the liturgy to what it was always meant to be: Catholics at Mass engaged in understanding and praying the liturgy with heart and mind, and this active engagement expressed in their reciting and singing the parts of the Mass proper to them, rather than sitting (or

5. For further discussion of this apostolic letter and its critique of activism, see Chapter 4 of *Resurgent in the Midst of Crisis*.

6. Through the 1960s and 70s, activists with bad taste and a poor grasp of human psychology exhausted themselves in efforts to coerce the people in the pews into what William F. Buckley Jr. wryly called "hyperactive participation" (*Nearer, My God: An Autobiography of Faith* [New York: Doubleday, 1997], 97).

7. See *Nicomachean Ethics*, Bk. 10, ch. 7. This Aristotelian (and, truth be told, Platonic) doctrine was unanimously accepted by all the Fathers of the Church, leading to the conviction of the intrinsic superiority of the contemplative life consecrated wholly to God over the active life of external works—something the Magisterium itself has taught.

kneeling, as the case may be) as passive observers, saying their own private prayers. That is, personal devotion is to enhance one's full, active and conscious participation at Mass, not substitute for it.[8]

Actuosa bespeaks a profoundly (one might even say totally) active response that goes beyond superficial sayings or gestures, beyond the moving of the mouth or hands, to the motions of the heart. *Participatio actuosa* involves the whole man, mind, memory, imagination, external senses, vocal chords. People are to be fully engaged with all their faculties of body and soul, in this regard quite like a ballet dancer or a Shakespearian actor. *Actuosa* essentially says: be as active as you can be in the activity of divine worship, which is first and foremost interior (after all, only intellectual beings can worship—brute animals, plants, minerals, are excluded from that noble activity) and becomes external when and as appropriate for each category of participant.[9]

Notice this wonderful truth: everyone can do everything in the Mass *interiorly,* even though external actions are notably and necessarily differentiated. For example, only the priest elevates the host, while only the laity come forward to receive Communion. Externally we are differentiated, as is just and right for a hierarchical Mystical Body such as the Church that visibly mirrors the hierarchical order of the human body itself and of the cosmos. But interiorly we are united by the one font and apex of all that we are, all that we do, and all that we suffer. The external diversity is at the service of the interior unity, just as the difference of sexes is for the sake of the unity and fruitfulness of marriage.[10]

The great theologian whom I hope future generations of Catholics will matter-of-factly refer to as "the Doctor of the Liturgy,"

8. Foreword, Fr. Samuel F. Weber, O.S.B., *The Proper of the Mass for Sundays and Solemnities* (San Francisco: Ignatius Press, 2014), xi.

9. Of the ample literature on the meaning of *participatio actuosa,* I particularly recommend Msgr. Richard Schuler, "Participation," *Sacred Music,* vol. 114, n.4 (Winter 1987): 7–10, available online.

10. This reflection helps us to see, once again, the profound disharmony introduced by extraordinary ministers of Holy Communion. When the laity assume this clerical function, a clash arises between the external action proper to the clergy, which is to come down from the altar to give the divine food and drink to the faith-

Joseph Ratzinger, calls to our attention a particularly modern problem:

> That which is truly great grows unnoticed, and silence at the right moment is more fruitful than the constant activity that only too easily degenerates into spiritual idleness. In the present age, we are all possessed by a strange restlessness that suspects any silence of being a waste of time and any kind of repose as being negligence. We forget the real mystery of time, the real mystery present in growth and activity. That mystery involves silence and stillness. Even in the religious sphere we tend to expect and hope for everything from our own activity. We use all kinds of exercises and involvements to evade the real mystery of interior growth before God. And yet in the religious sphere receptivity is at least as important as activity.[11]

Louis Bouyer's definition is therefore perfectly on target: "Participation in the liturgy is the reception of sacramental grace through a living faith illumined and enflamed by the liturgy itself."[12] Note how this definition highlights grace, faith, receptivity, illumination, and ardor—the spiritual ingredients of holiness. As Ratzinger says:

> The real "action" in the liturgy in which we are all supposed to participate is the action of God Himself. This is what is new and distinctive about Christian liturgy: God Himself acts and does what is essential.[13]

Cardinal Malcolm Ranjith expands on this point:

> This kind of participation in the very action of Christ, the High Priest, requires from us nothing less than an attitude of being

---

ful, and the action proper to the laity, which is to come forward towards the altar to receive that food and drink. The actions are contrary and complementary. The invasion of laity into the sanctuary establishes them as a separate social caste, a privileged group of "assistants," whose activity reinforces the impression that the priesthood is utilitarian and the laity are passive.

11. Joseph Ratzinger, *Dogma and Preaching,* trans. Matthew J. O'Connell (Chicago: Franciscan Herald Press, 1985), 78.

12. Louis Bouyer, *The Liturgy Revived: A Doctrinal Commentary of the Conciliar Constitution on the Liturgy* (Notre Dame, IN: University of Notre Dame Press, 1964), 106.

13. Ratzinger, *The Spirit of the Liturgy,* 173.

totally absorbed in Him. . . . Active participation, thus, is not a giving way to any activism but an integral and total assimilation into the person of Christ who is truly the High Priest of that eternal and uninterrupted celebration of the heavenly liturgy.[14]

Conscious Participation

Even with the common misunderstanding of "actual" cleared out of the way, it is a curious fact that the integral expression from *Sacrosanctum Concilium* 14 is rarely quoted: "Mother Church earnestly desires that all the faithful should be led to that *full, conscious, and active* participation in liturgical celebrations which is demanded by the very nature of the liturgy."[15] Whatever happened to "full" and "conscious"?

The experience of several decades of attending Mass in both "forms" of the Roman Rite (and both celebrated with rubrical fidelity and a reverent spirit) has convinced me that there is paradoxically a far greater possibility of not consciously paying attention to the Mass in the vernacular, precisely because of its familiarity: it becomes like a reflex action, the words can go in and out while the mind is far away. The vernacular is our everyday comfort zone, and so it does not grab our attention.[16] This is why when we are in a

---

14. Malcolm Ranjith, "Toward an *Ars Celebrandi* in Liturgy," *Adoremus* Online Edition, March 2009, vol. 15, n. 1, printing the transcript of his talk at the Gateway Conference in St. Louis, November 8, 2008.

15. In the original: "*Valde cupit Mater Ecclesia ut fideles universi ad plenam illam, consciam atque actuosam liturgicarum celebrationum participationem ducantur, quae ab ipsius Liturgiae natura postulatur.*"

16. The oft-noted problem of "zoning out" during readings is a universal problem for which no liturgy has a foolproof solution—and yet, all things being equal, one might prefer a situation where one could follow along with the reading in one's daily missal, and then hear it read afterwards in English from the pulpit before the homily, as if often done in traditional communities. One's chances of getting something out of that reading would be significantly higher. At least, that's been my own experience over the years. The assimilation of the Word of God in its liturgical finality is greatly aided by the older Roman Rite's one-year reading cycle, the lections of which tend to be shorter and are even repeated a number of times during the year. For a defense of the old lectionary and a critique of the new, see Kwasniewski, "Reform of the Lectionary."

busy place where lots of people are speaking, we tend not to notice that they are even talking—whereas when we hear a foreign language, something other than our mother tongue, suddenly our attention is caught by it.

Of course, this lack of attentiveness can happen in the sphere of any language: as someone once put it, I can be doing finances inside my head while chanting the Credo in Latin—if I have been chanting it every week for years. But it nevertheless seems evident that this danger is significantly less present with the *usus antiquior*, for two reasons.

First, its very foreignness *demands* of the worshiper some effort to enter into it; indeed, it demands of the worshiper a decision about whether he really wants to enter into it or not. It is almost pointless to sit there unless you are ready to *do* something to engage the Mass or at very least to begin to pray. The use of a daily missal, widespread in traditional communities, is a powerful means of assimilating the mind and heart of the Church at prayer—and for me, following the prayers in my missal has amounted to a decades-long formation of my own mind and heart, giving me a savor for things spiritual, exemplars of holiness, ascetical rules, aspirations and resolutions. When I attend the *usus antiquior*, I am always much more actively engaged in the Mass, because there is more to do (I will come back to this point) and it seems more natural to use a missal to help me do it.

Second, the traditional Latin Mass is so obviously focused on God, directed to the adoration of Him, that one who is mentally *present* to what is happening is ineluctably drawn into the sacred mysteries, even if only at the simplest and most fundamental level of acknowledging the reality of God and adoring our Blessed Lord in the most Holy Sacrament. I am afraid to say that it is not clear at all that most Catholics attending most vernacular Novus Ordo liturgies are ever confronted unequivocally and irresistibly with the reality of God and the demand for adoration. Or, to put it differently, the old liturgy *forms* these attitudes in the soul, whereas the new liturgy *presupposes* them. If you do not already have the right understanding and frame of mind, the Novus Ordo will do very little to give it to you, whereas the *usus antiquior* is either going to give it to you in time or drive you away. When you attend the traditional Mass, you find yourself either attracted by something special in it, or put off by the demands it makes. Lukewarmness is not an option.

The word "conscious" is a relative term: consciousness is always correlative to its object, that of which we are or become conscious. When we consider what it is that occupies our consciousness, it is usually either something on which we are concentrating in play or labor, or something that gradually or suddenly impresses itself upon our senses and thereby seizes our mental attention. Now, we are bound to the liturgy in both ways. We can yield ourselves to it by a voluntary effort, which may, if we are blessed, result in "getting lost" in it playfully and arduously; or our attention can be caught by something in the liturgy itself—a word, sound, or melody, a span of silence, an action or series of actions—that draws our gaze, turns our ear, invades our smell, moves our affections.[17] These facts about human consciousness help us to see that the liturgy, although it exists to glorify God, should be comprised of elements that *move* us to the activity of glorifying God. A long and complex history of liturgical development achieved exactly such a result, which was the fruit of centuries of enthusiastic religious practice drawing upon universally communicative symbols of the sacred, filtered through and, one might say, wondrously garbled by, the parameters of special divine revelation.[18]

Consequently, one can never too much deplore the ascendancy of

---

17. On the connection between efficacious liturgical action (efficacious from the *ex opere operato* standpoint) and consistently patterned sensory stimulation, see Linda Graber, "Focus vs. Blur: Multi-Sensory Learning, Motivated Focus, and the Mass," published at *OnePeterFive* on January 15, January 25, and February 26, 2016.

18. What I mean by the last claim is that while Christian worship obviously makes use of universal sacred symbols (as the prolific and often insightful work of the so-called "Perennialists" emphasizes), it unpredictably modifies and curiously recombines them, sometimes even doing a certain violence to them, owing to the "scandal of the particular," Jesus of Nazareth, the incarnate *Logos*. Our worship, like our theology, rests (as Guardini and Ratzinger never tire of saying) on cosmos, history, and mystery. The first and last may be shared to some extent with other religions, but the middle term, which is conceptually and existentially centermost, is unique. Therefore the Faith and its liturgy can never be rationally extrapolated or constructed. For more on this point, see Chapters 2 and 3.

a utilitarian and functionalist attitude that largely robbed the Mass of its power to move us in manifold ways. Since those charged with the liturgical reform must have thought that moving people—deepening their spiritual lives—was the utility and function sought for in the liturgy, we are faced with a perplexing question: why did they end up removing so many of the active ingredients? The reason is that they were not just utilitarians and functionalists, which would have been regrettable enough, but also rationalists who underappreciated the potency of means of communication other than those operating at the level of fully conscious, propositional, rational thought.[19]

It is useful to be clear and forthright about this point, because so few people today would still agree with that kind of mentality. Liberals and charismatics both want to focus on the emotions, and they associate theological conservatism with a form of rationalism. But to get the emotions back into a liturgy from which the moving pageantry of centuries of heartfelt devotion has been largely eliminated, they have to bring in a whole lot of stuff which is nowhere in the official liturgical books. With the elements that once appealed to the whole man and his emotions having been stripped away, novel elements are invented and inserted. This, of course, breeds ever more subjectivity, heterogeneity, and ultimately heterodoxy in the liturgy. To escape this madness we must return to an objective liturgy that is capable of addressing the whole person from all the depth of tradition, and which evokes and conveys the totality of the Christian mystery in veiled and complex ways.

St. Thomas Aquinas states, somewhat surprisingly: "the essences of things are unknown to us," *rerum essentia sunt nobis ignotae*.[20] For Thomas, even the essence of a fly cannot be fully known to us.[21] There is a tension between the Aristotelian account of our intellects

19. The "old ICEL" translation shows how they stripped out the adjectives again and again—no poetic language allowed!

20. St. Thomas Aquinas, *De veritate*, q. 10, a. 1: "Because the essences of things are unknown to us, but their powers are known to us through their acts, we frequently use the names of powers or potencies to signify essences."

21. *On the Apostle's Creed*, art. 1: "Our knowledge is weak to such a point that no philosopher would be able to investigate perfectly the nature of a single fly."

knowing the essences of things and the inaccessible depth of essence that Josef Pieper talks about in his evocative book *The Silence of St. Thomas*. If we do not have total mastery of any natural essence, much less can we expect to have it of a supernatural mystery. Just as the essences of natural things are hidden from our minds, and the substance of Our Lord in the Blessed Sacrament is hidden behind the veil of accidents, so the essence of the Holy Sacrifice of the Mass is beyond the realm of appearances and yet is glimpsed through them when they are not standing in the way.

Full Participation

So much for "conscious." What about "full" participation? Again, as surprising as it may seem in the wake of tendentious criticisms, the traditional Latin Mass allows the faithful a *fuller* participation in worship because there are more kinds of experience to participate in, verbal and non-verbal, spiritual and sensuous—indeed, there is far more *bodily* involvement, if one follows the customary practices. This last point deserves close attention.

At a Low or High Mass, depending on the feast, one might make the sign of the cross eight times:

- "In nomine Patris, et Filii, et Spiritus Sancti";
- "Adjutorium nostrum in nomine Domini";
- "Indulgentiam, absolutionem, et remissionem...";
- "Cum Sancto Spiritu" (end of the Gloria);
- "Et vitam venturi saeculi" (end of the Credo);
- "Benedictus qui venit" (in the Sanctus);
- if the absolution is repeated at the Confiteor before Communion;
- at the final blessing.

To this, some add the sign of the cross at the elevation of the Host and of the Chalice. And of course, the triple sign of the cross is made twice—once at the Gospel, and once at the Last Gospel.

Moreover, one will end up striking the breast up to 18 times(!):

- thrice at the "mea culpa" of the servers' Confiteor;
- thrice at the Agnus Dei;
- thrice at the second Confiteor;

- thrice at the "Domine, non sum dignus";
- thrice at the Salve Regina ("O clemens, O dulcis, O pia");[22]
- thrice at the "Cor Jesu sacratissimum, miserere nobis."

All these beatings of the breast are no small matter, since, as St. Thomas teaches, venial sins are forgiven when one does this action with a contrite heart.[23]

Traditionally-minded Catholics learn to make a slight bow of their heads at every mention of the name of Jesus, at doxologies, at phrases in the Gloria ("Adoramus te," "Gratias agimus tibi," and "Suscipe deprecationem nostram"), and at the "simul adoratur" of the Credo, and to bow more fully at other times during the liturgy, such as when the priest is passing by or when the thurifer is incensing the people.[24] We go one step further than bowing by genuflecting at the "Et incarnatus est" of the Creed—*every time* the Creed is said or sung, not just on Christmas and Annunciation, as in the Novus Ordo. We genuflect as well at the final blessing and at the words "Et verbum caro factum est." There are also other special

---

22. The prayers after Low Mass are not part of the Mass as such. Nevertheless, they fit into the larger point of this chapter, namely, that those who attend the *usus antiquior* regularly are exposed to a panoply of ways and occasions of participating that no longer exist in the Novus Ordo. The Low Mass and the High Mass each offers certain ways of entering into the spirit of the liturgy that are blocked off in the Novus Ordo.

23. At *In IV Sent.* d. 16, q. 2, a. 2, qa. 4, sc. 1, Aquinas writes: "There are many remedies against venial sins; for example, beating of the breast, sprinkling with holy water, extreme unction, and every sacramental anointing; a bishop's blessing, blessed bread, general confession, compassion, the forgiveness of another's faults, the Eucharist, the Lord's Prayer, and other sorts of light penance." The beating of the breast (*tunsio pectoris*) is the first example that comes to St. Thomas's mind: there is something rather obvious about it as a sign of repentance. Aquinas gives a fuller explanation in *Disputed Questions on Evil*, q. 7, a. 12: "There are other things that cause the remission of venial sin . . . for while they do not cause grace, they do stimulate the mind to consider something which stirs up the fervor of charity; and also it is piously believed that [on the occasion of their use] divine power works inwardly by stirring up the fervor of love. And in this way, holy water, the bishop's blessing, and other sacramentals of this kind cause the remission of venial sin. There are still other things that cause the remission of venial sin by stirring up the fervor of charity solely by way of reflection—for example, the Lord's Prayer, striking the breast, and the like."

occasions during the liturgical year when everyone is called upon to genuflect.

While the postures of the faithful at certain times in the Mass are not as regimented as in the Novus Ordo, a Low Mass will typically have the faithful kneeling for a long time (from the start all the way to the Gospel, and from the Sanctus all the way through the last Gospel), which is a demanding discipline and really keeps one's mind aware that one is in a special sacred place, taking part in a sacrifice. At a Sunday High Mass, there will be quite a lot of standing, bowing, genuflecting, kneeling, and sitting, which, together with the signs of the cross, the beating of the breast, the bowing of the head, and the chanting of the responses, amounts to what educators call a TPR environment—Total Physical Response. You are thrown into the worship *body and soul,* and, at almost every moment, something is happening that puts your mind back on what you are doing. The Novus Ordo has eliminated a lot of these "muscular" elements in favor of merely aural comprehension and verbal response, which, by themselves, constitute a fairly impoverished form of participation, and surely not a full one.

Most distinctive of all, perhaps, is the immensely peaceful reservoir of silence at the very center of the traditional Latin Mass. When the priest is not reading the Eucharistic Prayer "at" you, but instead is offering the Canon silently to God, always *ad orientem,* it becomes much easier to *pray* the words of the Canon oneself in union with the ministerial priest, or, if one prefers, to give oneself up to a wordless

---

24. None of these bodily actions is *scripted* in the sense that a rubric requires the people to do them, since the *usus antiquior* is blessedly free of rubrics dictating how the people are (or are not) to participate at every moment. As a result, different people at worship do some or all of these actions, according to their knowledge or inclination, or even what they happen to notice as the Mass progresses, and no one minds this diversity. There is a healthy sense of freedom of movement a little reminiscent of what one may find among the Eastern Orthodox who may walk about during the liturgy lighting candles and venerating icons. The Novus Ordo, on the contrary, perversely takes for granted the Protestant innovation of cluttering open sacred space with benches or pews and turns sitting on them into a scripted pseudo-sacred action befitting its wordy worship.

union with the sacrifice. This makes the Canon of the Mass a time of *more intensely* full, conscious, and actual participation than is facilitated by the constant stream of aural stimulation in the Novus Ordo.

A Culture of Prayer

An observation I once saw fits in well with the foregoing analysis:

> One can still hold the new rite to be integrally Catholic, and yet consider that the culture of the extraordinary form, where the people are supposedly passive, tends to teach people to pray independently, while the culture of the ordinary form often tends to create a dynamic in which people just chat to each other in church unless they are being actively animated by a minister.[25]

Another way of putting it is to say that the traditional Mass allows for and, in a way, encourages a multitude of approaches to it. There is the person who sits and watches the ceremonial actions, which are beautiful in themselves and full of meaning. Another person likes to follow all the texts in the missal and make them his own. Still another closes her eyes and listens to the chants, the organ, the sound of censer chains clicking, and lets herself float on an ocean of silence. In the traditional Mass there is a sublime integration of music, text, ritual, and silence, a coherent unity of elements, the simultaneity and hierarchical execution of which are a vivid reflection of the diverse and simultaneous layers of cosmic reality and of intelligible meaning—and which, on a purely practical level, respect and foster diverse ways of participation on the part of different members of the congregation. In a refreshing way, the old liturgy accords a certain freedom and dignity to the layman, whose baptism has equipped him to be a member of "a chosen race, a royal priesthood, a holy nation, God's own people" (1 Pet 2:9). His participation is not rigidly scripted in accord with a committee's determination (in the mid-1960s) of what "modern man" needs and how he is (and is not) to behave himself, as if he were perpetually

---

25. This comment appeared at *The Sensible Bond*, a weblog subsequently disabled.

enrolled in an ecclesiastical kindergarten.[26] Rather, the liturgy spreads out a lavish banquet of prayer from which everyone can take all that they please, in the way that suits them best.[27]

The vast difference between traditional and modern modes of participation goes to the very heart of the difference between confessional Catholicism and its contemporary reinterpretation, with its momentous implications for the spiritual lives of believers. Perhaps no one has articulated the point more lucidly than Alfred Lorenzer in his potent 1981 critique *The Council of the Bookkeepers*. As Stuart Chessman summarizes:

> Psychological analysis establishes the importance of symbols in the development of the human personality. Of the greatest importance is the "presentative" character of the symbol. In other words, the sensuous symbol offers itself to the observer as a whole, as something to be freely explored and understood. The author contrasts this with the didactic, rational, "discursive" nature of modern communications, especially, under modern civil society, of advertising. In the latter, opinions and ideologies are imposed upon the recipient. The loss of symbols creates a personality which cannot mature, and thus necessarily remains unemancipated and unfree.
>
> Now the Council and specifically the decrees on the reform of the liturgy substituted a didactic, discursive approach for the previous symbolic essence of the liturgy. The new function of the

26. Speaking of the 1960s, William F. Buckley Jr. notes: "It used to be that there were stretches of several minutes during the Mass when worshipers were, so to speak, on their own, left to follow the missal, in English or in Latin; or indeed to ignore the liturgical stagecraft and ponder, muse, inquire, worship. This was no longer possible" (*Nearer, My God,* 99). In a 1967 essay in *Commonweal,* Buckley referred to "the liturgical calisthenics devised by the Central Coach, who apparently judges it an act of neglect if the churchgoer is permitted more than two minutes and 46 seconds without being made to stand if he was kneeling, or kneel if he was standing, or sit—or sing—or chant—or anything if perchance he was praying, from which anarchism he must at all costs be rescued" (ibid., 98).

27. In ch. 39 of his *Rule,* St. Benedict notes that at the principal meal two main dishes are always to be prepared, so that those who, for any reason, may not partake of the one, may partake of the other. It is not "one size fits all." In a similar way, the traditional liturgy offers multiple points of entry or levels of access, all of them legitimate, and none of them enforced.

Mass was to deliver content to the assembled congregation. In so doing, the office of the priest or "presider" paradoxically acquired a greatly increased importance. In other words, far from fostering an allegedly "mature" laity, the Council actually had exactly the opposite consequence. This corresponds to modernity and its endless bombardment of its denizens by advertising.[28]

Our analysis has led us, therefore, to a conclusion that flies in the face of conventional wisdom. "Active participation," in the manner in which it is usually understood and implemented in the Novus Ordo sphere, actually fosters passivity, immaturity, and superficiality, while the Catholic who receives in a *seeming* passivity all that the traditional liturgy has to give, its dense universe of intertwined symbols offered peacefully to the free play of the participant, actualizes his potential for worship to a far greater extent. Consequently, the person who is looking for full, conscious, and actual participation should look for a traditional Latin Mass. There he will find, with due time and effort, a richness of participation more comprehensive, variegated, and fruitful than the reformed liturgy allows.

At root, I am striving to articulate something I have seen after 25 years of frequently assisting at both forms and doing my best to participate in each—namely, that I can *yield* myself more completely to, and derive more fruit from, the traditional Mass. I think the reasons for this are many and varied, but it is not merely a set of subjective reasons. There is more *in the liturgy itself* to connect to and be enriched by. As Cardinal Burke put it rather bluntly in an interview with Una Voce Austria: "[T]he difference between the two forms is very stark. The rich articulation of the Extraordinary Form, all of which is always pointing to the theocentric nature of

---

28. Published at *The Society of St. Hugh of Cluny,* January 26, 2017. The liturgical reform, says Lorenzer, "'ideologized' the liturgy and thus twisted, through substitute rituals, the old reciprocal relationship between presentative symbolism and sensual-symbolic forms of interaction into an indoctrination" (ibid.).

the liturgy, is practically diminished to the lowest possible degree in the Ordinary Form."[29]

One might draw a comparison with two different treasure chests. If both forms of the Mass, containing the Blessed Sacrament within their confines, can be compared to the Ark of the Covenant, nevertheless the Novus Ordo is a sleeker, more modern, smaller treasure chest that is less ornamented and offers a less jewel-encrusted setting for the Sacrament, while the traditional Mass is a capacious old treasure chest with the riches of many centuries deposited in it. At first acquaintance, some may even find it oppressively and randomly adorned, but this reaction tends to go away as one understands better the meaning and beauty of the contents. I am reminded of the difference between the old papal tiaras and the space-age tiara gifted to Paul VI. The contrast between them is quite like the contrast between the forms.

To this extent, therefore, the classical Roman Rite, as such, offers *more* to actively participate *in*—and the main reason it does not strike people this way is that they have not yet been able to access those riches. This could be the result of many factors: simple lack of opportunity; poor catechesis; misconceptions of the "preconciliar Mass"; a lack of general intellectual culture; being turned off by cranky traditionalists. Nor can we exclude indifference to the unknown, hesitation before the unfamiliar, and laziness before the demanding. Conversely, when people who are striving to be devout Catholics and to plumb the depths of the Church's liturgy discover in the *usus antiquior* a liberating, exciting, even revelatory experience of worship, we could not really say that this is very surprising; after all, this is the liturgy that nourished saints, theologians, and mystics for many centuries.

This being said, the *ex opere operantis* dimension enters in, of course: a prayerful Catholic who gives his all to the Mass can subjectively derive more fruits from a Novus Ordo Mass than a distracted person who, attending a traditional Mass, daydreams about baseball or office politics. A person's holiness can make up for any number of external defects or deficiencies. We know about the saints who

---

29. Transcript published at *The Radical Catholic*, December 11, 2014.

celebrated Mass in prison cells with a thimble of wine and a crust of bread. We also know about corrupt princes and prelates who celebrated Solemn High Masses with great majesty.

This correctly subjective consideration does not, however, cancel out the consideration of liturgical form as such and what it *objectively* offers to the participating subjects, nor does it entirely relativize the question of how *the forms themselves,* with their content, rubrics, and overall Gestalt, habituate the subjects—in a sense, how they are training the vines to grow. Thanks be to God that grace can so often surpass nature and culture, supplying for their absence; but thanks be to God as well for providing so many supports of nature and culture, smoothing the path to grace!

Through its inherent riches and through the attitudes of reverence and adoration it so strongly develops, the traditional liturgy makes available a superabundance of graces and disposes us to receive them more profoundly. In this sense, as good theologians have explained with customary carefulness, all Masses are *not* equal in every respect. It is *not* a matter of indifference which Mass we attend, how reverently it is celebrated, or what form it is; people can be better or worse off in regard to taking hold of the fruits of the Mass, and its impetratory power varies with the holiness of the clergy and, indeed, the holiness of the Church on earth at a given time.[30]

Someone who is ignorant of a better way, liturgically speaking, can still work out his salvation in fear and trembling, and avoid serious sin. But that is a minimalist way of putting it. If the question is "will this person's mind and heart be *as deeply formed* in the mysteries of Christ and the Church by an inferior liturgy as by a superior one, assuming equal attentiveness to both?," then the answer is surely "no." So there is good news and bad news. The good news is that salvation and some degree of holiness are possible in either case. The bad news is that poor liturgy means poor formation of the inner man, which clips the wings of the spirit and limits the height and breadth of the Church's mission.

Naturally, all such answers are said relatively. A priest stuck in a

---

30. See Ripperger, *Topics on Tradition*, 113–32.

prison cell reciting the Our Father can attain far greater holiness than a person in a beautiful church with a beautiful liturgy, but we would not want to say that everyone should be thrown in jail and have Mass with stale bread crumbs and drops of sour wine. Rather, the beautiful church and liturgy are there *for a reason,* to speak to our senses, our minds, our hearts—and you can be sure that the priest in jail, although submissive to God's holy will, would be grateful to be delivered from captivity and restored to a more fitting house of worship.

In an age of such great confusion as ours, characterized by an astonishing ignorance of tradition, a self-destructive contempt for the past, a modern theology of accommodationism at every level, and an unbounded hubris that dares to lay hands on what is most sacred and change it at whim, it can be extremely difficult to maintain one's interior peace and remain a peacemaker, with a charitable attitude at all times towards all men, especially those of the household of the Faith. We who dearly love the sacred liturgy, a most special gift of the Heart of Christ, will have to struggle with this challenge all our lives, but it is our way of participating in His Passion, and there is a Resurrection at the end of it—both in time, as Our Lord mercifully restores His Church here and there, and in eternity, where the Church in her heavenly perfection is altogether holy, without spot or wrinkle or blemish.

Meanwhile, in this vale of tears, ignorance is *not* bliss; ignorance will prevent a lot of souls from seeking or achieving perfection (of any degree). Rather, we need to pray for wisdom to know what is best, that we may see everything else in its light, and for charity, that our knowledge—as well as our sufferings—may be infused with love, especially for those who, through no fault of their own, are skimming the surface of the Christian mystery rather than being immersed in it. *Miserere nostri, Domine, quia peccavimus tibi.*

When I shared with a friend my opinion on the superior *participatio actuosa* fostered by the traditional Mass, he objected that my stance seemed to rule out even the possibility that the *usus antiquior*

could be improved in this regard. I replied that it was not my intention to assert that conclusion. Perhaps improvement in regard to this laudable goal—properly understood, of course—would be possible, slowly, over much time, and in response to the promptings of saints or of the faithful themselves.

What I *am* convinced of is that assembling a committee of trigger-happy liturgical "experts" whose brains are stuffed with debatable scholarship and ideological agendas is no way to improve *anything* that has been handed down to us, and I am equally convinced that even as it now stands, the *usus antiquior,* celebrated by and for well-informed Catholics, allows for the realization of the principal goals of *Sacrosanctum Concilium* far better than the Novus Ordo does—even assuming Reform of the Reform-favorable circumstances, which, needless to say, seldom obtain.

Nor should it seem strange that this would be so. After all, most of the members of the original Liturgical Movement thought that the solution to the problem of liturgical deracination and devotional subjectivism was not to change the Church's rites but to educate the people in the rites we have inherited. Even *Sacrosanctum Concilium* goes out of its way to say: "There must be no innovations unless the good of the Church genuinely and certainly requires them; and care must be taken that any new forms adopted should in some way grow organically from forms already existing" (§23). Regardless of what the Constitution's drafters may have *wished* it had said, the promulgated text expresses a fairly conservative stance—one that was massively contradicted by subsequent developments.[31]

---

31. We see a similar problem with John Courtney Murray's postconciliar interpretation of *Dignitatis Humanae.* He helped formulate the document, but in the end, it does not say exactly what he wishes it said nor what he went around afterwards claiming that it did say. Without pretending to solve the enormous difficulties presented by this document, one may safely say it does not embrace the Lockean privatization of religion and idolatry of toleration, and therefore does not endorse the American understanding of the separation of Church and State. Similarly, in regard to the conservatism of *Sacrosanctum Concilium,* I do not deny that the document contains moments of insane rupture, e.g., the suppression of the

After all, it was no less than Pope Paul VI who, in a General Audience of November 26, 1969, openly endorsed and defended the ousting of Latin and the repudiation of Gregorian chant, in spite of manifest conciliar teaching to the contrary—teaching that he, in company with over 2,000 bishops, had approved only a few years earlier. Such contempt for an ecumenical council can hardly be found in the annals of Church history. With such disobedience or hubris in the shepherd, it is no wonder his pontificate was marked and marred by such disobedience and contempt in the flock. It could be seen as a form of divine poetic justice.[32] "In the suffering of love there is a certain fitness that gives dignity and even beauty to pain: but here there was none. Here was not only betrayal, but distortion and mockery; it was as if John, and not Judas, had betrayed Our Lord."[33]

One of the first objections raised against Catholics who love the traditional Latin Mass and labor for its broadest possible restoration is that we are viewing the past through rose-colored glasses and that, in reality, things were terribly bad before the Council and urgently needed changing. The problem with making this claim (or refuting it, for that matter) is that the relevant evidence one might draw upon is vast and diversified beyond belief, with many conflicting elements. Nevertheless, while admitting for the sake of argument

---

office of Prime. But no matter how you look at it, right side up or upside down, this Constitution cannot be turned into a blueprint for the Novus Ordo Missae that rolled off the production line some seven years later. A strict application of the desiderata might have yielded something like the 1965 interim missal or the current Anglican Ordinariate liturgy. There were loopholes, to be sure, and dirty work in the business of expunging all the non-scriptural footnotes in the eleventh hour before the final vote of the Council Fathers, but the funny thing is that it was the *loopholes* that ended up dominating the implementation, rather than the clear (or semi-clear) principles and specifications. No one can deny this.

32. Some might be tempted to say: "The Pope is above a council, and he need not follow a council's promulgated documents at all; indeed, their very meaning is so totally subject to his judgment that one could never say that a pope was rejecting or disobeying a council, since it has authority only by his consent, and he can withdraw that consent." This is an irrational ultramontanism that no Catholic who respects tradition, the magisterium, or the papacy should ever countenance.

33. Kent, *Brother Michel*, 232.

that there were problems prior to the Council, I think it is safe to say there is one supremely obvious difference between the period before the heyday of liturgical rupture (ca. 1964–1970) and the period after.

Before this period, Catholics around the world were known for their widespread attendance at Mass, and it seems that a great many people were trying to be devout, or at least respectful, during Mass. Families attending Low Mass together, praying the rosary or reading devotional books, may not have been the pinnacle of *participatio actuosa*, but then again, as the Liturgical Movement pointed out, many places had never implemented what St. Pius X had called for—namely, that Mass be sung, that the people sing the chants and dialogues of the Mass Ordinary, and that they become familiar with the actual prayers of the liturgy. Still, there was a distinctively Catholic thing that Catholics did every Sunday (and the more pious, more often than that); they *knew* that this was the Holy Sacrifice of the Mass, that Jesus was really and truly present in the Eucharist, and that you could not receive Him if you were in a state of mortal sin.

Mass attendance was already decreasing in the mid-to-late sixties, for social and cultural reasons known to all, but after the liturgical rupture embodied in the Pauline Missal, attendance fell precipitously.[34] The situation we have on our hands today, with only a small percentage of the baptized still going to church at all, has its birth in this period of liturgical experimentation, insolence, disruption, and confusion. A decline had already set in prior to the Novus Ordo Missae, but it was the outrageous shock of substituting a new rite of worship for an age-old bearer and transmitter of Catholic identity that confirmed definitively the modernizing madness of the institutional church. This was the death knell. To paraphrase Joseph Ratzinger, if this is how the Church treated her most valued possession, her mystical treasures, what other betrayals could be expected

34. Participation in fact declined across *all* Christian denominations at this time, and for analogous reasons: generally, Christians gave in to the temptation to accommodate their teaching and way of life to the modern *Zeitgeist*; specifically, many Protestant groups undertook ill-considered revisions to their religious rituals, with some even adopting the mistakes of the Catholic Church in the name of ecumenism. All of this was bound to have similar effects across the board, given the flaunting of both natural law and divine law.

from her? Would anything remain stably in place? Could doctrine itself survive the onslaught? Should we bother to "buy" anything such a self-doubting and even self-destructive Church has to offer?

This is why some, rightly in my opinion, consider the two Synods on the Family under Pope Francis to be the logical continuation and completion of the conciliar reforms. The years during and after the Council were preoccupied with changing ritual and discipline as widely as possible, while doctrine seemed to be left untouched, but all along the modernists have been preparing as well as they could for an opportunity to "renovate" the doctrine as well. Given the freedom to do so, there is almost *nothing* in the Faith that they would not modify or deconstruct, even as almost nothing in the Mass was left intact. It takes centuries to build, and only a few moments to tear down.

Even with a liturgy entirely in the vernacular, Catholics today *by and large* seem barely aware of those basic truths of the Faith mentioned above—and again, it is not reasonable to say the problem is *merely* poor education. As I have argued in this book and elsewhere, the very form of the liturgy does not convey those truths as fully or effectively. If you rarely hear aloud (or read in your missal) prayers indicating that the Mass is a true and proper sacrifice, if you rarely see visible tokens in deference to this mystery, then can we say that the Eucharistic liturgy is being true to itself, true to its very nature and purpose? In short, the reformed liturgy was as much a repudiation of *Sacrosanctum Concilium*'s principles as the traditional liturgy was capable of fulfilling them if only consistent formation of the people had been patiently pursued.

In this sense, I am certainly of the opinion, which has been discussed at length by Alcuin Reid, that authentic liturgical formation is the golden key to *participatio actuosa,* and that without this formation, no amount of fiddling and fidgeting with the liturgy is ever going to make a real difference, a profound difference, in how the people participate. They will be devout or semi-devout spectators at the *usus antiquior,* bored or semi-bored spectators at the Novus Ordo. For this reason, too, a growing number today are of the opinion that the traditional liturgy, which carries within it so very much to participate in, is the ideal point of departure for the spiritual revitalization of Christian worship that Pope John XXIII seemed to have numbered among his objectives for Vatican II but that Paul VI thwarted with his myopic modernizations.

We come full circle. Does this mean there can be no improvements in the liturgy handed down by our forefathers? That conclusion would not seem to follow from anything argued here. On the contrary, the liturgy should continue to develop organically, because that is both a sign and a cause of its vitality. Eventually, the old Missal should accommodate some of the most beloved of the more recent saints, such as St. Pio of Pietrelcina, who was passionately devoted to the Tridentine Mass. All the same, it is eminently reasonable that, after the maelstrom of the past fifty years, change does not seem to be high on the list of priorities for lovers of the sacred liturgy. Truly organic development takes time, plenty of time, and no one need be in a rush.[35] The improvements most desperately needed in the Church today are those that will take place in our minds and hearts when we throw ourselves anew into the Church's treasury of worship and so learn how to be Catholic once more. Fundamentally, *we ourselves* are the ones who need reform, not the liturgy.

---

35. As an author somewhere says, the liturgy should change so slowly that the Mass of one's childhood should be and seem recognizably the same as the Mass of one's old age. One should be able to keep using one's beloved daily missal as the decades pass.

Sanctis qui sunt in terra eius, mirificavit omnes voluntates meas in eis.
As for the saints in the land, they are the noble, in whom is all my delight.
<small>PSALM 15:3</small>

9

A Perpetual Feast of All Saints

I N THE YEARS WHEN I was first getting to be familiar with the traditional Latin Mass, I remember being struck by how many references there are to "all the saints" in the daily, seasonal, and sanctoral prayers, and, in general, just how permeated it is with the *cultus* of the saints. The liturgy came alive in my eyes as, so to speak, a perpetual Feast of All Saints. It seemed so fitting to me that the liturgy by which the saints were produced, the liturgy that nourished and sanctified them, so richly celebrates their glory and beseeches their prayers. I saw that the memory of the saints is kept alive *here,* in the solemn sacrifice, the point of contact between heaven and earth, in a mysterious communication between the Church Triumphant and the Church Militant, like a Jacob's Ladder on which imperfect souls rise up in prayer and already perfected souls descend in their loving intercession. The saints and angels are familiarly present throughout the old rite, which points to their intrinsic relationship to the very essence and effects of the Holy Sacrifice of the Mass.[1]

This realization was connected with another: due to its stability, coherence, and unity, the traditional Mass is characterized by St. Augustine's succinct definition of peace: *tranquillitas ordinis,* "tranquility of order." Is not peacefulness one of the most obvious traits of the Mass of Ages? With a few seasonal exceptions, the Order of Mass remains fixed, repeated day after day, while the propers, the readings, collects, antiphons, are like the glinting surface of a great calm lake stirred by a mild breeze. *Locum refrigerii, lucis, et pacis*: the liturgy imitates, and thus creates in the soul, the *tranquillitas ordinis* of the heavenly Jerusalem. By their simplicity and beauty

---

1. On this point, see Kwasniewski, "Reform of the Lectionary," 299–301.

and a variety that never threatens the total unity of worship, these changing parts of the Mass draw attention to the liturgy's changeless core, the solemn prayer raised by Jesus Christ the High Priest to His heavenly Father, the prayer of sinful man to the God of our salvation. "He must increase but I must decrease" (Jn 3:30): this is what we are taught by the very *format* of the ancient rite, where the real presence of Christ, in His true and proper sacrifice, always stands front and center.

All the different "options" and the overwhelming variety of material in the modern Roman Rite distract one's attention from things of greatest and everlasting importance, which always ought to remain the same, enabling the worshiper to penetrate ever more deeply into the changeless mysteries.[2] Because the ancient Roman Rite is much more *the same* than *different* from day to day, it is easy for a layman with his missal to see the inner connection between, on the one hand, the various feasts of the saints and of Our Lord and Our Lady, and, on the other hand, the ever-present life of Christ, "the same yesterday, today, and forever" (Heb 13:8), as reflected in the actions and words of the priest. The ancient rite's elements revolve around the sacrifice of the Cross like planets around the sun, in the company of the Mother of God, saints, and angels who are everywhere present in the liturgy. The ancient rite imitates the glorious diversity-in-unity of the heavenly Jerusalem, of which it is truly a foretaste, "the most beautiful thing this side of heaven."

In the traditional Mass, the priest and the servers alike say: "I confess to Almighty God, to Blessed Mary ever Virgin, to Blessed Michael the Archangel, to Blessed John the Baptist, to the Holy

---

2. "The *reinvented liturgy* delights in providing options which serve further to fracture its unity. Options are a secular preoccupation. The Divine Office, the prayer of the Church directed to be offered to God each day, always had as its unifying principle repetition at every hour of the Collect of the Mass to mark its function as the embellishment of the Church's sacrifice. This rule has gone by the board" (Michael Baker, "It's the Council that's the Problem," published at *Super Flumina*, June 22, 2016).

Apostles Peter and Paul..." Taking into account the still-prevalent custom of the Confiteor right before communion, we find this constellation of saints—the Mother of God, St. Michael, St. John the Baptist, St. Peter, and St. Paul—invoked *three times* in the Mass. Of course, Our Lady and SS. Peter and Paul, with St. Andrew and St. Michael, are invoked or commemorated a number of other times in the Mass, as well. In the Novus Ordo, on the other hand, impoverished in this respect as in so many others, everyone (priest and people alike) says at the same time, and only once: "I confess to Almighty God and to you, brothers and sisters...therefore I ask blessed Mary, all the angels and saints and you, brothers and sisters...." Notice the pronounced shift from the *personal*—Mary, Michael, John, Peter, and Paul—to the *impersonal,* the *abstract*: "all the angels and saints." At first glance, it might seem nice that the whole heavenly court is being invoked. On a second look, however, it shows a process of depersonalization and the accompanying loss of immediate meaning. It is like the difference between saying "Love all mankind, because everyone is your brother or sister" and saying "Love your neighbor Joe who irritates you, and your neighbor Sally whose dog never stops barking, because both of them are children of God." When one confesses to *St. Michael,* to *St. Peter and St. Paul,* one invokes particular real historical and heavenly patrons, patrons with a special authority and role in the variegated drama of salvation. In spite of our lowliness, we are in communion with them as fellow members of the Mystical Body of Christ. They are hearing our humiliating confession; they, personally, are going to pray for us. When one confesses to everybody, one confesses, in a way, to nobody. It might be added that in many cases, frequenters of the Novus Ordo will not even hear the stripped-down Confiteor at all, because the priest is allowed to choose a different option for the "penitential rite," including the pseudo-troped Kyrie: "You were sent to heal the contrite of heart..."—another of the innovations that make of the Novus Ordo not a form of the Roman Rite but a new rule of prayer loosely based upon the Roman Rite.

In general, the saints are intimately bound up with the core of the old liturgy—right where they belong, in the presence of their Lord and Teacher, their divine exemplar. The liturgy shows forth this "cloud of witnesses" by honoring them and begging their intercession, always under and in light of Jesus Christ, the sole Mediator. It gives them their due position by connecting the propers, readings, and prayers to the very saints themselves, rather than pushing the saints off to the side to make room for a bloated lectionary that plods along in sovereign indifference to the saints, complemented by the streamlined Bauhaus design of a liturgy with no required antiphons. The classical liturgy *monstrates* the relationship of the Head of the Church to His members in glory, thereby fostering the living communion of saints. The Novus Ordo effectively wipes this dimension out. The saints are only vestigially present in it, as a kind of add-on to a structure that has been stripped of their names and memories. The readings have little to do with the saints, thereby separating Scripture from the saints who *lived* Scripture, whose lives were the very *proof and meaning* of Scripture. What is the purpose of the Bible, if not to instruct us in holiness? It is only a book, a mass of paper and ink, if it does not yield sanctity of life. The word-as-written, the bookish word, replaces the word-as-lived, the word enfleshed in the saints. And what is this? It is Protestantism—not surprising for a liturgy that was designed with Protestant advice and ecumenism in mind. As is widely known, a Novus Ordo Mass that utilizes Eucharistic Prayer II (the fast-lane anaphora that never clearly speaks of the Mass as a true and proper sacrifice) was found perfectly acceptable by Protestant consultants in the late 1960s.

Let us consider the feast of the Conversion of St. Paul on January 25. In the Novus Ordo, this feast is a big enough deal to be honored by a special lesson and Gospel. Thus, at least in the case of feasts (in the technical sense in which the Novus Ordo calendar employs the term "feast"), if we add the rare touch of a schola to sing the propers of the Mass, the flaw just mentioned would not be present. However, what *is* missing? The beautiful presence of St. Paul *in the liturgy itself.* In the ancient rite, Saints Peter and Paul are there with us, praying with us and for us. Their memory is never allowed to fade, nor does it pass from our view. They are the greatest of the apostles, the foundations of the Church: the Rock of the Church and the Apostle to the Gentiles. It is supremely fitting that they should be explicitly present, quietly, unobtrusively, but nevertheless in a manner that reflects their centrality in the mystery of the Church. To what am I referring? The following prayers in the traditional Mass, all of which mention Peter and Paul: (1) the Confiteor, said twice or thrice; (2) the *Suscipe sancta Trinitas*; (3) the Roman Canon; (4) the *Libera nos*; and (5) the oration in the Leonine prayers after Mass, if they are recited. Saints Peter and Paul will have been invoked as many as seven times each.

The saints show up in surprising ways in the old Roman liturgy, signs of its long and sometimes meandering development over time. For example, on Sexagesima Sunday, the epistle focuses on the many sufferings of St. Paul, and the Collect expressly invokes his aid: "O God, who seest that we put not our trust in anything that we do: mercifully grant that by the protection of the Doctor of the Gentiles we may be defended against all adversities." On Thursday of the third week of Lent, when the station church in Rome is that of SS. Cosmas and Damian, the liturgy itself commemorates them in the Collect: "May the blessed solemnity of Thy Saints Cosmas and Damian glorify Thee, O Lord: whereby Thou hast, in Thine ineffable providence, given to them everlasting glory and to us Thine aid." Owing to the great devotion to her in olden times, St. Anastasia is commemorated on her *dies natalis*—which happens to be Christmas![3] The virgin martyr St. Agnes, likewise beloved to the Christians of Rome, has the unique privilege of a primary and a secondary feast standing a week apart, the first on January 21, the second on January 28. The traditional rite is full of such colorful, "irregular" touches, the comforting signs of age-old devotion to the saints. Nearly all of them were stripped out of the standardized, rationalized rites of the liturgical reformers, who seem to have been allergic to things ancient, organic, complex, unpredictable, or subtle.

One of the most notable features of any traditional liturgy, including the ancient Roman Rite, are the multiple layers of reference, rubric, and ceremonial. Often many things are going on simulta-

---

3. Her commemoration occurs at the second Mass of Christmas, the Mass at Dawn (*Lux fulgebit*).

neously, with different people exercising different roles and following a line proper to them, as happens in the reality of the cosmos, with its hierarchies of angels and men, and its web of interconnected organisms, particles, forces, and systems. We stand mysteriously in the presence of the Holy Trinity, Our Lord Jesus Christ, His Blessed Mother, the angels and saints, in a massive density of majestic fellowship and fervent love, to which the whole of God's creation ministers. The importance, the need, the beauty of this richness of hierarchical presence cannot be overemphasized. The rationalistic dumbing-down of the liturgy strikes at this multiplicity and complexity—an insult hurled at the nature of reality and an affront to the intelligence of man, as if humans were simpletons who can pray only on one level, in one dimension, with one object and purpose. But anyone who has breathed the atmosphere of a truly ancient liturgy knows that this is not only factually false, it is theoretically pernicious, inasmuch as it distorts the nature of prayer, liturgy, worship, and—I will even say—misreads the capacities and exigencies of human consciousness itself.

The old Roman rite often features several collects, secrets, and postcommunions, several layers of commemorations. The mellifluous chant proceeds while the priest (and the people) are saying other prayers. The Introit soars while the prayers at the foot of the altar are recited, and as the priest ascends the altar, the haunting melody of the Kyrie begins.[4] This is all to the good. The more we are surrounded by and immersed in prayer, the better we are formed, the more our heart's aspirations are given voice. We are carried away, in spite of the resisting gravity of fallen nature, into prayer, recollection, meditation, repentance, conversion.

---

4. Note that in a *Missa cantata* (just now I am not considering the *Asperges* as part of the Mass properly speaking) the first audible words of the priest in the sight of all the people are the solemn chanted words: *Gloria in excelsis Deo.* This one simple phrase elegantly enunciates the purpose of the entire preparatory and penitential movement up till that point, while announcing the central mystery that will follow—*omnis honor et gloria,* when the Son offers Himself in a perfect oblation of love, giving perfect honor and glory to the Most Holy Trinity. In contrast, who can know what flood of pedestrian verbiage may betoken the start of a Novus Ordo Mass, as the celebrant attempts to engage the people in a relevant tête-à-tête?

We enjoy a tremendous freedom of spiritual expansion and expression, yet, paradoxically, most aspects of the ancient rite are far more fixed and far less fluid than in the Novus Ordo—and this, too, reflects reality and the exigencies of the soul, because things of infinite density, like the Roman Canon or the common of the saints, ought to be repeated since they can never be exhausted; and the Scriptural antiphons and readings for virgins, martyrs, bishops, doctors, also ought to be repeated because the soul profits more from learning the *meaning* of Scripture than from being exposed to gobs of sheer text. The same rationalism that led to the stripping down of the prayers led to a multiplication of texts, whose glaring didacticism shows that the intention is to educate the ignoramuses. Did the reformers really want the Christian people saturated with the Word of God? Why then did they abolish the Prologue of John's Gospel, read after almost every Mass, to the point that Catholics practically had it memorized? Having Scripture "by heart" like this is worth far more than a tidal wave of pericopes washing over the heads of the faithful week after week, year after year.

As we have seen, the old rite of Mass *constantly* joins our prayers to those of the saints, and asks God for blessings *through their intercession.* The mystery of the communion of saints is omnipresent—an emphasis on the Church as *koinonia* or *communio* that the Second Vatican Council is said to have rediscovered, just when it was about to vanish from our public prayer. The forgers of the new rite abolished, as much as they felt they could, prayers to God through or by means of the intercession of the saints. We see the saints gone from the Confiteor, gone from the Offertory, gone from the *Libera nos,* and depleted in the body of collects. What a vast impoverishment! What a shameful repudiation of hallowed practices handed down to us in spite of wars, famines, plagues, and machinations! Here, as in other respects, we see the manner in which the new rite is *anti-dogmatic,* undermining Catholic belief by systematic omission.[5] Numerous aspects of the Faith are no longer fairly or fully

---

5. For more discussion of such points, see Kwasniewski, *Resurgent in the Midst of Crisis,* especially Chapter 6, "Offspring of Arius in the Holy of Holies."

represented (that is, in a consistent and noticeable way), but have been silently dropped or downgraded, with the result that the majority of today's Catholics are in a state of ignorance or error in regard to fundamental Catholic doctrines that used to enjoy bold and unequivocal expression in the sacred liturgy (*lex orandi, lex credendi, lex vivendi*). In the wake of almost half a century of the suppression of traditional liturgical elements, our fellow Catholics do not know what is missing from the modern re-interpretation of the Mass and therefore what *they* are missing by attending it.

The Catholic calendar suffered incalculable damage in the reform. Much of the damage came from a kind of furious desire to purge the calendar of saints or to limit their presence, just as we have seen within the Order of Mass. There is an almost rabid smushing together of distinct feast days. For example, why were St. Timothy and St. Titus (January 24 and February 6 on the old calendar) made to share the same feast day (January 26 on the new)? Is not the fact that they are named recipients of canonical letters in the New Testament enough to justify separate commemorations? When you put two together in this way, you make it more difficult to "know" and to honor either one distinctly. An even more glaring and scandalous example is the forcing together of the feasts of Michael, Gabriel, and Raphael (September 29, March 24, and October 24 on the old calendar).[6] Here we have *the only angels whose names are revealed to us in Scripture,* compacted together on one day of the calendar, September 29! This was an act of men who were losing their faith or who had already lost their faith in the angels and in their presence in the life of the Church. In the traditional liturgy and calendar, the angels

---

6. It is true that the feast of St. Michael is (or rather, his feasts are) very ancient while those of the other two archangels are more recent. But this points to legitimate development in the Church's calendar; once all three archangels are honored, it is strange to collapse them back down into a single day.

are much more obviously and integrally present, as is just and right.[7] Most of the 1962 Prefaces refer *by name* to various hierarchies of angels, whereas many of the 1970 Prefaces are content with a vague gesture: "and so, with all the angels and saints…" Such vagueness significantly changes the character of this juncture in the liturgy, where we are entering into the heavenly courts to join the ranks of angels in their praise of the eternal Son of God, the Lamb of God slain upon the altar of sacrifice. Given the corporate consolidation of the archangels, the vague gesturing of the Confiteor and the prefaces, and the removal of references to the angels elsewhere in the liturgy, is it remotely surprising that a robust belief in the angels, or the *active* invocation of them, has evaporated among the Catholic faithful? Church leaders also jettisoned Pope Leo XIII's magnificent prayer to the Archangel Michael when they dustbinned the prayers after Low Mass. How absurd this excision is can be gathered from the same pope's oft-repeated assertion that the Church in modern times is facing a new and more subtly aggressive persecution from the proponents of ideologies such as naturalism, rationalism, and liberalism, with Satan leading the charge.

Similarly, was it really necessary to remove saints' days from Lent, because it might confuse the worshiper and lead his mind away from the meaning of Lent? This worshiper must be of singular mental dullness to find it distracting to have one prayer connected with the Lenten season and a second prayer in honor of a particular saint. The meaning of Lent is brought out most when we reflect on the lives of the saints, who, once again, made Lent *real,* who *lived* Lent as perfectly as it can be done. If we think about penance in general, we shall get nowhere; if we think about the penance of the saints, how they mortified the flesh, what they suffered, what they accomplished, *then* we shall be moved, exhorted, driven onwards in our pursuit of the austere holiness to which Lent calls us.

The old calendar has a richness to it which grows on one the more one attends daily Mass. It leads the mind to the very first martyrs of the Church; it exalts the Fathers and Doctors; it proclaims

7. See Peter Kwasniewski, "A Brief Introduction to the Angels," *The Latin Mass* vol. 16, n. 2 (Spring 2007): 34–39.

great saints who have reinvigorated the world down through the ages. These saints become one's friends, and one's communion with them grows as each year their feasts are dutifully celebrated.[8] This happens precisely in function of the way that the ancient liturgy *commemorates them*—namely, by bringing them *to the fore* in the prayers and readings.[9] How do we get to know Our Lord better? One way, and a very important way at that, is to get to know His friends, His companions, His followers. The basic insight of many popular ecclesial movements—namely, that Christianity is premised on convivial and sincere friendship—has been for centuries encapsulated in the very form of the liturgy. The traditional liturgy really makes you want to *meet* these holy men and women.

Ironically, for all the Second Vatican Council's talk of modern man's needs, one especially *pressing* need—namely, the need for friendship in a world increasingly individualistic, competitive, isolating, and lonely—was undermined on the supernatural plane by the purging and marginalization of the saints. Even when they are mentioned, the saints are not woven deeply or consistently into the fabric of the Novus Ordo. The new liturgy is more like an empty hall, a church stripped of statues, icons, stained glass, with nothing left but whitewashed walls. That is the *feeling* or atmosphere it creates, even though there are still a few references to saints and angels. The references are not integrated, they do not form a whole—a problem related to the more pervasive problem of the lack of *inner unity* in the new rite, the order of which is linear, discursive, and modular, not circular, intuitive, and organic.

Reading St. Thomas's *Commentary on the Sentences of Peter Lombard*, I noticed that he makes an argument based on the Collect for Easter Sunday. I went to look at my Baronius Missal and found that,

---

8. The plethora of "optional memorials" in the new rite has created a situation in which many saints are frequently not commemorated at all. I have known priests who, as a matter of principle, always bypass optional memorials. To use a friend's wry expression, the saints are "optioned out of existence."

9. See Chapter 9 of *Resurgent in the Midst* for further discussion of this point.

indeed, the prayer we use today in the *usus antiquior* is identical to the one he quoted back in the 1250s.

At times during Mass or when reading the Fathers and Doctors of the Church, I am powerfully struck by the thought of just how vast a legacy of history, culture, and prayer is embedded and preserved in the traditional Roman liturgy. Our prayers and ceremonies go back in many instances to the first millennium of the Church. The traditional Roman Rite speaks in the same language, breathes the same atmosphere as the Fathers and Doctors and a mighty host of saints, and brings us into their presence.

Most of us are under the influence of the misnomer "Tridentine Mass"—a phrase that, although defensible, suggests to some people that this liturgical form was fashioned in the era of the Council of Trent. As students of liturgical history know, however, the reality is quite different: the substance of the Missal of Pius V had already been present for many centuries, and, in fact, as far back as the time of St. Gregory the Great (d. 604), we will find the core of the Roman Rite already there.[10] As Fr. John Hunwicke has pointed out, the Roman Canon is so ancient that its theology of consecration predates the controversy over the divinity of the Holy Spirit, and therefore lacks an *epiclesis* of the sort that the Byzantine liturgy, to combat this heresy, inserted at a later date. The Roman Canon operates on the older belief that whatever the Father approves and ratifies will be accomplished—including the making-present of the sacrifice of His Son under the consecrated bread and wine. The Father wills it, and it is done.[11]

What is the value of simply doing what our forefathers did? What is the value of participating in a Mass that is, in so much of its wording and ceremonies, the same as the one prayed by St. Thomas Aquinas or St. Francis of Assisi, St. Robert Bellarmine or St. Thérèse of Lisieux? What is the value of holding in one's mind and heart, or

10. Hence the preference of some for calling the *usus antiquior* the "Gregorian Rite."

11. Fr. Hunwicke deserves the nickname "Roman Canonist" for his many fine articles in defense of the antiquity, primacy, purity, and rightness of the Roman Canon for the Western liturgical rites that owe their origin to Rome, and his pointed critiques of the dire innovation of introducing multiple Eucharistic prayers.

whispering on one's lips, or singing with one's voice, prayers that go back, unchanged, for century after century after century? Dom Gregory Dix speaks movingly about the steady prayer entered into by so great a cloud of witnesses:

> [There is] a certain timelessness about the eucharistic action and an independence of its setting, in keeping with the stability in an ever-changing world of the forms of the liturgy themselves. At Constantinople they "do this" yet with the identical words and gestures that they used while the silver trumpets of the Basileus still called across the Bosphorus, in what seems to us now the strange fairy-tale land of the Byzantine Empire. In this twentieth century Charles de Foucauld in his hermitage in the Sahara "did this" with the same rite as Cuthbert twelve centuries before in his hermitage on Lindisfarne in the Northern seas. This very morning I "did this" with a set of texts which has not changed by more than a few syllables since Augustine used those very words at Canterbury on the third Sunday of Easter in the summer after he landed.[12]

While it might be difficult to express this subtle value in words, it is not difficult to see why such prayer, across centuries, across continents, across cultures, depth calling out to depth, age to age and saint to saint, has such an enormous appeal to young people who are discovering or re-discovering the Faith. There is strength in knowing that we are holding on to a giant indestructible rope that connects us to countless holy men and women before us, all of whom are now in heavenly glory, for which this very same liturgy prepared them on earth. There is consolation in feeling that, in the midst of a world of constant change, indeed, a modern world of almost neurotic mobility, displacement, and waste, the most important things do not change, indeed will never change. There is immense peace in returning, week after week, to readings, prayers, antiphons, ceremonies, that have survived every war, famine, plague, and persecution, and carry with them the aura of agelessness, the ardor of adoration, the savor of sanctity, the sweetness of psalmody. One comes to Mass, and one finds that it is truly, simply,

---

12. Gregory Dix, *The Shape of the Liturgy* (London/New York: Continuum, 2005), 745.

purely the Mass—as it was, as it should be, as it will be until the end of time.

> Ever in me is your present; in me your ephemeral life can redis-cover its surest meaning, because ever in me is the fidelity and the patience of Divine Love and its promise. You who are worn out by the whirl of time and things, you who have been torn to pieces, divided further and lost; come and see, I will gather you together again, unify you, calm you, for I am always the same; I am the lan-guage with which your fathers and mothers prayed. . . . I am the long and still fresh memory of people when they remember God.[13]

Yes, there have been changes in the liturgy over time, but these changes are like ripples on the surface of a vast sea, tranquil in its depths. The identity and integrity of the liturgy come down even to us, each generation cherishing what was handed on while embel-lishing it with offerings of their own devotion.

Even when we cannot put it into words, this reality, this sense of immense depth and spaciousness, of the collapsing of time and dis-tance as we enter into communion with an innumerable host of worshipers, is part of the indefinable experience of attending the traditional Latin Mass. Blessed be Jesus Christ, "the same yesterday, today, and forever," who has embodied His everlasting love in a lit-urgy that is its unclouded mirror.

> I remembered God, and was delighted, and was exercised, and my
>   spirit swooned away.
> My eyes prevented the watches: I was troubled, and I spoke not.
> I thought upon the days of old: and I had in my mind the eternal
>   years.
> And I meditated in the night with my own heart: and I was exer-cised and I swept my spirit.
> Will God then cast off for ever? or will he never be more favour-able again?
> Or will he cut off his mercy for ever, from generation to genera-tion?
> Or will God forget to shew mercy? or will he in his anger shut up

---

13. Jean Borella, *The Sense of the Supernatural,* trans. G. John Champoux (Edinburgh: T&T Clark, 1998), 62.

his mercies?

And I said, Now have I begun: this is the change of the right hand of the most High.

I remembered the works of the Lord: for I will be mindful of thy wonders from the beginning.

And I will meditate on all thy works: and will be employed in thy inventions.

Thy way, O God, is in the holy place: who is the great God like our God?

(Psalm 76:4–14)

☩

Catholics who assist at the traditional liturgy of the Church come to love one monumental fact about it: its stability, regularity, constancy. With a few exceptions due to local calendars or unannounced votive Masses, one can come to any *usus antiquior* liturgy and know within moments which Mass in the missal is being celebrated—and then know, with certainty, exactly how that Mass will unfold for the remaining half-hour or hour, since everything is fixed in place.

What a consolation to know that the celebrant is not being asked to exhibit the state of his mind in extemporaneous remarks, or his pastoral judgment in choices between this or that prayer! *The Mass is simply the Mass*—older, greater, stronger, and steadier than any of us mere mortals, and we gratefully submit ourselves to its lofty spiritual pedagogy and accumulated wisdom. We, including the clergy, are not the drivers but the passengers. The driver is Christ our Lord, and never once in the liturgy (except perhaps in a homily gone awry) are we confronted with a jarring disjunct between the principal celebrant and His intelligent instrument.

Those who have practiced the ancient prayer of *lectio divina* know how much one benefits from the slow assimilation of a chosen text. One must mortify the desire to read too much or to skip all over the place. One often has to re-read and re-read a passage before it opens up and discloses its treasure. In just the same way, the one-year lectionary of the traditional *Missale Romanum* affords the worshiper time to absorb a certain set of luminous biblical passages, well chosen for their liturgical purpose. Meeting these texts repeatedly, one puts them on like a garment, or assimilates them like food and drink. One begins to think and pray in their phrases.

What happens with the lectionary happens, in turn, with the entire liturgy. The fixity of the *usus antiquior* from top to bottom, from collect to postcommunion, from Psalm 42 to the Prologue of John, facilitates a liturgical *lectio divina* that can range over the words of the entire missal, in both its repeated (Ordinary) and changing (Proper) parts.

To have the light and warmth of contemplation, you first need the fire of prayer; to fuel prayer, you need the wood of meditation; and to have meditation, there has to be *reading*. Reading presupposes something fixed and stable to be read, internalized, remembered, pondered. Any improvisation at this level, or any overwhelming quantity of text or a constantly changing text, will tend to thwart the slow and steady building of memory, the shaping of the imagination, and the fertilizing of the intellect. If you throw too much wood on the fire, you put it out. If the wood is green, the fire smokes. And if there is no kindling and no match, the fire cannot be started.

All of these things have to be in place: the right ingredients in the right order, with the right proportions and the right timing. Fifteen hundred years of slow and highly conservative liturgical development produced the right content, the right order, the right proportions, and the right timing. Because the new liturgy has vastly more content and the way things play out is subject to the choices of celebrant and musicians, the proportion of parts is quite malleable and liable to enormous imbalance, and the pacing or feel of the liturgy is not comfortingly invariable and focused.

This, then, is the fundamental problem with *praying* the new liturgy: it is too pluriform, too gigantic, and too mutable to sustain a meditative or *lectio divina* engagement with the texts, chants, and gestures. One cannot simply surrender to it and take on its identity, since the wills and intellects of various secondary agents are too much in play, making its identity like the chameleon's color. "Will the real Novus Ordo please stand up?"[14] One cannot rest in some-

---

14. As my adolescent son remarked, apropos this liturgical problem: "Friendship requires that your friend stays more or less the same. If he was always acting

thing that is always changing. To paraphrase Heraclitus: "You can never step in the same Novus Ordo twice."[15]

In the traditional liturgy, the daily stability of the Mass and its relatively limited selection of readings, together with the recurrence of all the psalms in the weekly cursus of the Divine Office, strongly supports a liturgical *lectio divina* that is decisive in deepening the spiritual life of clergy and laity. In particular, one profits from the immensely powerful correlation of the antiphons and readings of the Office with those of the Mass.[16] On the other hand, it would be hard to deny that there are correlations between the revised liturgical books, the customary crowd-oriented *ars celebrandi,* the lack of ascetical-mystical life in so large a part of the clergy, and the shallowness, if not heterodoxy, of preaching. These things tend to reinforce one another, and there is little to oppose them from within the form of the liturgy itself, which is too multifarious, too sprawling, and too subject to the piloting of the "president."

Moreover, the overwhelming fixity of traditional liturgical forms makes the times when there *are* differences in the prescribed liturgy all the more striking. The omission of Psalm 42 and the doxologies

---

differently, you couldn't get to know him or rely on him. I think it would be hard to be friends with a schizophrenic person."

15. I am aware that this is not true of the Oratorians and a few other privileged communities where the *usus recentior* is celebrated with a reliable consistency of traditional options. These communities account for less than 1% of the religious landscape.

16. I speak here from personal experience. Although I had already attended the *usus antiquior* Mass and had fallen in love with it at Thomas Aquinas College in California, I really came to know it well when, at the International Theological Institute in Austria, I was able to attend a daily 6:00 a.m. Low Mass for several years (something, alas, that has not been possible over the past decade—and how I miss it!). Going through that cycle day by day profoundly formed me and won me over completely to the old prayers and calendar. I believe it would do the same for any serious Catholic who was given the grace of such consistent exposure. Later on, as I began to pray the old Divine Office, the connections between it and the Mass were a cause of continual delight and strengthened my life of prayer. I know that a similar discovery happened for the Benedictine monks of Norcia years ago when they realized that there was too much of a disjunct between the traditional monastic office and the Novus Ordo Missae. In order to achieve an internal "reconciliation" of all their daily prayer, they chose the Vetus Ordo as their communal rite.

during Passiontide makes us feel we are being stripped and humiliated with Christ. The *dona eis requiem* of the Agnus Dei at the Mass for the Dead reminds us (as do so many other details of the Requiem Mass) that we are offering up our prayers for the repose of the souls of the faithful departed and not thinking of ourselves, of the needs of the living.[17] At special moments in the year, genuflections are called for during the course of a Tract or a Gospel, such as during the octave of Epiphany or during Lent.[18] Peculiarities take over the Divine Office on All Souls and in Holy Week. Changes like these in an otherwise monolithic and highly determined pattern can be shattering in their psychological effect. It is like a great composer who knows how to use a touch of sharp dissonance that makes the prevailing consonance all the more powerful, or a great painter who adds a touch of bright red to an otherwise subdued canvas. The old liturgy shows a masterful grasp of how human psychology works.

The same rationalistic instinct that multiplied the quantity of texts also abolished almost all such unique features and differentiations, so that there was a simultaneous flattening of rites into uniformity and an uncontrolled expansion of material in the lectionary

17. This in contrast to post-conciliar funerals and Masses for the dead, which are almost entirely focused on the living who are present, due to the assumption that the deceased requires no prayers and is already rejoicing with all his friends and relatives in heaven. The traditional Requiem Mass severely orders the entire service to the benefit of the deceased soul, which is why it was particularly loathed by the reformers, both in the sixteenth century and in the twentieth.

18. Among the most moving and beautiful signs of the latreutic or adorational function of the readings in the *usus antiquior* are those times in the course of the liturgical year when the priest, ministers, and faithful genuflect during a passage that speaks of some reality that *cries out* for the total response of the believer, in body and soul. On Epiphany and during its octave, when the priest reads or chants that the Magi fell down and worshiped Christ, he, and everyone with him, bends the knee in silent adoration. In Lenten Masses the priest kneels at the Tract *Adiuva nos*; on Palm Sunday, the Finding of the Holy Cross, and the Exaltation of the Holy Cross, they do so at the words *ut in nomine Jesu omne genu flectatur* of the Epistle; and on a number of other occasions, such as at the third Mass of Christmas, when the Prologue of John is read; at the end of the Gospel for Wednesday of the Fourth Week of Lent (Jn 9:1–38); during the Alleluia before the *Veni, Sancte Spiritus* sequence; and at votive Masses of the Holy Spirit.

and missal. Sadly, we can note that both the uniformity and the expansion are characteristic of industrial methods of mass production. Indeed, the word "mass" in contemporary English has two meanings: the density of matter and a widespread group of similarly-minded individuals. The modern Mass exhibits excess of material as well as a democratic leveling of difference within that material. This phenomenon is most of all manifest in the revised lectionary, which, although many times larger than the old one-year lectionary, nevertheless contains less of the total breadth of Scripture's actual message because of its studied avoidance of passages that might "offend" or be "misunderstood."[19]

But we have reason today to be of good cheer, for these problems are more and more widely acknowledged, and the only sensible solution to them—the restoration of the fullness of traditional Catholic worship—is gaining ground, despite semi-official resistance. What will happen when the last barriers fall down is not difficult to predict. The traditional liturgy—both the *Missale Romanum* and the *Divinum Officium*—is ideal for the life of prayer to which we are all called by God, and to which our baptism invisibly impels us. As a locus of *lectio divina,* the classical Roman Rite stirs us to ponder and linger over particular phrases of Scripture or particular liturgical prayers hallowed by tradition and to make them the basis of a most fruitful meditation and preparation for Holy Communion. This magnificent liturgy will continue to gain ground, one prayerful soul after another, one seminarian, priest, or bishop at a time, one altar and parish to the next.

Thanks be to God that He, in His everlasting mercy, has not seen fit to abandon us into the hands of our enemies, as our sins no doubt deserve, but has safeguarded the traditional liturgy all through these decades, rescuing a portion of His flock from modernism and working wonders to restore, all around the world, the integral prac-

19. See my article "A Tale of Two Lectionaries: Quality versus Quantity," published on January 16, 2017 at *New Liturgical Movement,* and the further references given therein.

tice of the Faith. It is ours, now, to respond with gratitude, yielding our minds and hearts to the wisdom of the ages, and carrying forward these treasures with a missionary zeal that does not rest content with the good we have, but strives to spread and multiply that good in our day and among our fellow Catholics. There are a hundred different ways we can do this, from ambitious to minuscule, in the public square and in the home, but our work is clearly marked out for us: we must be missionaries of the Mass, as were countless Dominicans, Franciscans, and Jesuits in the age of exploration. Not losing hope in the face of the setbacks sure to come, not resting from our labors due to victories hidden in the hand of God, we will persist in honoring, invoking, and emulating the saints, our elder brothers and sisters—and, please God, one day join them in the perpetual Feast of All Saints in heaven.

Benedictus es in templo sancto gloriae tuae:
et superlaudabilis, et supergloriosus in saecula.
Blessed art Thou in the holy temple of Thy glory: and
exceedingly to be praised, and exceeding glorious for ever.
DANIEL 3:53

In loco isto dabo pacem.
In this place I will give peace.
HAGGAI 2:10

10

The Peace of Low Mass
and the Glory of High Mass

Pope John Paul II's encyclical letter *Fides et Ratio* opens with a stirring image:

> Faith and reason are like two wings on which the human spirit rises to the contemplation of truth; and God has placed in the human heart a desire to know the truth—in a word, to know himself—so that, by knowing and loving God, men and women may also come to the fullness of truth about themselves.

One could adapt this image in a liturgical way: silence and song are like two wings on which our spirit rises to the praise of God. If one wished to characterize the Low Mass in a single word, that word might be peace; if one were searching for a word to describe the High Mass, it might be glory. These are the two facets of the mystery proclaimed in the song of the angels: "*Glory* to God in the highest, and *peace* on earth to men of good will" (Lk 2:14). God on high deserves to receive the homage of what is most beautiful and most sublime, which we see in a *Missa cantata*, even more in a Solemn High Mass, and most of all in a Pontifical Mass. It is no less true that the Son of God entered our midst as the Son of Man, with a quiet humility reflected in the quiet prayer and noble simplicity of the Low Mass.[1] Whether high or low, full of splendor or full of silence,

---

1. Note that I say "*noble* simplicity," which cannot be manifested by a stripped-down liturgy that has substituted simplism, superficiality, and banality for the purity, intensity, and "thickness" of traditional liturgy, which speaks more forcefully of the numinous and the ineffable and thus reaches souls at a deeper level more successfully.

the traditional Mass puts one in a state of prayerful attentiveness and leaves one in a state of simple adoration.[2]

Sung Mass was—and, in a certain sense, still is—the normative liturgy of the Roman Rite. Even as Byzantine liturgies are sung as a rule, so too was the Roman liturgy, once upon a time; its sung form long antedated the development of the recited Mass, and it remains the ideal, as far as the Magisterium is concerned.[3] High Mass in the *usus antiquior* is manifestly like the worship of the heavenly Jerusalem as conveyed in the imagery of the Book of Revelation: there is singing as well as a massive silence; every part of the liturgy is accentuated, given its full due.

> Be mindful from whence thou art fallen: and do penance, and do the first works. (Rev 2:5)
> *Confiteor Deo omnipotenti... Kyrie, eleison...*

> And they sung a new canticle, saying: Thou art worthy, O Lord... (Rev 5:9)
> *Tu solus sanctus, Tu solus Dominus, Tu solus Altissimus...*

> Go, and take the book that is open, from the hand of the angel who standeth upon the sea, and upon the earth. (Rev 10:8)
> *Lectio Epistolae beati Pauli Apostoli... Sequentia Sancti Evangelii...*

> The four living creatures had each of them six wings; and round about and within they are full of eyes. And they rested not day and night, saying: Holy, holy, holy, Lord God Almighty, who was, and who is, and who is to come. (Rev 4:8)
> *Sanctus, Sanctus, Sanctus Dominus Deus Sabaoth...*

---

2. Of course, having to take care of little children can distract us, but even parents get to pray occasionally at the traditional Mass, and appreciate how it orders, quiets, and animates their souls and the souls of their children who grow into it over time.

3. For a fuller presentation of this point, see my articles at *OnePeterFive*: "'Song Befits the Lover': Understanding the Place of Gregorian Chant in the Mass," September 2, 2015; "Why Gregorian Chant? And Why Sung by the People?," September 4, 2015; and "How We Should Sing—And Why People Don't Sing," September 7, 2015. In Chapter 6 of *Sacrosanctum Concilium,* the Second Vatican Council held up the chanted Latin Mass as the ideal.

And when he had opened the seventh seal, there was silence in heaven, as it were for half an hour. (Rev 8:1)
Te igitur, clementissime Pater…

And I saw: and behold in the midst of the throne and of the four living creatures, and in the midst of the ancients, a Lamb standing as it were slain… And singing the canticle of Moses, the servant of God, and the canticle of the Lamb… (Rev 5:6; 15:2–3)
Agnus Dei, qui tollis peccata mundi…

When we see this magnificent drama of salvation unfolding in front of us and within us, we assist at the commingling of the cosmos and the court of heaven. We are seized with wonder at divine mysteries and place ourselves in awe before God. As bread strengthens the heart of man and wine bringeth joy, so the bread of silence and the wine of song confirm and console us in our exile, as we go up to the house of the Lord, the city of the great King.[4] *Cantabiles mihi erant justificationes tuae in loco peregrinationis meae.* "Thy justifications were the subject of my song, in the place of my pilgrimage" (Ps 118:54).

It is all the more to be regretted, therefore, that the Low-Mass-as-norm mentality continues to be strong and to hold people in its grip.[5] A friend wrote to me that in her local Latin Mass community, about forty attend the Sunday High Mass, whereas the Low Mass is packed with faithful. They like the fact that it is earlier in the morning, offers quiet time for praying privately, and does not last too long. This reaction, in turn, could signify several things.

First, it cannot be denied that people of the Western world (perhaps especially Americans) tend to be impatient with ceremonial or religious ritual and would rather fulfill their obligation as efficiently

---

4. Cf. Ps 103:15; Ps 121; Ps 47:3; Mt 5:35.

5. The predominance of the Low Mass has a complex history. The medieval development of private Masses made perfect sense for monastic priests or priests not otherwise tasked with a public celebration of the liturgy, but when the practice spilled over into the sphere of parochial Masses, it may be seen as a kind of abuse. Other cultural factors enter in as well, such as the Irish dependence on Low Mass in a time of persecution, which hardened into a preference that was carried into the United States of America by immigrants. See Thomas Day, *Why Catholics Can't Sing*, revised and updated ed. (New York: Crossroad, 2013).

as possible. Sung in full from the *Liber Usualis,* the great interlectional chants—I refer to the Gradual and Alleluia, or Gradual and Tract, or Paschal double Alleluia—would undoubtedly seem like a sojourn in Purgatory for some. The sung Mass is a feast for the senses and the spirit, but it requires more work to pull it off and more leisure to appreciate it.

A second and related problem is the atrocious lack of musical education among clergy and laity, which discourages the attempt to sing the Mass. Sometimes, it is true, the musical resources are simply lacking. But the problem may also arise from a combination of unreasonable expectations and a degree of laziness. The chanted Mass does not have to sound professionally recordable. It is enough that all that should be sung is sung, with the correct texts and approximately the right melodies.

Third, and most deeply, the clinging to Low Mass is a sign of human beings starved and starving for silence and a kind of solitude. Many are attracted to the traditional Latin Mass precisely because it is, and comes across as, an unhurried, earnest, intimate encounter with God, like Moses before the burning bush, a form of worship that is totally given over to Him and induces in the worshiper a filial fear, a hushed reverence before the Lord of heaven and earth.

> Contemplation is a gaze of faith, fixed on Jesus. "I look at him and he looks at me": this is what a certain peasant of Ars in the time of his holy curé used to say while praying before the tabernacle. . . . Contemplation also turns its gaze on the mysteries of the life of Christ. Thus it learns the "interior knowledge of Our Lord," the more to love him and follow him.[6]

The very posture of the priest and the long moments of silence emphasize that this is all about Him, not about us, except inasmuch as we belong to Him. Indeed, this form of the Mass is so theocentric that it seems, in a manner of speaking, not to care what we think or feel—which is a tremendously liberating thing. How freeing it is to enter a church, kneel, and get swept away in the great prayer of the

---

6. *Catechism of the Catholic Church,* n. 2715.

Eternal High Priest, an offering that is so much greater and loftier than oneself and one's wretchedness, yet to which one is still invited to contribute the widow's mite, knowing that Christ will accept it and multiply it.

All of this is provided by *both* the traditional Low Mass *and* the High Mass, but not by a reformed liturgy that seeks above all to establish contact with the congregation at hand and to mobilize it for action. There, the individual worshiper is put on the spot, made the object of appeals and the subject of demands, and hurried along to communion time, while being habituated to feeling comfortable around the sacred. There is little if any habituation in the fear and wonder that should be our dispositions towards the *mysterium tremendum et fascinans,* confirming the connection made by the psalmist: *Viam pacis non cognoverunt; non est timor Dei ante oculos eorum.* "The way of peace they have not known: there is no fear of God before their eyes" (Ps 13:3).

If we strongly prefer the Low Mass even on Sundays and Holy Days and feel a lack of enthusiasm for the High Mass, it is at least worth asking ourselves whether we might not be praying enough *outside of* Mass, with the result that the Low Mass has become for us a daily or weekly vitaminized dose of prayer, potent enough to make up for a way of life that is not sufficiently nutritious. In the life of one who is bound to the Lord by various cords of love—for instance, Lauds or Vespers or other shorter hours of the Divine Office,[7] *lectio divina,* spiritual reading, Eucharistic Adoration, or the Rosary, to name the most notable—the Holy Sacrifice of the Mass is free to be truly what it is: a pinnacle, the *fons et culmen vitae Christianae,* a time for "pulling out all the stops."

As we know, the "four-hymn sandwich" that dominates almost all Novus Ordo parishes today is not a new invention of the rebellious 1960s but derives from the permission to sing vernacular hymns at Low Masses in the decades *preceding* Vatican II. In order to solve this problem of communal sentimentalism, which stood in tension with the liturgy's public, formal, objective character and

7. Or the Little Office of the Blessed Virgin Mary.

with the people's genuine participation *in the liturgy as given,*[8] the Council itself called for the use of Gregorian chant, Renaissance polyphony, and newly-composed music that would look to these great models and emulate their qualities. Tragically, we remained in the rut of the four-hymn sandwich, except that the schmaltzy Victorian style of yore was replaced by a pseudo-folk or light-rock style. No formal change occurred, merely a material substitution. All the underlying assumptions and expectations stayed the same, and the call to invest oneself in the liturgy as such, so that one could truly live a *vita liturgica,* went unheeded.

It is, of course, possible to outfit a Low Mass with music that possesses the proper qualities by singing chants (*Adoro te, Ave verum corpus,* etc.), picking the right organ music, and using tasteful hymns, but all this is still a far cry from the High Mass or the Solemn Mass, which is the liturgy-as-music and music-as-liturgy.

If today we do not take seriously enough the difference between *singing the Mass* and *singing at Mass,* or between an exalted public celebration and a pared-down private celebration, we will be in danger of replicating a new form of 1950s Catholicism that risks toppling down again like a house of cards through a failure to embrace the *fullness* of our liturgical tradition.[9] As much as possible, the sacred liturgy needs to be celebrated *in full,* in its ritual and musical integrity, if we hope to see a revival worthy of our tradition and a lasting cure for the rationalism and utilitarianism that have crept into nearly every aspect of modern life. The liturgy must be seen not only as truth, but as the *splendor* of truth, the manifestation of God's *glory.*

The attitude of St. Hugh of Lincoln (1135/40–1200) was marvelously impractical, as he always placed an emphasis on slowing down for God and giving Him the utmost, regardless of pressing business.

8. See Guardini's fine insights on this matter in the opening chapter of his book *The Spirit of the Liturgy.*

9. I am *not* saying that 1950s Catholicism was not stronger and healthier than the Catholicism of today. Denial of this would be idiotic. But I am concerned about certain regrettable habits or patterns already in place in the 1950s that provoked some of the radicalism, indifference, and apostasy that followed.

Hugh indeed never lost sight of the fact that a bishop is first and foremost the chief liturgical minister. He would never permit the least slovenliness in singing the Office. Once he was assisting at Mass with another bishop, Hugh de Nonant of Coventry. They were then to dine with the King. Not to delay the royal dinner, the Bishop of Coventry wanted a Low Mass and began to read the Introit of a Confessor, *Os justi,* in his speaking voice. Hugh would have none of it and began to chant the Introit with all the notes of the Proper. Like St. Dominic who sang his daily Mass, Hugh seems to have followed an excellent principle, the reverse unfortunately of that obtaining today: don't *say* Mass if you can *sing* it. One can imagine his judgment of the numerous parishes where the Mass is not sung, even on Sundays and great feasts.[10]

Without a doubt, weekday Low Masses or "private" Masses have immense meditative beauty and an indispensable place in the spirituality of the priest and the faithful. We should be grateful that this custom developed, which so well suits the desire and the need for a daily enactment of the Sacrifice of Calvary. But we must not allow this providential simplification to marginalize or replace the solemn fullness of the original sung form of Mass, by which our communal worship on the Lord's Day and the great feasts of the Church's year is fittingly elevated, so that we may enter into the Lamb's High Feast using all of our powers of body and soul, and drawing upon all the gifts of our faith.

A friend and I were talking about the difference between sight in the liturgy and sound. If a liturgy *looks* silly, as it invariably does when the priest is facing the people but addressing God, one can always close one's eyes and retreat into the interior castle (or at least make the attempt). But if there is endless blather and/or loud muzak, one cannot close one's ears—and it would be rude to plug them with one's fingers or reach for the wax earplugs. Put simply, the *sound* of

---

10. From the delightful book *Neglected Saints* by E.I. Watkin (New York: Sheed & Ward, 1955), 63–64.

the liturgy is more unavoidable and more determinative than the *sight* of it.

The modern liturgy is more or less designed to be a non-stop talkie from start to finish. Either the priest is talking or the lectors are talking or the people are making responses or songs are being sung.[11] There is nary a moment to absorb what has been uttered, to reflect on what has been sung, or to prepare for the next step, whatever it might be. One feels like the unfortunate pupil of an overbearing governess who never stops lecturing him about how he must tie his shoes, wash his face, do his long division, and write in his copybook with a regular cursive.

Let us face it: a recited vernacular Mass, with the priest going on and on and on in a rambling monotone, can have a soul-deadening effect. Because everything is said aloud and facing the people, it is the opposite of a traditional Low Mass, which is said quietly and facing the Lord. Because there is so little singing and so little silence, it is also the opposite of a traditional High Mass. At the Novus Ordo Neither-High-Nor-Low Mass, one drowns in an ocean of dull verbiage.[12] No wonder the Church is dying in the Western world: how could it survive such waves of boredom, worse in their own way than any iconoclasm? The words of St. John Climacus are eerily applicable to many celebrations of the Novus Ordo:

> Talkativeness is the throne of vainglory on which it loves to show itself and make a display. Talkativeness is a sign of ignorance, a door to slander, a guide to jesting, a servant of falsehood, the ruin of compunction, a creator of despondency, a precursor of sleep, the

---

11. Even in 1967, William F. Buckley, Jr. spoke of "the fascistic static of the contemporary Mass," a line he recalls in his later book *Nearer, My God*, 98. His critical remarks on "hyperactive participation" are worth reading: see 96–107.

12. By abolishing a clear distinction between the completely sung Mass and the completely recited Mass, the Novus Ordo has been prolific in illegitimate offspring: the Mass where nothing is sung but the Alleluia before the Gospel; the Mass where the Kyrie is recited and the Gloria sung, or vice versa, or where the rest of the Ordinary is sung but the Creed is always recited; the compromise Mass where an Introit is chanted *before* Mass begins, because the Introit's proper place is usurped by a random hymn; the high-level hybrid Mass where everything is sung except for the readings; and so forth.

dissipation of recollection, the abolition of watchfulness, the cooling of ardour, the darkening of prayer.[13]

Young Catholics who are serious about their faith crave the silence and spaciousness of the traditional liturgy, the way it moves slowly, breathes, opens out, respects and demands one's own prayer, made in one's own way and at one's own pace. It is so liberating to attend a Mass where the focus is somewhere else, beyond, and you catch up as you can, without being addressed or cajoled. It is merciful to our weaknesses and yet plays to our strengths.

Priests who must celebrate the Ordinary Form should do everything they can to avoid this death by verbosity! They should pray the Roman Canon *sotto voce,* so that it is barely audible and preserves its dignity, rather than being announced like the daily news so that it loses its sacrality. They should chant as much of the Mass as they can, and see to it that a choir or schola chants the Ordinary and the propers. They should protect and promote liturgical silence. Only in these ways can the Ordinary Form avoid being a form of torture to the ears of body and soul.

With fifty years of sonic saturation behind us, we can appreciate far better the age-old wisdom of Holy Mother Church, who bid that her High Mass be sung from start to finish and her Low Mass be, throughout much of its course, as quiet as a whisper.[14] In a solemn

---

13. St. John Climacus, *The Ladder of Divine Ascent,* trans. Archimandrite Lazarus Moore (New York: Harper & Brothers, 1959), Step 11, available at http://www.prudencetrue.com.

14. A reader may wonder what I think about the so-called "Dialogue Mass," that is, having the people in the pews at a traditional Latin Low Mass speak all the texts that would either be said by the servers or sung by the faithful at High Mass. This is a question that, in the words of the Gospel, divides "father against son and son against father, mother against daughter and daughter against her mother, mother-in-law against her daughter-in-law and daughter-in-law against her mother-in-law" (Lk 12:53).

Against it, one might argue that it teaches people the wrong notion of active participation, since many of the prayers to be recited aloud are, in fact, private prayers of preparation, and perhaps we would benefit more from treating them as our own private prayers of preparation, in silence (see Jacques and Raïssa Maritain's warning to liturgical enthusiasts of the 1950s in their book *Liturgy and Contemplation*). One should not equate Psalm 42 with the Kyrie or Gloria, or with

Mass or a *Missa cantata*, almost everything is either chanted or done in silence; only the Confiteor before Communion (if there is one) and the "Domine, non sum dignus" are spoken. This means about 99% of the liturgy's audible words are chanted. In a Low Mass or a *Missa recitata*, much is spoken by the celebrant *sotto voce* or silently, so that it is perfectly obvious to worshipers that the priest is speaking intimately to the Lord, not addressing a message to them. As a result, it is easier for the laity themselves to pray—they are borne along the river of prayer that flows from the priest's lips. Thus, tradition presents us with the marvelous spectacle of two forms of worship, one of which alternates ecstatically between song and silence, while the other is absorbed in a colloquy of love that dares not profane itself with the voice of everyday speech. Both are admirably suited to foster prayer: the prayer of the community, the prayer of contemplation, the prayer of the heart.

With the Novus Ordo, all this has been banished. Where have the chanted propers, the chanted Ordinary, the chanted priestly prayers, gone? Where has the profound silence gone? In a typical weekday celebration, 95% of the liturgy is spoken out loud, towards the people as an audience. It is talk, talk, talk, a wearisome march through texts that are not even particularly notable for their literary qualities (unlike, in this respect, the Anglican Ordinariate liturgy, which is free to draw upon some of the best English prose ever put on paper). No wonder it has so little impact on the soul: it neither creates the space required for assimilation nor exults and woos with the song of the divine lover. It is, as it were, neither cold nor hot,

---

the responses to public dialogues. In this there may be a democratic leveling of responses. Perhaps, too, it is an attempt to imbue Low Mass with a kind of publicity and involvement that is foreign to its spirituality and proper rather to the High Mass; it might even be one cause among many of the derailment of efforts to restore High Mass to a place of honor. There is, moreover, a peculiar beauty and power in a Low Mass that is whispered by the priest at a side altar early in the morning, and this grace should never disappear from the life of the Church.

On the other hand, I have seen the Dialogue Mass work well in the (admittedly rare) circumstances of a congregation of students conversant with Latin, who by taking the liturgy's words upon their lips acquire a greater intimacy with its prayer. Nor should it be overlooked that even in a Dialogue Mass there is plenty of silence; it does not have to lose the prayerfulness characteristic of the quiet Low Mass.

neither speechless nor lyrical; it is lukewarm—and we know what happens to the lukewarm.

Song is the realm of the lover, the mourner, and the bacchante, of heightened experience, of exultation and nobility, of beauty finding its voice. Silence is the realm of mystics in the grip of ineffability, genius concentrating on a problem, poets reminiscing and reaching for a word, the simple man confronted with realities vastly greater than himself, like love and death. Speech, for its part, is the realm of the ordinary, the matter-of-fact, the realm of commerce and politics. This is why both sung liturgy and silent liturgy are glorious, effective, and rich, each in its own way, while spoken liturgy is pale, feeble, and impoverished, a failure off the blocks. We are looking at a phenomenological difference that goes to the very heart of worship—what we are doing, towards whom, by whom, and why.

Psychology warns us against the naïve belief that our theories correspond to reality, and never is this more true than in the transition from liturgical theory to contemporary praxis. The Novus Ordo has occasioned gigantic scholarly defenses that sprawl across many volumes of text, but none of this matters in the least for the actual experience of worship. No matter how many books of theory are written, the fundamental *mode* of a liturgy conveys a message more obvious than any explanation. The person who enters a church and is caught up in the music and ceremonial of a High Mass or challenged to silent prayer by a Low Mass, both of which are obviously directed away from him towards the numinous Other, is experiencing divine worship, pure and simple. The person who enters a church and is literally confronted by a speaker emitting copious quantities of speech is experiencing a self-help seminar, regardless of whom the text is addressed to.

With the phrase "the Word of God and the wordiness of man,"[15] I sought to expose the contrast between *verbal* worship, which all Christian worship necessarily is, and *verbose* worship, which is antithetical to the spirit of the liturgy. As Ratzinger shows, the defining feature of our prayer is that it comes from and returns to the

---

15. The title of Chapter 2 in *Resurgent in the Midst of Crisis.*

Logos.[16] But since this *Logos* is the infinite, transcendent, eternal *Logos* of God, our prayer, too, should reflect these attributes in some way, if it is to be a faithful reflection and communicator of this Word. A single Gregorian chant, a Gradual between the readings, more profoundly conveys the *Logos* than hours of readings, homilies, lectures, or catechisms. A few minutes of adoring silence during the Canon of the Mass more profoundly conveys the *Logos* than the entire content of the Oxford English Dictionary or Strong's Concordance. As a society we are addicted to words, images, and sounds, but we have forgotten their origin and their purpose. The language of liturgy is not mere speech, with which our world is inundated, but *elevated* speech, namely, fair song and numinous silence, of which there is a dire ever-worsening shortage. These fraternal twins bring peace, that is, the tranquility of order; they bring contemplation, which is a foretaste of the beatific vision; they bring unity to our scattered thoughts and our broken lives. The wordiness of fallen human beings—encouraged, alas, by the rubric "in these or similar words" of the neo-Roman missal, as well as by its openings for commentary and announcements—does not bring peace, contemplation, and unity.

We can recognize here the prescience of Marshall McLuhan, who, intuiting that the medium *is* the message, knew that bringing microphones and speakers into churches could have no other effect than to undermine the liturgy.[17] The *medium of the Mass* is its first and

---

16. E.g., *The Spirit of the Liturgy,* 140, 148–56; "Image of the World and of Human Beings," in *A New Song,* 120–22. It is one of Ratzinger's favorite themes, enabling him to connect rationality, beauty, and transcendence.

17. Alfred Lorenzer noted the exhibitionist or commercial psychology resulting from the combination of the microphone and *versus populum*: "Nothing of what the celebrant does or omits is hidden from the 'spectator.'... Not only does the microphone make public every rustling and every breath; the image the public sees is closer to the setup in front of a TV chef than to the liturgical forms of even the Calvinist churches" (cited by Stuart Chessman at *The Society of St. Hugh of Cluny,* January 26, 2017). Lorenzer astutely connects this extroversion with electric lighting: "The restorers have contributed their own form of spatial destruction, specific to their trade: the very last corner of the church vaulting is illuminated by electricity, so that the interior has entirely lost its atmosphere. The original mixture of light has been replaced by electric sources, which run along the ledges like absurd garlands of light. And naturally the altars are bare" (ibid.).

abiding message to the faithful, within which everything else finds its place, acquires its color or tone. Liturgical song ennobles all that it touches, turning the wood of words into the gold of glory. Silence endows all that it envelops with a spirit of tranquility and a transcendence of orientation that allows words to keep their primordial freshness, as if they were coins never worn by constant handling. Of the three sisters, speech is the mode that risks profanation and buffoonery. Is it not famously awkward to speak at the most terrifying or wondrous moments, in an intimate embrace before or after a long parting, in a time of excruciating crisis, insoluble anguish, or unexpected victory, when one is face to face with the inscrutable, the inexorable, the immeasurable? Speech can do nothing in these situations except make a fool of itself or bring discredit to its subject. Far better to sink into silence or find a music that, with uncanny modulations, goes beyond the realm of speech into that which is intuited, felt, or mused on. This is just what traditional liturgy does: it sinks gratefully and calmly into silence, or it finds a chant that conveys the inner "visage" of the words in a manner subtle and penetrating.

The most perfect exemplification of this dialectic of music and silence is the traditional Solemn High Mass, of which the *Missa cantata* is an echo. The new Liturgical Movement should be striving for nothing less than a Solemn High Mass every Sunday in every parish. I recognize that this goal is far, very far away, but it must be our goal. Priests who know neither the peace of the Low Mass nor the glory of the High Mass should wait no longer; now is the time to learn to celebrate the Low Mass, and after that, the *Missa cantata,* so that these riches may be introduced to their people! Catholics are starved and hungering for real liturgy—liturgy in which the silences and the music *make integral sense,* rather than seeming like random add-ons. Speech has been bossing around her sisters far too long. It is time for liturgical silence and liturgical song to take their proper places in the life of the Church, for the life of the world.

George Frideric Handel is so well known for his multitudinous Italian operas and English oratorios that it can be easy to forget he was a native German-speaker for whom both of those languages were

acquired in the course of a colorful, productive, and largely successful career. It is somewhat surprising, then, that he set to music so
few German texts.

One lovely exception is the set of *Nine German Arias* (HWV 202–
210). The text of the aria "Süße Stille, sanfte Quelle" (HWV 205),
written by Barthold Heinrich Brocke in 1721, particularly caught my
attention. Here it is in translation:

> Sweet silence,
> soft source of calm tranquility,
> when, after this time
> of vain labor,
> I see in my mind's eye
> that rest which awaits us in eternity.

To me, this poem perfectly captures the feelings one has at a quiet
Low Mass. Though an ardent advocate of the High Mass and the
Solemn Mass, I also know from long and grateful experience how
the Low Mass, early in the morning on workdays, can be an oasis of
spiritual rest in the midst of our secular labors, a foretaste of that
eternal resting in God that we long for if we are awake and alert to
His reality and our destiny. As Belloc says, we glimpse here a totality, an archetype:

> Now in the morning Mass you do all that the race needs to do and
> has done for all these ages where religion was concerned; there you
> have the sacred and separate Enclosure, the Altar, the Priest in his
> Vestments, the set ritual, the ancient and hierarchic tongue, and
> all that your nature cries out for in the matter of worship.[18]

For a number of years I had the opportunity to assist at a calm,
almost whispered Low Mass each Saturday morning. The balm of it
is fresh in my memory.

It is so still in the church that I am strangely aware of silent things
like sunlight pouring through the stained glass windows, specks of
dust dancing in the air, my own breathing and heartbeat. I hear the
birds singing outside the church as the daylight grows, or drops of

---

18. Hilaire Belloc, *The Path to Rome* (Chicago: Henry Regnery Company, 1954),
49. He speaks, perhaps, with a touch of hyperbole, but one understands what he is
driving at.

water dripping from the eaves. As the age-old and ageless dialogue of the priest and servers wafts over me, I feel my soul grow calm in the presence of the Lord: the "still, small voice" of God speaks to me through the sacred liturgy. I understand better what Dom Guéranger once wrote: "The Holy Spirit has made the liturgy the center of his working in men's souls."

> Here Love spoke to him, poured Its riches upon him, demanded his love, and received it in return. In this interchange the need for words had long since passed; his soul plunged into silence, as a diver into a deep sea, rising to the surface slowly, slowly, after a prolonged submersion so profound that all activity was stilled and even breath ceased.[19]

The Novus Ordo never allows for this kind of experience. After decades of attending it in the best possible circumstances, with priests of unquestionable orthodoxy and piety, appropriate sacred music, a correct *ars celebrandi,* and so forth, I regret to say that the profound tranquility, the simplicity, silence, and otherworldliness so characteristic of the traditional Low Mass, have proved ever elusive. I think the main reason is that the Novus Ordo is always demanding you to *do* something, *speak* or *sing* or *move* or whatever it may be, bombarding you with stimuli directed at your person and expecting you to react to it. If you are not doing something, you ought to be. You are never left at peace for long. It is like having a schoolmarm who is always there poking you awake from your daydream and demanding that you get back to your long division problems: no time to waste! We've got work to do!

We modern Westerners are so inured to (one might even say seduced by) activism, we sometimes end up losing in our feverish work the graces we could have obtained in peace of soul, "waiting on the Lord."[20] What we need the most is to let ourselves simply *be*

---

19. Kent, *Brother Michel,* 105.

20. Belloc says that one of the benefits of a quiet morning Mass is that "the surroundings incline you to good and reasonable thoughts, and for the moment deaden the rasp and jar of that busy wickedness which both working in one's self and received from others is the true source of all human miseries" (*Path to Rome,* 47–48).

in the presence of the Lord, abiding with Him, breathing with His breath, watching for Him to show Himself in some small but extremely precious way, the call to go further up and further in, the overture to a new phase of love. It is hard to express what I am talking about to someone who has not experienced a truly prayerful Low Mass—and for those who have experienced it, no explanation is necessary.

Even if one has assisted at thousands of traditional Masses, the liturgy itself is so rich, so many-layered, that it unfolds before the gaze of faith new beauties we had never noticed before, new insights we had never thought of. And so it was for me one summer, in regard to the keeping of secrets at Mass.

Once in a while, usually on a summer weekday, it happens that no one else is available to serve the *usus antiquior* and it falls to me to don cassock and surplice for service at the altar. It is hard to describe my feelings on these occasions. Normally my perch is either up in the choir loft directing the schola or down in the pews following along in my missal. I do not often have the opportunity to see the Mass "close up" as a server does, and it always moves me deeply—not to mention the fact that kneeling for so long on a hard floor, keeping my back straight, is a good penance.

Now, it used to bother me that, whenever I was serving, I could not know what the priest was praying in the "Secret" of the Mass, except for the unvarying *per omnia saecula saeculorum.* But that summer, I noticed, as if for the first time, the immense beauty of the priest saying the "Secret" silently. Since this is a prime example of the kind of practice liturgists in the middle of the twentieth century considered a corruption to be stamped out (and so it was: its successor in the Novus Ordo, the *oratio super oblata,* is always said aloud), it seems worthwhile to ponder it more carefully.

The thick silence of that particular prayer, right before the great offering of the sacrifice (and at a moment when I have been habituated by the Novus Ordo to expect to *hear* something), made me realize with a new vividness how the Mass is a prayer *directed to God* first and foremost, to such an extent that my hearing and following of this prayer is secondary. The priest was not addressing it to me, but to God—and as I experienced this orientation of the prayer, it humbled me, focused me, purified me of a subtle remnant of self-interest that would take offense at not understanding everything. "It is good to hide the secret of a king" (Tob 12:7).

Someone might raise an objection: "St. Thomas Aquinas says that we worship God not for His sake, since He gains nothing from our prayers, but for our sake, that we may be perfected by ordering ourselves to Him. And so it is crucial that we understand what we are saying; otherwise, why not have the entire Mass be a completely silent act of adoration culminating in communion? Surely, things are said aloud in order to be grasped *by us,* since God Himself has no need of our words." As a Thomist, I agree with this point. I would never say that we should have no idea of what is going on or of what is being prayed in the liturgy. This is why much of the Mass, whether Solemn, High, or Low, is sung or spoken aloud, and this is why, in an age of near-universal literacy, daily missals are an excellent aid, highly to be encouraged. My own spiritual life has been watered and fertilized by years of following along in my now-battered missal, which, together with the singing, the postures and gestures, and simply watching and listening, has been an incomparable apprenticeship to the sacred liturgy, the Church's school of prayer par excellence. My students are well aware that I frown upon the pseudo-mysticism of those who, too lazy to use a missal (at least for the propers!), just sit there at Mass, allowing their thoughts to wander sleepily while they satisfy, if such it may be called, their Sunday obligation. This is not the lofty apophaticism of Dionysius the Areopagite but the passivity of a lump of rational clay unwilling to put itself into the potter's hands for mental and spiritual transformation.[21]

---

21. Undoubtedly, there are times when people need to put the book down and just *be* in God's presence. The point is that those who live in a literate society and are capable of engaging the riches of the liturgy are obliged to spend some time and effort getting to know it, otherwise they will not be able to defend themselves from the charge of false priorities or laziness. I would wager that most people who assist at the traditional Latin Mass are in no position to dispense with the aid of a

Consequently, I think it is important for the faithful to follow the prayers; and the Secrets are very rich prayers that deserve to live in our hearts.[22] But that does not change the fact that the *way* in which the Secret is customarily prayed in the *usus antiquior* sidesteps us altogether, leaves us behind. My point is not about the liturgy as such or as a whole; it is about a particular aspect, namely, that some things in the liturgy are done in secret, in silence, hiddenly, because they are directed to God alone, as if one is whispering a confidence or a tender word to one's beloved—and this is absolutely fitting and terribly important for us moderns who think we are (or ought to be) the center of attention. In stark contrast to *versus populum* celebrations, which have made the priest an announcer and the people an audience, the Secret prayer at the Mass, said *ad orientem,* with no man for audience, is a powerful symbol of what Cardinal Burke has called "the theocentric character of the liturgy."[23]

The earlier appeal to St. Thomas is, in any case, disingenuous, since Aquinas himself defends the custom of praying *secreto* in the Mass—a custom that, by the glorious thirteenth century, was already universally established:

---

daily missal. Even for one who is fluent in Latin, there can be the challenge of hearing the readings or prayers, a challenge sometimes resulting from a lack of projection and articulation on the part of the clergy, and sometimes from the size or disposition of the building or the noise of a fussing child.

22. A sense of the richness of the Secret prayers may be gathered from four examples: "May these holy mysteries, O Lord, cleanse us by their powerful virtue and make us come with greater purity to Him who is their source" (First Sunday of Advent); "May our offering on this day's festival be acceptable to Thee, O Lord, we beseech Thee, that, by Thy grace abounding, through this most holy exchange we may be found like unto Him in whom our nature is united to Thee" (Midnight Mass of Christmas); "Look graciously, O Lord, upon the offerings of Thy Church, in which are no longer offered gold, frankincense, and myrrh, but He, who by these same gifts was signified, is sacrificed and received, Jesus Christ, Our Lord" (Epiphany); "May the Sacrifice which we offer up in Thy sight, O Lord, be consumed by that divine fire which, through the Holy Spirit, enkindled the hearts of the disciples of Christ Thy Son" (Ember Friday of Pentecost).

23. Raymond Leo Cardinal Burke, "The Theo-Centric Character of Catholic Liturgy," *The Thomist* 75 (2011): 347–64.

There are other words which the priest alone recites, namely, such as belong to his personal office, "that he may offer up gifts and prayers for the people" (Heb 5:1). Some of these, however, he says aloud, namely, such as pertain to priest and people alike, as do the "common prayers"; other words, however, belong to the priest alone, such as the oblation and the consecration; consequently, the prayers that are said in connection with these have to be said by the priest in secret.[24]

After that summer, I have become ever more grateful that we are at times left out of the secret, which reminds us of all the mysteries in life, in the world, in the Church, that we do not understand and will never understand in this life, and perhaps not even in the life to come. I have always been struck by a prayer in the Liturgy of Saint John Chrysostom that the priest offers silently prior to the *epinikios hymnos* (Sanctus):

> You are God ineffable, inconceivable, invisible, incomprehensible ... we give thanks to You, and to Your only-begotten Son, and to Your Holy Spirit, for all that we know and that we do not know, the manifest and the hidden benefits bestowed upon us.

We are reminded that, in Milton's words, "they also serve who only stand and waite"[25]—or, in the case of a worshiper at Mass, kneel and wait. We are waiting for the full revelation of God, which will not come all at once, on our terms, but in roundabout ways, surprising us like a thief in the night, in unexpected illuminations and unsought graces.

In general, my experience over the past twenty-five years has taught me that even if I do not understand why something is done in a certain way in the classical Roman Rite, I ought to be patient and not judge the liturgy to be defective just because it does not pass muster in the court of my all-too-rational laws. The Lord scolded Job from the whirlwind for daring to demand a justification of His ways, and the Lord might scold us, too, for taking the same

---

24. *Summa theologiae* III, q. 83, a. 4, ad 6.
25. Sonnet "On His Blindness."

arrogant approach to the liturgy, when it, too, is at work on a plane higher than our thoughts and deeper than our desires. It is more humble to believe, and far more likely to be true, that *I* am defective for failing to grasp the meaning and purpose of this or that aspect of the Church's prayer, or that, faced with the dense objectivity of the liturgy and the profundity of its mysteries, I should not *expect* to understand it all in this life.

In short, I do not and dare not measure the liturgy; the liturgy measures me. Yes, we all know that liturgy develops over time and that small corruptions can creep in; but never, until the pride of Pistoia and its revival in the Consilium did Catholics dare to suggest that the very shape of the liturgy and the manner of offering it were *fundamentally flawed.* This radical rationalism—be it of the eighteenth century, when it was edifyingly crushed, or of the twentieth, when it was scandalously favored—is the revolutionary break, the moment of towering hubris, the internal rupture. As this rupture played out in the postconciliar era, the Secret, the Canon, the Embolism, and other such prayers were no longer allowed to be ritualized secrets, theocentric not only in their content but in their very execution; everything had to be extroverted, audible, comprehensible, anthropocentric not only in execution, but too often in content as well.

Traditionalists today recognize, with some melancholy, how right Pope Pius VI was to condemn, over 200 years ago, the Synod of Pistoia (1786), with all its pomps and works. That pope identified part of the Pistoian program as "recalling [the liturgy] to greater simplicity of rites, by expressing it in the vernacular language or by uttering it in a loud voice," on which he commented: "as if the present order of the liturgy received and approved by the Church had emanated in some part from the forgetfulness of the principles by which it should be regulated." To this view Pope Pius VI memorably applied the following pontifical appraisal: "rash, offensive to pious ears, insulting to the Church, favorable to the charges of heretics."[26]

Thanks be to God that there always were, still are, and will always

---

26. Bull *Auctorem Fidei*, August 28, 1794, Denzinger (43rd ed.), n. 2633.

be those who know that such reforms, whether hailing from the Enlightenment's heyday or prompted by Vatican *periti*, are a colossal mistake, a capitulation to a fleeting and prematurely aging modernity, and that the God "who giveth joy to my youth" is still being invoked every day, on every continent, by those who hold fast to the Mass of Ages, the Mass of the saints, the Mass of silence and of song.

Lignum vitae est his qui apprehenderint eam,
et qui tenuerit eam beatus.
She is a tree of life to them that lay hold on her:
and he that shall retain her is blessed.
PROVERBS 3:18

11

Homage to Our Lady, Queen of the Liturgy

I N PRAYING THE ROSARY and assisting at the old Mass, I have come to see seven points of likeness between them. The Rosary, a devotion from the Middle Ages, inhabits the same spiritual world as the Mass we receive in perfected form from that same period of flourishing faith. The Rosary is a microcosm of the liturgy's mysteries and displays the same unerring knowledge of the requirements of human nature.

1. *Useful repetition.* As all normal human beings know, and as apparently the liturgical reformers did not know, repetition is exceedingly useful and important in human discourse—as demonstrated in the rhythmic lines of poets, the intimate conversations of lovers, the lofty visions of mystics, the arias of opera composers, and the frequent requests of little children to hear the same story over again. We repeat that which is lovely to those who are beloved to us. The Rosary exemplifies this practice, but so does the traditional liturgy, whether the Mass or the Divine Office.[1] The many repetitions here reinforce, amplify, and give expression to the thoughts and feelings of the heart.

It was a cruel exercise of rationalism to slice out supposedly "useless" repetitions like the many kissings of the altar, the many utterances of *Dominus vobiscum,* the double Confiteor, the nine-fold

---

1. The psalms, in particular, are full of repetitions; one need only think of Psalm 135, with its constant refrain *quoniam in aeternum misericordia eius,* "for his mercy endures forever." Obviously such repetition was and always will be useful, or the psalms would not have been inspired by God in this way. The liturgy, and all Christian prayer, imitates Scripture in this regard.

Kyrie, the signs of the Cross, the multiple prayers before communion, and the twice-repeated threefold *Domine, non sum dignus.* I wonder if those responsible for this deformation had the sorry lot to be neglected children who did not hear poetry or stories repeated often enough.

The only kind of repetition Our Lord forbids is mindless or manipulative repetition, when one repeats vocables without mindfully intending anything thereby, or repeats words as incantations that can exercise power over some other object (including the gods, in the silly way that some pagans thought of them). Traditional Catholic piety uses repetition in an entirely different way, for the honor of God and the benefit of the soul, even as Our Lord repeated His prayer in the Garden of Gethsemane.[2]

2. *Focus on mysteries, not on activity.* The Rosary is "Our Lady's Psalter": it is, so to speak, the poor man's 150 psalms. But this poor man is each of us, all of us; we are poor beggars who kneel before God's throne, seeking His mercy and blessing through the hands of His Holy Mother. The prayers of the Rosary are themselves rich beyond measure, inexhaustible, the wellspring of a life of prayerful union with Jesus.

Some time after the Rosary's initial appearance, meditation on the mysteries of the life of Jesus and Mary was added as a framework for the decades. Notice how the Rosary makes us slow down and focus our attention on *divine mysteries*, not on the external apostolate or a frenzied activism. It is aimed more at *being* than at *doing*. The traditional Latin Mass, too, is blessedly free from our age's strange preoccupation with utility, instant results, and new-evangelization-everything. The Rosary and the Mass *form* us, deeply nourish us, and envelop us in the mysteries of Our Lord, through which we are saved. This is the prerequisite for doing anything at all for God's kingdom—and it is the goal of any work we can do.

3. *Focus on the Lord and His Mother, not on the people.* The Rosary, even when recited in a group, is still a "vertical" prayer: it is not about the group, or caught up in it, or focused on ministering

---

2. Mt 26:44: "And leaving them, he went again: and he prayed the third time, saying the selfsame word."

to its real or perceived needs, or attempting to coax or cajole some particular response. Like the Mass, it does *in fact* bring people together, it ministers to our needs, and it elicits responses. But its attention, its purpose, its entire orientation lie elsewhere.

This is perhaps the single most noticeable and praiseworthy aspect of the traditional Mass: at every point except the homily, the Mass is manifestly an act of worship directed to Almighty God, Father, Son, and Holy Ghost, an exercise of the priesthood of Christ and a sacrifice of His Body and Blood. It is clearly *not* a social get-together in which celebrant and congregation face one another and refreshments are served.

4. *A school of discipline.* Although there is nothing wrong with reciting the Rosary seated, many people pray it kneeling. This is tough on the knees and the back; it is not for nothing that kneeling is considered a penitential posture in the Eastern churches, and that Catholics traditionally kneel in the sacrament of Penance. The Rosary is a prayer that invites and, to a certain extent, demands, discipline: discipline of the body, and even more, of the soul. Whenever it goes off wandering, you have to pull your attention gently but firmly back to prayer. It is a prayer of perseverance: you have to stick with it, come what may. The devil certainly does not want you to continue to pray the Rosary. At least in my life experience, the Rosary is not a prayer you "get" right away; you have to grow into it, with trust in Our Lady's promises.

The traditional Latin Mass is a veritable bootcamp of spiritual discipline. At a Low Mass, it is the custom, at least in the United States, to kneel through almost the entire thing from start to finish. I cannot describe what a help this has been for my lazy self. At High Mass, too, there is plenty of kneeling, and the entire liturgy is longer—no rushing here, and yes, God is more important than anything else you or your family might be doing at this time, so get over your impatience. If you have a bunch of children, the challenges mount.[3] The Rosary and the old Mass demand—*and* reward—discipline.

---

3. See my article "*Ex ore infantium*: Children and the Traditional Latin Mass," *New Liturgical Movement*, March 2, 2015, and the links provided there.

5. *The use of tangible signs along with vocal and mental prayer.* I am convinced that one of the simple reasons we like the Rosary is that it involves a physical object: a set of beads, grouped into patterns, with medals and a crucifix. Catholics ought to like physical things, because God loves them. He brought the material world into being as one of His ways of communicating with us and one of the ways in which we can communicate with Him.

So the Rosary is not just a bunch of words (the curse of verbosity), nor is it just a Mount Everest of mental prayer (the curse of *devotio moderna* gone awry), but a harmonious triad: the repeated words, the orderly mysteries, and the beads. There is something for every part of us—and, to be honest, part of us will sometimes stand in for the rest of us. There are days when it seems a man's fingers are doing the praying more than his lips or his mind. We need to be humble enough to be carried by our own hands.

The comparison with the traditional Latin Mass is not far to seek. It is much more saturated with physical signs of the sacred, from start to finish, giving us more "pegs" to hang our prayers on. It blessedly allows a great latitude for meditation: one is not constantly being expected to do this, say that, "all together now!" There is silence to rest in, chant to expand with, ceremonial to watch, time and space to pray, and, when God favors us, a timeless connection with Him that nothing else can bring. The old Mass is not too cerebral or verbose, as if it were a lecture aimed at morally improving the faithful (often a vain effort, even at the best of times). It is an act of worship to which one can yield oneself, in which one can find God.

The well-thumbed daily missals of those who assist at Mass, and the veils worn by women, are, like the Rosary beads, tangible reminders of what we are doing. It is enough to glance at an antiphon or a page from the Order of Mass to bring our wayward thoughts back to the central mystery.

6. *It is received as something basically unchanged for centuries.* The Rosary has been around for a long time—and we dare not fool with it.[4] We do not suggest a "reformed Rosary" from which all "useless

---

4. Of course, the Luminous Mysteries are a sort of innovation, but the *idea* of using alternative mysteries from the life of the Lord goes back many centuries and

repetition" has been removed. We do not turn its received form inside-out to make it more acceptable or amenable to Modern Man. We do not scrap it as a medieval accretion or a superseded relic of credulous Mariolatry. No: we keep it, we cherish it, we preserve it, we hand it down unchanged to our children.

The logic, the attitude, the spirituality is the same when it comes to the Holy Mass. In its classical form, the Roman Rite in Latin has been developing organically for 1,500 years—with its development slowing down in recent centuries because it had achieved perfection of form, perfectly proportioned to the glorification of the Triune God and the needs of the worshiping community. We are humbly privileged to receive this immense treasure. We love it and we will hand it down to our children.

7. *Our Lady is invoked, by name, many times.* This is obviously true in the Rosary, which makes this devotion a healthy corrective to the Protestant rationalism that would reduce prayer to addressing God alone, ignoring His Mother and the saints, thereby insulting Him and sinning against His providential dispositions.

In like manner, the traditional Mass fittingly exalts Our Lady by mentioning her many times—in the unchanging prayers alone, 10 or 11 times, depending on the day.[5] In this frequent honoring of the Holy Theotokos, the Roman Rite shows its kinship with all other authentic

is recommended by the very apostle of the Rosary, St. Louis Marie Grignion de Montfort. Hence, I respectfully disagree with my traditionalist brethren who reject these mysteries, and I would suggest that they need to familiarize themselves with the breadth of the Rosary tradition. This is *not* to say, however, that Catholics *must* adopt the Luminous Mysteries; even John Paul II presented them as optional. It is curious, however, that they are *not* presented as optional in the Rosary brochures made by mainstream Catholic companies. This is a smaller instance of the same error that was perpetrated in earlier decades with regard to the reformed liturgy, where the progressive options (such as having no Latin or chant) were presented as requirements, and legitimate options were deemed forbidden or inopportune.

5. The variation is caused by the difference between a Low Mass and a High Mass. Here are all the places where the Holy Name of Mary is mentioned: (1–2) in the priest's Confiteor; (3–4) in the server's Confiteor; (5) in the Creed; (6) in the "Suscipe, sancta Trinitas" of the Offertory; (7) in the Roman Canon; (8) in the "Libera nos" after the Lord's Prayer; (9–10) in the Confiteor before communion; (11) in the Salve Regina of the Leonine prayers after Mass; (12) in the collect after the Salve Regina.

Christian liturgies, such as the Divine Liturgy of St. John Chrysostom. In contrast, the architects of the new Order of Mass sought to downplay Our Lady for "ecumenical" reasons. Her Holy Name, the terror of demons and the consolation of sinners, is reduced to 1 *to* 4 *mentions*; in practice, at daily Mass, a single mention only.[6]

The traditional liturgy, like the Rosary, never tires of recalling the memory and invoking the intercession of the all-glorious Mother of our God and Lord, Jesus Christ.

Perhaps part of the reason for the Rosary's continuing popularity is that it nourishes the spiritual life in many of the ways the traditional Latin Mass used to do (and still does, wherever it exists). This may also explain the natural fit between attending a Low Mass and praying the Rosary. While praying the Rosary during Mass may not be the ideal form of interior participation in the riches of the sacred liturgy, we know that the Church nevertheless does not prohibit or discourage it at a Low Mass, and I am simply pointing out that there is a *kinship* between the quiet offering of the public prayer of the Church and the quiet praying of the chaplet of Our Lady. There is consolation in this fact. For, if I am correct, the praying of the Rosary is preparing a large contingent of Marian Catholics to rediscover and return to the ancient Mass, so deeply and purely Marian in its spirituality. Something quite like this, of course, was happening in a spontaneous and organic way in the Franciscan Friars of the Immaculate, until its fresh vitality was brutally suppressed in the name of postconciliar uniformism. We see a parallel in the nefarious efforts made after the Council to suppress Marian devotion. Both forms of iconoclasm, the anti-liturgical and the anti-Marian, are born of Satan's hatred of the Incarnation.

Hail, Queen of the Most Holy Rosary! Hail, Our Lady of Victories! Pray for us sinners in this vale of tears, and obtain from Thy Son the longed-for restoration of the great and beautiful liturgy of the Roman Church. Amen.

---

6. In the Novus Ordo, the name of Mary is mentioned (1) in the Eucharistic Prayer; (2) in the Creed, where called for by the rubrics; (3) *if* the optional Confiteor is used, which is not common in daily Masses; (4) if the rarely-used Fourth Eucharistic Prayer is employed, there is an additional mention of Mary at the start of it.

Homage to Our Lady, Queen of the Liturgy

Every time we pray the Fifth Glorious Mystery, we ponder the Queenship of Mary. It is worth our while to ponder why she is, and is called, our Queen. Always feeling much safer when relying on a worthy authority, in this case I shall lean on Blessed Columba Marmion, who writes in his Rosary meditations:

> What is the purpose of all the mysteries of Christ? To be the pattern of our supernatural life, the means of our sanctification, the source of all our holiness. To create an eternal and glorious society of brethren who will be like unto Him. For this reason Christ, the New Adam, has associated with Himself Mary, as the new Eve. But she is, much more than Eve, "the Mother of all the living," the Mother of those who live in the grace of her Son. And since here below Mary was associated so intimately with all the mysteries of our salvation, at her Assumption into heaven Jesus crowned her not only with glory but also with power; He has placed His Mother on His right hand and has given her the power, in virtue of her unique title of Mother of God, to distribute the treasures of eternal life. Let us then, full of confidence, pray with the Church: "Show yourself a Mother: Mother of Jesus, by your complete faith in Him, our Mother, by your mercy towards us; ask Christ, Who was born of you, to give us life; and Who willed to be your Son, to receive our prayers through you."

Abbot Marmion observes that Jesus honors His mother not only with glory, as we celebrate on the feast of her Assumption into heaven, but also with *power,* as we celebrate on the feast of her actual rulership, *sub et cum Christo,* over angels and men and, one may dare to say, the entire created order.[7]

It requires little experience with devotional books to lament the fact that, especially in the past 150 years, Catholics have tended to sentimentalize the cult of the Virgin Mary, in ways that make it

---

7. When it comes to these various aspects of Our Lady, some confusion was introduced into the liturgical calendar by the reformers. On the *usus antiquior* calendar, the octave day of the Assumption, August 22, is the feast of the Immaculate Heart of Mary; May 31 is the feast of Our Lady's Queenship, as the end to the Marian month of May; July 2, the feast of the Visitation. On the *usus recentior* calendar,

rather difficult to imagine her as powerful. Yet she is our queen, our empress, a victorious warrior who has crushed the serpent's head. Where Mary reigns as queen, her Son reigns as king, for they are inseparable in the plan of salvation; where she reigns not, where her reign is ignored or denied, His royal reign is hampered, for His very identity is obscured and negated. Whoever has a weak or tepid view of Mary and her God-given authority over creatures will have a weak view of her Son and his properly divine authority over creatures. If she is made into a shy, wilting, fearful maiden, her Son will become a teary-eyed, slightly effeminate man, a dishonor done to Him by far too many holy cards and religious paintings.

That Our Lady stood under the cross when nearly everyone else fled, and in the darkness of faith offered up her most precious treasure, her own flesh and blood, to the heavenly Father, shows that she must have had the strongest human heart in the history of the world, with the greatest supernatural heroism. There is no martyr, confessor, virgin, or anchoress, no wife, mother, or widow whose virtues the Blessed Virgin did not possess in superabundance, in accordance with the grace of her divine Motherhood, which is the root and perfection of all her privileges. As our Eastern brethren proclaim in ecstatic prayer:

> Mighty conquering warrior, Mother of God, thy servants whom thou hast freed from ills offer up to thee songs of thanksgiving, and with thine unconquerable power, deliver us from all affliction, that we may cry unto thee: "Hail, Bride unwedded!"[8]

These regal and militant images can, of course, become a false portrait if they are taken in an excessively worldly sense. The Virgin Mary is our gentle and gracious Mother, humble and self-effacing, attentive to God alone, a "little flower" of exquisitely hidden beauty.

August 22 was changed to the Queenship of Mary, May 31 to the Visitation, and the memorial of the Immaculate Heart takes place the day after the feast of the Most Sacred Heart of Jesus. While any of these moves is defensible in the abstract, one may still question the wisdom of so many changes at once, based on the personal preferences of a committee, which is to say, not a compelling reason.

8. From the Kontakion that concludes the Byzantine Akathist to Our Most Holy Lady Theotokos.

And yet, taking *either* set of images and using it exclusively, as Catholics have tended to do with the "Mother dearest, meek and mild" type of language, is to miss something essential about the awesome reality of the Holy Theotokos as the archetype of all of God's creations, the most resplendently holy, noble, worthy, and powerful person God has ever made—one fashioned in His wisdom before all the ages and destined to reign forever over the Mystical Body of Christ, the innumerable hosts of angels, the vast throng of men and women saved from the jaws of death by her indomitable faith and unconquered fortitude.

When we meditate on the Queenship of the Theotokos, we venerate the might and power of her holiness—and the intimate virtues of her Immaculate Heart that made and forever make such might and power possible and real.

Holy Mary, Mother of God, Queen of heaven and earth, pray for us now and at the hour of our death, Amen.

A medieval poem to Our Lady, *Ave rosa sine spinis,* cleverly weaves its devotional exclamations around the words of the angelic salutation (in its original, shorter version, before the Most Holy Name of Jesus was added, and the petition *Sancta Maria, Mater Dei*).

> 1. AVE rosa sine spinis,
> Te quam Pater in divinis
> Majestate sublimavit,
> Et ab omni vae servavit.
>
> 2. MARIA stella dicta maris,
> Tu a Nato illustraris
> Luce clara deitatis,
> Qua praefulges cunctis datis.
>
> 3. GRATIA PLENA te perfecit
> Spiritus Sanctus dum te fecit
> Vas divinae bonitatis
> Et totius pietatis.

4. DOMINUS TECUM: miro pacto
Verbo in te carne facto
Opere trini conditoris:
O quam dulce vas amoris.

5. BENEDICTA IN MULIERIBUS:
Hoc testatur omnis tribus;
Coeli dicunt te beatam
Et super omnes exaltatam.

6. ET BENEDICTUS FRUCTUS VENTRIS TUI,
Quo nos semper dona frui
Per praegustum hic aeternum
Et post mortem in aeternum:

7. Hunc, Virgo, salutis sensum,
Tuae laudis gratum pensum,
Conde tuo sinu pia,
Clemens sume, O Maria. AMEN.

As I studied this text, I was struck by the way in which everything it says about the Blessed Virgin Mary applies analogously to the traditional liturgies, Eastern and Western, of the Church.

1. *HAIL, Rose without thorns, thou whom the Father by His majesty in heaven hast elevated and preserved from all woe.* The organically developed liturgies of the Church deserve our veneration; they are splendid roses, beautiful in their symmetry, lushness, color, and fragrance of holiness, without the thorns of rationalism, utilitarianism, anthropocentrism, and other baneful ideologies.

2. *MARY, known as the Star of the Sea, thou art illuminated by thy Son with the bright light of divinity, by which thou shinest bright with all thy gifts.* Over the rising and falling waves of tempestuous centuries, the liturgy has been like a fixed star, immutable in its apostolic essence but growing, expanding, in its expression of that sacred core, so that the light of Christ may shine forth ever more clearly and illuminate the world. This shining is undisturbed by the caliginous machinations of committees.

3. *FULL OF GRACE: the Holy Spirit perfected thee when He made thee into a vessel of divine goodness and of all mercy.* The Holy Spirit is the principal agent of genuine liturgy and its gradual develop-

ment from age to age. By His gentle brooding the Church's worship of God is perfected as a vessel of divine goodness and of all mercy, precluding the acceptance of radical rupture. How privileged we are to drink from this pellucid font!

4. *THE LORD IS WITH THEE: the Word became flesh in thee in a wondrous way by the action of the Creator who is Three in One: O, how sweet is the vessel of love!* Through the liturgy, the Word becomes flesh in our midst, and O, how sweet is the pure vessel of this Eucharistic love! As with Mary, the traditional liturgy echoes and magnifies the Word of the Lord, without human compromise, without omitting the hard sayings, without deflecting adoration from the Real Presence and the mystery of the sovereign Sacrifice.

5. *BLESSED ART THOU AMONGST WOMEN: all peoples bear witness to this. The heavens call thee blessed and high above all others.* How blessed among women is the Virgin in whom the Lord has done great things—the marvel of His Incarnation! Blessed, too, among prayers, high above all others, is the solemn, objective, and rational worship of the Church's traditional liturgy, which exalts those who partake of it by lifting them above the private limits, idiosyncrasies, and opinions of their age or place. All missionized peoples once bore witness to this universal blessing. May God grant it to be so in a future age.

6. *AND BLESSED IS THE FRUIT OF THY WOMB: grant that we may enjoy Him always, as a foretaste here, and after death, eternally.* Our Lord Jesus Christ, Eternal High Priest, Victim, Altar, Thou givest Thyself to us in Holy Communion as the price of our redemption, the food of our pilgrimage, the earnest and foretaste of our eternal bliss! Canst Thou do anything more for us that Thou hast not already done? Thou art far more generous with us than we could ever deserve. We owe it to Thee to be faithful stewards of Thy manifold gifts, beginning and ending with the sacred liturgy, lest we be found unworthy servants who squandered Thy treasury.

7. *O merciful Virgin Mary, lay up in the holy refuge of thy Heart and mercifully receive this disposition to salvation and the pleasing duty of thy praise. Amen.* For us, the liturgy is a holy refuge, the heart of our Catholic life, where we raise up to God the sacrifice of praise and fulfill our vows to the Lord. By the Virgin's prayers may He gra-

ciously accept our oblation, which we offer in union with all the saints of the Catholic Church across the ages.

Towards the end of my book *Resurgent in the Midst of Crisis,* I spoke of a threefold amnesia, namely, the postconciliar forgetfulness of the traditional liturgy, of Catholic social teaching, and of Thomas Aquinas.[9] I should like to reiterate here my claim that these three things do indeed belong together, not accidentally, but by a kind of inner bond or tendency, such that a sincere seeker who begins with one of them would be drawn to discover the others, if the opportunity were not denied him or impeded by hostile forces.

This inner bond is not a result of the rules of logic; it may best be described as a personal dynamism rooted in the Incarnate Word and the history of the Catholic Church that flows forth from His pierced side.

What is the center of a Catholic's existence? The Holy Eucharist. "He who eats my flesh and drinks my blood has eternal life..." (Jn 6:54). The Mass, above all other prayers, is the activity that defines a Catholic as such. *As the Mass is, so will the Catholic be.* Weak, anemic, bland, and trendy liturgy will produce weak, anemic, bland, and trendy Catholics, many of whom will fall away from sheer boredom, distracted by the allurements of consumerism. Those who remain will be shaped by the *ars celebrandi* like clay in the potter's hands. But if the Mass is potent, weighty, full of spiritual salt, and defiantly countercultural, so will its participants be: fed on Light, they are ready to oppose the rulers of this present darkness. They are ready to enthrone Christ as King in their souls—and as King of the universe, of every nation, people, government, and culture, including America's. And they are ready to listen to the Popes who, over the past 700 years, have singled out St. Thomas Aquinas as the theologian par excellence of the Catholic Church, the teacher from whose wisdom all may freely drink, the servant of truth who will lead them to the feet of the one and only Teacher, Jesus Christ.

9. See *Resurgent,* 183–97.

Homage to Our Lady, Queen of the Liturgy

We come full circle: St. Thomas, who rested his head against the tabernacle in prayer; who was given the grace to see more deeply than any other man into the astonishing mystery of the Most Holy Eucharist; who masterfully formulated the doctrine of political authority and the correct relationship of Church and State—this undoubting Thomas always brings us back to Christ, the King and High Priest of our confession, the supreme Legislator, Liturgist, and Laudator.

A true, heartfelt adherence to tradition is expressed in a triple reverence: first, for all the Fathers and Doctors, especially St. Thomas, who stands at their head; second, for the sacred liturgy they prayed and handed down to us with an observant love that extended to the tiniest details; third, reverence for the Christian society they aspired to build and, having built it, defended to the hilt. Take away any one of these things, and you take away the basis of the others. The traditional liturgy, with its archaic wisdom, noble pageantry, and sublime beauty; the avid study of St. Thomas Aquinas, teacher of the universal Church; Catholic social doctrine in its full integrity, based on the social kingship of Christ: these three things stand or fall together.

Is it a coincidence that these three all at once nearly disappeared after Vatican II and even became the object of bitter enmity and persecution? It is not for me to say what came first or what caused what, as the particular circumstances behind the debacle, all the intellects and wills, thoughts and volitions, are nearly infinite. All I see is that these three pillars did stand together, and they have fallen together, with the arguments given against each one of them looking suspiciously similar in logic and content to the arguments given against the others. Is it any surprise that, after their fall, the Church is in a state of almost total chaos, liturgically, doctrinally, socially, in spite of superficial "signs of hope" we hear so much about?

In my last book, however, I neglected to speak of the hidden cord that binds this identifying triad of Catholicism together: devotion to the Blessed Virgin Mary. Such devotion is the foundation on which true ecclesial reform can and must be built, and without it, there is never reform, but only deformation, depersonalization, decline into corpse-like bureaucracy and the empty mouthing of formulas. Where there is true devotion to Our Lady, there is also a deep love of the Church, a total commitment to the spread of the Gospel, and hence, a true openness to the social dimension of the Faith as well as to its theological inheritance. A Marian Catholic is, in the social realm, a supporter of the kingship of Christ, as befits a subject of our heavenly Queen; a Marian Catholic is, in the intellectual realm, a disciple of St. Thomas Aquinas, because Holy Mother Church has declared him her Common Doctor, and Mary is the Seat of Wisdom and the model of obedience to authority; a Marian Catholic is, in the liturgical realm, a lover of silence, contemplation, and beauty, as was the Virgin of Nazareth.[10] One who would give himself entirely in prayer and praise to the Blessed Virgin Mary would necessarily be moving towards this triad of goods, and thus, be advancing the reign of the great King over all the earth.

10. See Chapter 3.

Act of Reparation for Sins against Our Lord in the Sacred Liturgy

O LORD JESUS CHRIST,
Sovereign High Priest of the New and Eternal Covenant,
Who didst ordain Thine Apostles
to make present Thy Holy Sacrifice,
Who through them didst entrust to Thy Church
the memorial of Thy saving Passion,
Who didst make the sacred mysteries of Thy love
the font and apex of our life in Thee,
Who didst bestow Thy Spirit to guide Thy Church
into the fullness of truth-namely,
into that right worship in spirit and in truth
that Thy Father desirest of all men:

Thou hast ensured that holy things
be offered and received worthily and reverently
by establishing for us, century by century,
a sacred liturgy free from all error,
savoring in the highest degree of that holiness and devotion
which raises the mind to God.

Upon Thy beloved Bride
Thou hast lavished
robes of beauty,
jewels of eloquence,
a diadem of glory,
that she may ever be the living image of Thy beauty,
chanting Thy words and glorifying Thy Name,
secretly communing in Thy favors
and showing forth to the world
Thy surpassing wonders.

Lord Jesus, wicked and violent men
have grievously spurned this gift of Thine.
They have profaned Thy temple,
wasted Thy sanctuary,
dismantled Thy tabernacle,
and treated Thy divine liturgy
as Thou wast treated in Thy bitter Passion,

when they stripped off Thy garments
and made Thee into a laughing-stock,
humiliated in the sight of all.

While Thou hast never forsaken Thy Church
nor allowed her tradition to perish,
yet how many, claiming to act in Thy Name,
have forsaken Thee, the fountain of living water,
and have digged to themselves broken cisterns
that can hold no water
and give no life.

Have mercy on us, we beseech Thee,
for the countless sins, offenses, and negligences
committed against Thee in Thy sacred liturgy.

Have mercy on us for the violence done
to this majestic work of Thy merciful love;
for the arrogant rejection of this precious gift
of Thy Most Sacred Heart;
for the ignorance and hubris of would-be reformers
who dared lay hands on Thy heritage.

Have mercy on bishops, priests, deacons, and laity
who offer and receive unworthily and irreverently.

Have mercy on all Christians who know not what they do,
and do what they should not.

Have mercy on all of us who, knowing better,
have been guilty of lukewarmness in Thy service,
of cowardice in following Thy promptings
to adhere to what we see is better,
or of complicity in the profanations committed by others.

We are diminished, O Lord,
and brought low in all the earth this day for our sins.
We have scarcely prince, leader, or prophet,
rightful sacrifice, oblation, incense, or firstfruits.
Fully restore unto us, O Lord,
the heritage we have foolishly abandoned.

By Thy life-giving wounds,
by the fountain of Thy Precious Blood,
heal the wounds we have inflicted upon ourselves.

We desire to belong to Thee alone,
to please Thee alone,
to compass Thine altar,
hear the voice of Thy praise,
and tell of all Thy wondrous works.
We desire to love the beauty of Thy house
and the place where Thy glory dwelleth.

Accept us, O Lord,
in the spirit of humility and in a contrite heart,
and grant that our sacrifice of praise
may be pleasing unto Thee and fruitful for us.
Make us follow Thee with all our heart,
fearing Thee and seeking Thy Face.
Put us not to confusion,
but deal with us according to Thy meekness,
and according to the multitude of Thy mercies.

Do Thou give us grace to pay Thee
reasonable and acceptable homage,
to thank Thee for Thy innumerable gifts,
to make reparation for our crimes,
to offer prayers and supplications
for ourselves and the entire Church,
and most of all,
to adore and magnify Thy holy and exalted Name.
For Thou, King of Kings and Lord of Lords,
the unblemished Lamb
who taketh away the sins of the world,
art worthy to receive power, and divinity,
and wisdom, and strength,
honour, and glory, and benediction,
unto endless ages of ages.

Amen.

Dominus mihi astitit, et confortavit me . . .
et liberatus sum de ore leonis.
The Lord stood by me, and strengthened me . . .
and I was delivered out of the mouth of the lion.
2 TIMOTHY 4:17

Super aspidem et basiliscum ambulabis,
et conculcabis leonem et draconem.
Thou shalt walk upon the asp and the basilisk:
and thou shalt trample under foot the lion and the dragon.
PSALM 90:13

12

"Always Forward, Never Back"

EVERY LINE WRITTEN in these pages is born from my personal experience of the things of which I speak. I have sat through every possible permutation of the Novus Ordo, and some impossible ones. I have collaborated or argued with every type of priest or liturgist. I have seen the Reform of the Reform in action and made such contributions to it as I could. I have worked with bishops who promote all the best and bishops who ruthlessly stomp on tradition. I have participated in silent private Masses, magnificent Pontifical Masses, and more or less successful dialogue Masses. I try never to write about anything that has not been intimately and frequently a part of my life as a Catholic. This will, I trust, help explain the bitterness and harshness of some passages, the tolerance and pragmatism of others, and the melancholy triumphalism that permeates the whole—at once exultant over so many victories and chastened by the sight of so much devastation. It is a hard time to be thinking and writing about the liturgy, when so much is in flux, indiscernible and unpredictable, at the mercy of potentates and volunteers. I am thoroughly prepared to be surprised with the passage of each year at how many good things have sprung up and how many bad things have persisted or emerged from hibernation.

Dr. Eric de Saventhem (1919–2005), first President of the International Federation Una Voce, spoke these prophetic words in a speech in New York City in 1970—words all the more remarkable in the face of the escalating victories of philistinism and modernism, the threat of total devastation, and the hopelessness of the situation emerging at that time:

275

A renaissance will come: asceticism and adoration as the main-spring of direct total dedication to Christ will return. Confraternities of priests, vowed to celibacy and to an intense life of prayer and meditation, will be formed. Religious will regroup themselves into houses of strict observance. A new form of Liturgical Movement will come into being, led by young priests and attracting mainly young people, in protest against the flat, prosaic, philistine or delirious liturgies which will soon overgrow and finally smother even the recently revised rites.

It is vitally important that these new priests and religious, these new young people with ardent hearts, should find—if only in a corner of the rambling mansion of the Church—the treasure of a truly sacred liturgy still glowing softly in the night. And it is our task, since we have been given the grace to appreciate the value of this heritage, to preserve it from spoliation, from becoming buried out of sight, despised and therefore lost forever. It is our duty to keep it alive: by our own loving attachment, by our support for the priests who make it shine in our churches, by our apostolate at all levels of persuasion.[1]

All this has been fulfilled before our eyes, and there is not the slightest sign that the "new form of Liturgical Movement" will back down just because of new threats and intimidations and the premature swaggering of the anti-Ratzinger faction. Indeed, if history tells us any lesson, it is that unjust persecution makes the flame burn more intensely and then, as soon as opportunity arises, blaze out more vehemently.

And yet, so much more is waiting to be done; there is fire to be kindled on the earth, in every place, every community, every church—the fire of the Catholic Faith in its totality and integrity, its tradition and beauty. In this connection we might draw courage from the noble words of the Book of Nehemiah (2:17–18):

> Then I said to them, "You see the trouble we are in, how Jerusalem lies in ruins with its gates burned. Come, let us build the wall of Jerusalem, that we may no longer suffer disgrace." And I told them of the hand of my God which had been upon me for good, and

1. The full text is available at the FIUV website: http://www.fiuv.org/p/address-given-bydr.html

also of the words which the king had spoken to me. And they said, "Let us rise up and build." So they strengthened their hands for the good work.

When we returned to America in 2006 after living in Austria for almost eight years, my family and I spent a little time among friends in California and visiting some of the Missions along the way. At one of these Missions, I picked up a holy card of Blessed Junípero Serra that carried in bold letters the great missionary's motto: "Always forward, never back." This motto was strangely comforting to me at the time and helped me look forward to the future with trust in divine Providence.[2]

At the conclusion of an Italian-language Novus Ordo Mass at the Church of Ognissanti in Rome, commemorating the fiftieth anniversary of the first Italian Mass in history, Pope Francis used similar language, but in a quite different context and for a very different purpose:

> Let us thank the Lord for what he has done in his Church in these fifty years of liturgical reform. It was truly a courageous gesture for the Church to draw near to the people of God so that they are able to understand well what they are doing. This is important for us, to follow the Mass in this way. It is not possible to go backwards. We must always go forward. Always forward! And those who go backward are mistaken.

As we know, this was neither the first nor the last time the Holy Father has made this sort of impassioned remark. Fr. James Schall writes, with subtle criticism:

> On March 3rd, 2015, Pope Francis wrote a short letter to the Theological Faculty at the Catholic University of Argentina, an institution with which he is no doubt most familiar. Pope Francis is not a speculatively-orientated man. He sees theology in practical terms. Vatican II, he tells the Argentine Faculty, is a "re-reading of the Gospel from the perspective of contemporary culture." He does

---

2. The fact that Blessed Junípero's motto has been co-opted by today's liberals should not sour us against its true Catholic sense.

not say that it is a "re-reading" of contemporary culture from the perspective of the Gospel. The Council produced an "irreversible movement of renewal which comes from the Gospel. And now we must go forward." What, one wonders, does "forward" imply? The notion of "progress" for the sake of "progress" avoids the question of "progress to what?" or "forward to where?" To go "forward", we must first look backward to the Gospel. Chesterton said progress can only be made by looking backwards. The future is blank, but history contains real people, real choices for good or bad.[3]

Indeed, it is the Pope's frequent endorsement of creativity, innovation, and spontaneity, along with "making a mess," that might well cause any lover of tradition or proponent of the new Liturgical Movement to wince with embarrassment and regret. Unlike Pope Benedict, Pope Francis does not seem to have progressed in his way of thinking beyond the limited vision of the movers and shakers of the Second Vatican Council period, with its superficial optimism.

Let us give this Ognissanti rhetoric some careful thought. "Backwards" and "forwards" are inherently ambiguous metaphors. If we decide to stick with polyester vestments, guitars and pianos, banners, and wide fat candles offset asymmetrically by artificial flowers, are we not looking backwards into the 1960s/1970s? If we sing Gregorian chant, are we trapped in the Middle Ages—or are we singing a timeless music that is always and everywhere *Catholic,* as many popes have taught? Is Latin a "dead language of the past," or is it the sacred language of eternal Rome, through which we signify the apostolic truth and constancy of what we celebrate? Those who love traditional things are interested in *neither* "going backwards" *nor* "going forwards." We are interested in worshiping God worthily *in the present,* in continuity with the past, and for the future health of the Church.

Metaphysically, it is impossible to "go backwards." The past is unchangeable. It is not really possible to "go forward," either, since the future is in God's hands alone. All that we have is the present, the "now," and we must use this now wisely for the glory of God and

3. Fr. James V. Schall, S.J., "On Pope Francis and Understanding Theology," published at *The Catholic World Report,* March 30, 2015.

the sanctification of our souls. The only standard for us is not a distant past or a dreamy future, but what is right, good, appropriate, beautiful, *here and now*. This cannot be determined by any age or chronology, any ideology or -ism; it must be determined by sound principles that we receive from the Church and from her Tradition, which is living and active, like the Word of God of which it forms a part.[4]

In our liturgical and sacramental worship, Christ is signified as having come in the past, as being present to us now, and as yet to come in glory. He is Lord of all time, the Alpha and the Omega.

1. Our Eucharistic worship signifies Christ as a *past* reality, since He has already come into the world as the Word-made-flesh and has accomplished plentiful redemption. This may be called *the principle of tradition,* or the handing down of that which is already given: *hoc facite in meam commemorationem.*

2. The Mass signifies Christ as a *present* reality, the One who irrupts into our time and space in the miracle of transubstantiation, taking the gifts we give Him here and now and changing them into Himself. This we might call *the principle of inculturation,* the way in which the Word made flesh enters into every time, place, people, society, culture—not, however, to be conformed to it but to conform it to *Himself,* that it might be healed and elevated. As St. Augustine says, when we eat the Bread of Life worthily, we do not change this holy food into our substance; rather, we are changed into It, the more powerful overmastering the weaker. In like manner, John Paul II reminded the Church that the liturgy must be not only inculturated but also countercultural,[5] for it is, in truth, the more powerful force, unless we allow it to be shamefully subordinated to the world.

3. The Mass signifies Christ as one who, having come, and being in our midst, is awaited in His glorious coming to judge the living and the dead and to bring to completion the whole of history and

---

4. See the Dogmatic Constitution on Divine Revelation *Dei Verbum* (November 18, 1965), §10.

5. John Paul II, *Address to the Bishops of Washington, Oregon, Idaho, Montana, and Alaska* §4.

the entire cosmos, from prime matter to the loftiest seraphim. The very fact that we receive Him as waybread, as our strength and stay under the appearances of bread and wine, tells us we are waiting and longing for an indissoluble communion, the face-to-face vision of God. This tension towards the future may be called *the principle of transcendence,* by which the liturgy reminds us that we are destined for an act of worship that is not inherited from a past time or re-lived in present symbols but given immediately and eternally by the Lord Himself, when He manifests His glory to our purified gaze.

The necessary reference to the *past* makes us adhere to hallowed forms of commemoration, so that we would sooner die than have our inheritance violently taken from us, abused, reduced, or modified past recognition. The exigency of the *present* makes us attentive to the needs of the flock around us—including, of course, the need to be thoroughly connected to tradition so as to be *catholic,* that is, the same in all places and all times, since the past was once present, and all of history is present to God. The *future* perfection, which shows up the relativity of our earthly endeavors, makes us absolutists about heavenly glory alone. We would not, in other words, attempt to argue that this or that particular liturgical tradition is indispensable for the Christian life, as if everyone had to be Byzantine or Roman, although it is true that *some* authentically-lived tradition is indispensable for *each* person.

All three of these principles imply missionary outreach, although they are not ordered to outreach as their end; rather, evangelization flows from them when they are rightly believed and practiced. If we know and love tradition, it is an immense gift we will want to share. If we know and love people, we will share this gift with them in a way that draws upon their identity and challenges it to conversion. And if we know and love God, we will do all of this for His glory.

"Brethren, whatever is true, whatever is honorable, whatever is just, whatever is pure, whatever is lovely, whatever is gracious, if there is any excellence, if there is anything worthy of praise, think about these things" (Phil 4:8)—think about these things and cling to every expression of them, as much as you can, so that they remain alive and active in the world. This is our work right now. If we do it well, as Catholics, we will find that what we are doing is, not surprisingly, very much akin to what our ancestors and forefathers in the Faith have done. We will not be anxious about progress, which is ambivalent, or the future, which is in God's hands. We will neither go archaically backwards nor futuristically forwards. "I will go unto the altar of God, to God who giveth joy to my youth" (Ps 42:4).

The reader of Annibale Bugnini's memoirs comes upon a passage early on concerning a questionnaire sent around in 1948 to "almost a hundred liturgical experts in all parts of the world" by the editors of the Roman periodical *Ephemerides Liturgicae,* concerning "reform of the Missal, Breviary, calendar, Martyrology, and other liturgical books." Bugnini writes:

> This questionnaire, sent as it was by the editorial staff of a period-ical regarded as the semi-official voice of Roman liturgical circles, was the first alarm signal that something was stirring. In those days it was unheard of for anyone to challenge even a rubric or to use the word "reform." The questionnaire was therefore a bold move. In this case the proverb was proved true: "Fortune favors the brave."[6]

Although this motto is not repeated again in the almost 1,000-page book, nevertheless the spirit of the motto, if one may call it so, hov-ers everywhere. Bugnini presents himself countless times as the intrepid visionary who dares to take action whenever and wherever he can to push forward the "renewal" of the liturgy. The moment there is an opening, he takes it.

Today we look back sorrowfully, at times wrathfully, over the utter devastation caused by Bugnini and his accomplices, but we cannot dispute their mastery of the psychology of attack, alliance, subterfuge, feint, calculated compromise, redoubled attack. They were men who seized their opportunities and did not sit on their hands wondering when other people would do the job for them, or worse, waste their time on endless bickering and hairsplitting, in an

---

6. Annibale Bugnini, *The Reform of the Liturgy 1948–1975,* trans. Matthew J. O'Connell (Collegeville, MN: The Liturgical Press, 1990), 11.

attempt to get things "right." Like our political liberals, they could lay aside differences for the sake of gaining major objectives. I know an elderly monk, once a young student in Rome, to whom Bugnini candidly admitted in the early 1970s that the Pauline liturgical reform was only the first wave of the intended transformations. What the liturgists sought as the end game was the abolition of *any* predetermined liturgy and its replacement by a loose "structure" that local communities could fill with their own inculturated content. But they knew that they could not obtain this radical end without a compromise along the way, and that compromise was the Novus Ordo.[7]

In his commentary on the *Rule* of St. Benedict, Canon Simon quotes the same saying, but sees in it a larger spiritual lesson—one that all of us who are striving to recover and promote all things traditional, particularly the widespread celebration of the *usus antiquior,* would do well to heed:

> Probably a miracle will not be necessary to relieve our trouble. For, as we may repeat, the incapacity of men often arises from sloth or pusillanimity. They too often forget the simple truth that if a thing is to get done, we must do it. And when we have spent long hours in contemplating, in a spirit of false and foolish self-pity, the real or pretended difficulties of our duty, we have not changed the reality of things one whit: our duty is always our duty, and the will of God abides: we have only succeeded in weakening ourselves. "Fortune favors the brave": in this case fortune is the grace of God.[8]

It is ever so. One must do all that one can to accomplish the good. The battle is never over; one can never rest on one's laurels. In recent years, the tables have begun to turn, the tide is shifting—even

---

7. This explains the choler of progressives about a Vatican instruction like *Liturgiam Authenticam,* which represents an older way of thinking about liturgy, applied to the provisional Novus Ordo experiment in order to put an end to its vernacular deracination. The critics are right to this extent: the Novus Ordo is obviously not designed with stability or universality in mind, and so it seems an arbitrary limitation to expect it to conform to Tridentine standards of liturgical form.

8. G.A. Simon, *Commentary for Benedictine Oblates on the Rule of St. Benedict,* trans. Leonard J. Doyle (Eugene, OR: Wipf and Stock, 2009), 475.

in spite of more recent setbacks. Now is the acceptable time for the true liturgical renewal that never occurred after Vatican II, a renewal that will begin with the age-old tradition of the Church transmitted in the *Missale Romanum, Rituale Romanum,* and Divine Office that predate the mendacious machinations of the Council aula, and will end with the full, solemn, conscientious and devout celebration of these same rites, enriched with noble sacred art and music, and made fruitful by a deep formation of clergy and laity in the spirit of the liturgy.

It is up to us to do our part in this great work of liturgical renewal, which is to say, liturgical restoration and optimal celebration. Let us not grow weary, in spite of all obstacles, setbacks, and delays, or succumb to a kind of fatalistic resignation or quietism. Let us not indulge in foolish self-pity as we contemplate the real or imaginary difficulties of our duty. Duty will always be difficult, and the "world" within the Church will always be opposed to true reform.[9] Taking hold of every opportunity divine Providence gives us, using all our energy and every talent we have, we must take the steps and make the moves that will advance our side towards victory. Time is short, the stakes are high, and fortune favors the brave.

There is an old adage: *per aspera ad astra,* "through hardships to the stars." We never reach the heights without a climb through that which is uncongenial, that which challenges and stretches us. Trials come before triumph, purifications before perfection. This is true as much for movements as for individuals.

One day I was meditating on chapter 58 of St. Benedict's *Rule,* and I was struck by the way the holy patriarch recommends winning souls for monastic life.

> When anyone is newly come for the reformation of his life, let him not be granted an easy entrance; but, as the Apostle says, "Test the spirits to see whether they are from God." If the newcomer, therefore, perseveres in his knocking, and if it is seen after four or five days that he bears patiently the harsh treatment offered him and

---

9. I mean by this that even within the Church on earth there is always the world, in the sense of worldliness, the prudence of the flesh, the influence of the Evil One.

the difficulty of admission, and that he persists in his petition, then let entrance be granted him. . . .

Once the monk is admitted, his trials are not yet over:

> Let him [a senior monk] examine whether the novice is truly seek-ing God, and whether he is zealous for the Work of God, for obe-dience and for humiliations. Let the novice be told all the hard and rugged ways by which the journey to God is made.

This reminded me of something Fr. John Zuhlsdorf says: if we desire an increase in priestly and religious vocations, if we seek conversions to the Faith, we need "hard-identity Catholicism." We need to say clearly *everything* that we believe—consoling things (God is love) as well as astonishing things (Jesus is really, truly, substantially present in the Holy Eucharist), painful things (all of us will suffer our whole lives from disordered concupiscence and will need continual repen-tance), and things unpopular in a given society (marriage is an indissoluble union of man and woman, ordered to the begetting and educating of children). To know and live our faith, we need our tra-ditions, customs, and devotions *in full.* We need to make real demands on people—for otherwise *they* cannot possibly believe that *we* really believe the things our Bible and our Catechism say we do.

For fifty years, Church leaders have supported the softening or even suppression of the Faith's demands: be it effortless accessibility in the liturgy, less fasting and abstinence, fewer holy days of obliga-tion, little or no mention of hell or purgatory, almost no preaching on mortal sin and confession, ignoring the virtues of purity, chas-tity, and modesty, or countless other examples. We have been lulled to sleep, or driven to boredom, with "soft-identity Catholicism": nothing too harsh or off-putting, difficult or countercultural. This approach has been a monumental failure, as anyone familiar with Church history and Catholic spirituality could have predicted, and as increasingly dire statistics from around the world confirm.[10]

---

10. Individuals like Giuseppe Cardinal Siri (1906–1989) and Fr. Calmel did pre-dict it with utter clarity, since they had the wisdom to recognize the false principles. Regarding statistics, it is true that the Church is seeing growth in Africa, albeit not

St. Benedict's description, "zealous, obedient, and ready for humiliations," could be a spiritual charter for the new Liturgical Movement and especially for those who hold fast to the Church's tradition. We must be zealous, tirelessly promoting and defending the sacred liturgy and all that is holy, beautiful, and valuable across generations. We must also be obedient in all the ways that are essential and necessary. And these two qualities together will mean that we are sure to be put to the test regularly and will experience humiliations. "He has not promised pleasant things in this world to those that love Him, but hardships," says St. Remigius.[11] Yet these are the hardships that wean us from ourselves and attach us more and more to Him who is our salvation, life, resurrection, and joy. I find comfort and strength in the words of Roger-Thomas Calmel, O.P. (1914–1975), a priest who suffered much for his stalwart defense of the Faith:

> It is impossible to say "What's the use?" when one knows that it is *always* good to prove to God our love, the first proof of love being to persevere in the Faith and to keep Catholic Tradition. All the reasons we have for losing heart—the prolonged fight, the extensive betrayal, the increased isolation—should be considered only in the supreme light of faith. The greatest misfortune that could befall us is not to be bruised in the depth of our soul by the woes of the present times and the scandals from on high; it would be to lack faith and consequently to fail to see that the Lord makes use of the present distress to urge us to turn our gaze towards Him, to invite us to show Him more than ever our trust and love.[12]

---

without serious problems that will have to be faced sooner or later. But the historically Catholic populations of Europe and the Americas are declining precipitously. Only traditional communities are increasing in numbers, but they are, as yet, a small minority.

11. Cited in St. Thomas Aquinas, *Catena Aurea* on Mt 12:19 (Southampton: The Saint Austin Press, n. d.), 1:443.

12. "Apologia pro St. Pius V," an excerpt from Fr. Calmel's "Saint Pie V, un pape fils de saint Dominique," *Itinéraires*, April 1972, published at Angelus Online, February 2015; available at www.angelusonline.org.

> In all my troubles, I have never lost my faith, I have never
> despaired.   *Blessed Karl I of Austria* (1919)

As bleak as a landscape may be, there are always beautiful flowers
growing somewhere. We see this in a dramatic way in deserts: when
the infrequent rains come, dormant plants burst into blossom.

I remember looking at a book years ago on the eruption of
Mount St. Helens in Washington State. The book included photos
of the environment before the eruption, during it, and immediately
afterwards, when everything for miles around looked like a lunar or
Martian landscape: gray, barren, lifeless. Then the book had photos
of subsequent years at various intervals. Even in this desolation,
small plants began to grow again, insects and birds returned, and in
a remarkably short time, life was flourishing once more.

The Council and the liturgical reform were a ten-year volcanic
eruption that buried the heritage of the Church, killed off much of
her life, and left us with a hopeless mess. But life is stronger than
death, and God is more powerful than our mistakes. Slowly, the
landscape is coming alive again, as tradition pushes its way through
the layers of mud and debris, and beauty is restored to the world.

Working as a professor and choirmaster with young Catholics
over the years has given me great hope for the future. They are hungry for the sacred, for tradition, and for beauty, and they can and
will make a difference when their time comes. They fall in love with
Gregorian chant and Renaissance polyphony. They come to know
and love the priceless heritage of the Church. This heritage speaks
for itself, as it has always done; if it is simply allowed to exist, it
attracts souls to Our Lord and His Mystical Body. What a privilege
to act as "matchmaker" for this marriage! There is a powerful movement afoot among younger clergy and religious for restoring and
elevating the sacred liturgy. They are mostly silent and biding their
time, because they cannot be too vocal or public if they wish to
retain their positions and escape persecution. Although discour-
aged by officialdom and facing formidable obstacles, the movement
has on its side all the laws of theology, history, and sociology.

"Always Forward, Never Back"

Things will doubtless have to get worse before they get better, but the seeds of renewal are already widely scattered and germinating.[13] When their time to burst forth and bear fruit is at hand, we shall see a new fulfillment of the chronicler's words: "The workmen were diligent, and the breach of the walls was closed up by their hands, and they set up the house of the Lord in its former state, and made it stand firm" (2 Chron 24:13).

Always forward to Tradition—never back to modernism.

---

13. Some have compared our liturgical situation to the forty years Israel spent wandering in the wilderness for its sins of infidelity, but given that we have already passed the fifty-year mark from the first major misery, viz., the introduction of the vernacular around 1965, it is more realistic to think in terms of the seventy years of the Babylonian captivity.

Bibliography

This bibliography includes every book cited in these pages as well as additional books pertinent to the subject matter, but with no attempt at comprehensiveness even within the sphere of traditional Catholic literature. Citations of magazines, journals, blogs, online Vatican documents, or the works of Aquinas are not included. Books that I would recommend most highly ("must-reads") are marked with an asterisk.

Aillet, Marc. *The Old Mass and the New: Explaining the Motu Proprio Summorum Pontificum of Pope Benedict XVI.* San Francisco: Ignatius Press, 2010.

Amerio, Romano. *Iota Unum: A Study of Changes in the Catholic Church in the XXth Century.* Trans. John P. Parsons. Kansas City: Sarto House, 1996.

Augustine of Hippo. *Confessions.* Trans. Frank Sheed, ed. Michael P. Foley. Indianapolis: Hackett, 2006.

Augustine of Hippo. *Teaching Christianity* [*De Doctrina Christiana*]. Trans. Edmund Hill, O.S.A. Hyde Park, NY: New City Press, 1996.

Belloc, Hilaire. *The Path to Rome.* Chicago: Henry Regnery Company, 1954.

Benedict XVI. See Ratzinger.

*A Benedictine monk [Dom Gérard Calvet]. *Discovering the Mass.* Trans. Jean Pierre Pilon. London, UK: The Saint Austin Press, 1999.

*———. *The Sacred Liturgy.* London, UK: The Saint Austin Press, 1999.

*A Benedictine Monk. *In Sinu Jesu: The Journal of a Priest at Prayer.* Kettering, OH: Angelico Press, 2016.

Borella, Jean. *The Sense of the Supernatural.* Trans. G. John Champoux. Edinburgh: T&T Clark, 1998.

Bouyer, Louis. *The Liturgy Revived: A Doctrinal Commentary of the Conciliar Constitution on the Liturgy.* Notre Dame, IN: University of Notre Dame Press, 1964.

———. *The Memoirs of Louis Bouyer.* Trans. John Pepino. Kettering, OH: Angelico Press, 2015.

Bradshaw, Paul F. *The Search for the Origins of Christian Worship: Sources and Methods for the Study of Early Liturgy*, 2nd ed. New York: Oxford University Press, 2002.

Bruyère, Cécile, O.S.B. *The Spiritual Life and Prayer According to Holy Scripture and Monastic Tradition*. Trans. Benedictines of Stanbrook. Eugene, OR: Wipf and Stock, 2002.

Buck, Roger. *Cor Jesu Sacratissimum: From Secularism and the New Age to Christendom Renewed*. Kettering, OH: Angelico Press, 2016.

Buckley, William F., Jr. *Nearer, My God: An Autobiography of Faith*. New York: Doubleday, 1997.

Bugnini, Annibale. *The Reform of the Liturgy 1948–1975*. Trans. Matthew J. O'Connell. Collegeville, MN: The Liturgical Press, 1990.

Bux, Nicola. *Benedict XVI's Reform: The Liturgy between Innovation and Tradition*. Trans. Joseph Trabbic. San Francisco: Ignatius Press, 2012.

Caldecott, Stratford, ed. *Beyond the Prosaic: Renewing the Liturgical Movement*. Edinburgh: T&T Clark, 1998.

Cekada, Anthony. *Work of Human Hands: A Theological Critique of the Mass of Paul VI*. West Chester, OH: Philothea Press, 2010.

Chesterton, G.K. "Why I Am a Catholic." In *The Collected Works of G.K. Chesterton*, vol. 3. San Francisco: Ignatius Press, 1990.

Cicognani, Amleto. *The Saints Who Pray With Us in the Mass*. Enlarged edition. Kansas City, MO: Romanitas Press, 2017.

Crean, Thomas, O.P. *The Mass and the Saints*. San Francisco: Ignatius Press, 2009.

*Davies, Michael. *Cranmer's Godly Order: The Destruction of Catholicism through Liturgical Change*. Fort Collins, CO: Roman Catholic Books, 1995.

————. *Liturgical Time Bombs in Vatican II. The Destruction of Catholic Faith through Changes in Catholic Worship*. Rockford, IL: TAN Books, 2003.

————. *Pope John's Council*. Kansas City, MO: Angelus Press, 2007.

*————. *Pope Paul's New Mass*. Kansas City, MO: Angelus Press, 2009.

————. *The Roman Rite Destroyed*. Kansas City, MO: Angelus Press, 1992.

————. *A Short History of the Roman Mass*. Rockford, IL: TAN Books, 1997.

Day, Thomas. *Why Catholics Can't Sing*. Revised and updated ed. New York: Crossroad, 2013.

de Chivré, Bernard-Marie. *The Mass of Saint Pius V: Spiritual and Theological Commentaries*. Trans. Ann Marie Temple. Winona, MN: STAS Editions, 2007.

Bibliography

Delatte, Dom Paul, O.S.B. *The Rule of Saint Benedict: A Commentary.* Trans. Dom Justin McCann, O.S.B. Eugene, OR: Wipf and Stock, 2000.

*de Mattei, Roberto. *The Second Vatican Council—An Unwritten Story.* Trans. Patrick T. Brannan, S.J., Michael J. Miller, and Kenneth D. Whitehead. Ed. Michael J. Miller. Fitzwilliam, NH: Loreto Publications, 2012.

de Sainte-Marie, Joseph, O.C.D. *The Holy Eucharist—The World's Salvation. Studies on the Holy Sacrifice of the Mass, its Celebration, and its Concelebration.* Leominster: Gracewing, 2015.

Dix, Gregory. *The Shape of the Liturgy.* London/New York: Continuum, 2005.

Dobszay, László. *The Restoration and Organic Development of the Roman Rite.* Ed. Laurence Paul Hemming. London/New York: T&T Clark, 2010.

Durand, William. *The* Rationale divinorum officiorum *of William Durand of Mende: A New Translation of the Prologue and Book One.* Trans. Timothy M. Thibodeau. New York: Columbia University Press, 2007.

Elissa, Anna. *Mantilla: The Veil of the Bride of Christ.* Malang: Penerbit Dioma, 2016.

Ferrara, Christopher A., and Thomas E. Woods, Jr. *The Great Façade: The Regime of Novelty in the Catholic Church from Vatican II to the Francis Revolution.* Kettering, OH: Angelico Press, 2015.

Freeman, Kathleen. *Ancilla to the Pre-Socratic Philosophers.* Cambridge, MA: Harvard University Press, 1948.

Fortescue, Adrian. *The Mass: A Study of the Roman Liturgy.* Fitzwilliam, NH: Loreto Publications, 2012.

Gamber, Klaus. *The Reform of the Roman Liturgy: Its Problems and Background.* Trans. Klaus D. Grimm. San Juan Capistrano, CA: Una Voce Press and Harrison, NY: The Foundation for Catholic Reform, 1993.

Giampietro, Nicola. *The Development of the Liturgical Reform as Seen by Cardinal Ferdinando Antonelli from 1948 to 1970.* Fort Collins, CO: Roman Catholic Books, 2009.

Gihr, Nicholas. *The Holy Sacrifice of the Mass Dogmatically, Liturgically, and Ascetically Explained.* St. Louis: B. Herder, 1949.

Goodman, Dena. *The Republic of Letters: A Cultural History of the French Enlightenment.* Ithaca, NY: Cornell University Press, 1996.

*Guardini, Romano. *Sacred Signs.* Trans. Grace Branham. St. Louis: Pio Decimo Press, 1956.

———. *The Spirit of the Liturgy.* Trans. Ada Lane. New York: The Crossroad Publishing Co., n.d.

Guéranger, Dom Prosper, O.S.B. *Institutions liturgiques,* 2nd ed. Paris: Société genérale de Librairie catholique, 1878.

Hadot, Pierre. *Philosophy as a Way of Life: Spiritual Exercises from Socrates to Foucault.* Trans. Michael Chase, ed. Arnold Davidson. Malden, MA: Blackwell Publishing, 1995.

———. *Plotinus or The Simplicity of Vision.* Trans. Michael Chase, ed. Arnold Davidson. Chicago: University of Chicago Press, 1993.

Hazell, Matthew P. *Index Lectionum: A Comparative Table of Readings for the Ordinary and Extraordinary Forms of the Roman Rite.* N.p.: Lectionary Study Press, 2016.

*Houghton, Bryan. *Mitre and Crook.* New Rochelle, NY: Arlington House Publishers, 1979.

*Hull, Geoffrey. *The Banished Heart: Origins of Heteropraxis in the Catholic Church.* London/New York: T&T Clark, 2010.

Hünermann, Peter, ed. *Denzinger's Enchiridion Symbolorum: A Compendium of Creeds, Definitions, and Declarations of the Catholic Church,* 43rd edition. San Francisco: Ignatius Press, 2012.

Irwin, Kevin W. *Liturgy, Prayer, and Spirituality.* New York/Ramsey: Paulist Press, 1984.

———. *Responses to 101 Questions on the Mass.* New York/Mahwah: Paulist Press, 1999.

*Jackson, James W., F.S.S.P. *Nothing Superfluous: An Explanation of the Symbolism of the Rite of St. Gregory the Great.* Lincoln, NE: Fraternity Publications, 2016.

John Climacus. *The Ladder of Divine Ascent.* Trans. Archimandrite Lazarus Moore. New York: Harper & Brothers, 1959.

Jungmann, Josef, S.J. *The Mass of the Roman Rite: Its Origins and Development (Missarum Sollemnia).* Trans. Francis A. Brunner, C.S.S.R. Notre Dame, IN: Christian Classics, 2012.

*Kent, Michael [Beatrice Bradshaw Brown]. *The Mass of Brother Michel.* Milwaukee: Bruce, 1942.

Kinder, Terryl N. *Cistercian Europe: Architecture of Contemplation.* Grand Rapids: William B. Eerdmans; Kalamazoo: Cistercian Publications, 2000.

Knox, Ronald A. *The Hidden Stream.* New York: Sheed & Ward, 1953.

———. *The Pastoral Sermons.* Ed. Philip Caraman, S.J. New York: Sheed & Ward, 1960.

———. *The Window in the Wall: Reflections on the Holy Eucharist.* New York: Sheed & Ward, 1956.

Bibliography

Kocik, Thomas. *The Reform of the Reform? A Liturgical Debate: Reform or Return.* San Francisco: Ignatius Press, 2003.

Kowalska, Maria Faustina. *Diary: Divine Mercy in My Soul.* Stockbridge, MA: Marian Press, 2003.

Kwasniewski, Peter A. *Resurgent in the Midst of Crisis: Sacred Liturgy, the Traditional Latin Mass, and Renewal in the Church.* Kettering, OH: Angelico Press, 2014.

Laise, Juan Rodolfo. *Communion in the Hand: Documents and History.* Boonville, NY: Preserving Christian Publications, 2011.

*Lang, Uwe Michael. *Signs of the Holy One: Liturgy, Ritual, and Expression of the Sacred.* San Francisco: Ignatius Press, 2015.

*————. *Turning Towards the Lord.* San Francisco: Ignatius Press, 2004.

*————. *The Voice of the Church at Prayer: Reflections on Liturgy and Language.* San Francisco: Ignatius Press, 2012.

Larson, Anne M., ed. *Love in the Ruins: Modern Catholics in Search of the Ancient Faith.* Kansas City: Angelus Press, 2009.

Lewis, C.S. *God in the Dock: Essays on Theology and Religion.* Ed. Walter Hooper. Grand Rapids: William B. Eerdmans, 1970.

Mahrt, William Peter. *The Musical Shape of the Liturgy.* Richmond, VA: Church Music Association of America, 2012.

Manelli, Stefano M., F.F.I. *Jesus Our Eucharistic Love. Eucharistic Life Exemplified by the Saints.* New Bedford, MA: Franciscan Friars of the Immaculate, 1996.

Maritain, Jacques and Raïssa. *Liturgy and Contemplation.* Trans. Joseph W. Evans. New York: P. J. Kenedy & Sons, 1960.

Martindale, C.C., S.J. *The Words of the Missal.* New York: Macmillan, 1932.

Mohrmann, Christine. *Liturgical Latin: Its Origins and Character.* Washington, DC: Catholic University of America Press, 1957.

*Mosebach, Martin. *The Heresy of Formlessness: The Roman Liturgy and Its Enemy.* Trans. Graham Harrison. San Francisco: Ignatius Press, 2006.

Muggeridge, Anne Roche. *The Desolate City: Revolution in the Catholic Church.* Revised and expanded. New York: HarperCollins, 1990.

*Nichols, Aidan, O.P. *Looking at the Liturgy: A Critical View of Its Contemporary Form.* San Francisco: Ignatius Press, 1996.

O'Connell, Canon J. B. *The Roman Martyrology,* 1956 ed. Westminster, MD: The Newman Press, 1962.

Ottaviani, Alfredo Cardinal, and Antonio Cardinal Bacci. *The Ottaviani Intervention: Short Critical Study of the New Order of Mass.* Trans. Anthony Cekada. West Chester, OH: Philothea Press, 2010.

Pearce, Joseph. *Literary Converts: Spiritual Inspiration in an Age of Unbelief.* San Francisco: Ignatius Press, 2000.

Pickstock, Catherine. *After Writing: On the Liturgical Consummation of Philosophy.* Oxford: Blackwell, 1998.

Pieper, Josef. *In Tune with the World: A Theory of Festivity.* Trans. Richard and Clara Winston. South Bend, IN: St. Augustine's Press, 1999.

Pristas, Lauren. *The Collects of the Roman Missals: A Comparative Study of the Sundays in Proper Seasons before and after the Second Vatican Council.* London/New York: Bloomsbury T&T Clark, 2013.

Ratzinger, Joseph. *Dogma and Preaching.* Trans. Matthew J. O'Connell. Chicago: Franciscan Herald Press, 1985.

*———. *A New Song for the Lord: Faith in Christ and Liturgy Today.* Trans. Martha M. Matesich. New York: Crossroad, 1997.

———, with Vittorio Messori. *The Ratzinger Report.* Trans. Salvator Attansio and Graham Harrison. San Francisco: Ignatius Press, 1985.

*———. *The Spirit of the Liturgy.* Trans. John Saward. San Francisco: Ignatius Press, 2000.

*———. *Theology of the Liturgy: The Sacramental Foundation of Christian Existence.* Volume XI of *Collected Works.* [Includes *The Spirit of the Liturgy.*] Ed. Michael J. Miller. San Francisco: Ignatius Press, 2014.

Reid, Alcuin, ed. *A Bitter Trial: Evelyn Waugh and John Carmel Cardinal Heenan on the Liturgical Changes.* San Francisco: Ignatius Press, 2011.

———, ed. *From Eucharistic Adoration to Evangelization.* London/New York: Burns & Oates, 2012.

*———, ed. *Liturgy in the Twenty-First Century: Contemporary Issues and Perspectives.* London/New York: Bloomsbury T&T Clark, 2016.

———, ed. *Looking Again at the Question of the Liturgy with Cardinal Ratzinger.* Farnborough: Saint Michael's Abbey Press, 2003.

*———. *The Organic Development of the Liturgy,* 2nd ed. San Francisco: Ignatius Press, 2005.

———, ed. *The Sacred Liturgy: Source and Summit of the Life and Mission of the Church.* San Francisco: Ignatius Press, 2014.

———, ed. *T&T Clark Companion to Liturgy.* London/New York: Bloomsbury T&T Clark, 2016.

Ripperger, Chad. *Topics on Tradition.* N.p.: Sensus Traditionis Press, 2013.

Robinson, Jonathan. *The Mass and Modernity: Walking to Heaven Backward.* San Francisco: Ignatius Press, 2005.

Roy, Neil J., and Janet E. Rutherford, eds. *Benedict XVI and the Sacred Liturgy.* Proceedings of the First Fota International Liturgical Conference (2008). Dublin: Four Courts Press, 2010.

Rutherford, Janet E., ed. *Benedict XVI and Beauty in Sacred Music.* Proceedings of the Third Fota International Liturgical Conference (2010). Dublin: Four Courts Press; New York: Scepter Publishers, 2012.

Rutherford, Janet E., and James O'Brien, eds. *Benedict XVI and the Roman Missal.* Proceedings of the Fourth Fota International Liturgical Conference (2011). Dublin: Four Courts Press; New York: Scepter Publishers, 2013.

Sammons, Eric. *Be Watchful: Resist the Adversary, Firm in Your Faith.* Cincinnati: Saragossa Press, 2016.

Sarah, Robert Cardinal, with Nicolas Diat. *God or Nothing: A Conversation on Faith.* Trans. Michael J. Miller. San Francisco: Ignatius Press, 2015.

*Sarah, Robert Cardinal, with Nicolas Diat. *The Power of Silence Against the Dictatorship of Noise.* Trans. Michael J. Miller. San Francisco: Ignatius Press, 2017.

Saward, John. *Cradle of Redeeming Love: The Theology of the Christmas Mystery.* San Francisco: Ignatius Press, 2002.

Scheeben, Matthias Joseph. *Mariology.* Trans. T.L.M.J. Geuker. St. Louis: B. Herder, 1946.

Schneider, Athanasius. *Dominus Est—It is the Lord: Reflections of a Bishop of Central Asia on Holy Communion.* Trans. Nicholas L. Gregoris. Pine Beach, NJ: Newman House Press, 2008.

Senior, John. *The Remnants: The Final Essays of John Senior.* Foreword by Andrew Senior. Forest Lake, MN: The Remnant Press, 2013.

*Shaw, Joseph, ed. *The FIUV Position Papers on the 1962 Missal.* Third edition. N.p.: Foederatio Internationalis Una Voce, 2015.

Simon, Canon G.A. *Commentary for Benedictine Oblates on the Rule of St. Benedict.* Trans. Leonard J. Doyle. Eugene, OR: Wipf and Stock, 2009.

*Sire, H.J.A. *Phoenix from the Ashes: The Making, Unmaking, and Restoration of Catholic Tradition.* Kettering, OH: Angelico Press, 2015.

Snyder, Edward. *The Three Pillars of Faith in the Real Presence: Ordination, Offertory, Consecration.* Fitzwilliam, NH: Loreto Publications, 2015.

Speaight, Robert. *The Property Basket: Recollections of a Divided Life.* London: Collins and Harvill, 1970.

Strunk, Oliver, ed. *Source Readings in Music History.* New York: Norton, 1950.

Swain, Joseph P. *Sacred Treasure: Understanding Catholic Liturgical Music.* Collegeville, MN: Liturgical Press, 2012.

Topping, Ryan N.S. *Rebuilding Catholic Culture: How the* Catechism *Can Shape Our Common Life.* Manchester, NH: Sophia Institute Press, 2012.

Twomey, D. Vincent, S.V.D., and Janet E. Rutherford, eds. *Benedict XVI and Beauty in Sacred Art and Architecture.* Proceedings of the Third Fota International Liturgical Conference (2009). Dublin: Four Courts Press; New York: Scepter Publishers, 2011.

Ward, Maisie. *Gilbert Keith Chesterton.* London: Sheed & Ward, 1944.

Watkin, E.I. *Neglected Saints.* New York: Sheed & Ward, 1955.

Weber, Samuel F., O.S.B. *The Proper of the Mass for Sundays and Solemnities.* San Francisco: Ignatius Press, 2014.

Williamson, Hugh Ross. *The Great Prayer: Concerning the Canon of the Mass.* Leominster: Gracewing, 2009.

Woods, Thomas E., Jr. *Sacred Then and Sacred Now: The Return of the Old Latin Mass.* Fort Collins, CO: Roman Catholic Books, 2008.

Zundel, Maurice. *The Splendour of the Liturgy.* New York: Sheed & Ward, 1939.

Vann, Gerald, O.P. *The Paradise Tree.* London: Collins, 1959.

INDICES

Index of Subjects

* This index does not include entries for which almost every page would have to be listed, such as "*usus antiquior*" or "traditional Latin Mass."

Index of Subjects

bowing, 126, 153, 201–2; *see also* genuflection
breviary, *see* Divine Office
Byzantine liturgy, xxi–xxiv, 40n12, 65, 68, 74n35, 78, 80–81, 106, 159, 202n24, 225–26, 236, 264, 280

calendar, 82, 117n4, 147, 170, 176n2, 218, 222–23, 228, 230n16, 263n7, 281; *see also names of saints and seasons*
candles, xxii, 99–100, 121, 202n24, 278
canon law, xxv, 136–39, 141–42, 152, 164
capitalism, 38–39, 77
Cartesian mentality, 38, 128n15
catechesis, 30, 42, 48n25, 95–96, 153, 206, 246, 284
Catholic social teaching, *see* social doctrine
celibacy, xiii, 276
ceremonial, xxii, 11, 13, 17, 31, 40, 42, 47, 56n6, 60, 66, 75, 98, 108, 132, 147, 171, 177, 192, 203, 219, 225–26, 237, 245, 260
chalice, xxiii, 10n19, 19, 73, 162, 167, 200
change in liturgy, *see* organic development
chant, *see* Gregorian chant
charismatic(s), 105, 161, 199
chasuble, 121, 142; *see also* vestments
cherubic hymn, 106
children, and liturgy, 24, 26, 42, 44, 98, 101, 110, 126–27, 156, 170, 173–74, 180, 187, 213n35,

236n2, 251n21, 257–59, 261, 284
Christ the King, *see* kingship of Christ
Christ the High Priest, *see* priesthood of Christ
Christmas, 54n2, 56n6, 117n4, 201, 219, 231n18, 252n22
Christology, 123
churchmen, 56n7, 60n12, 141, 150
clericalism, 66n24, 108
collect, 93, 215, 216n2, 219–21, 224–25, 229, 261n5
collectivism, 47–48, 84, 109, 148, 232
commemoration of saints, *see* saints, veneration of
committee, liturgy by, xx, 11n20, 15, 48n25, 56, 74n35, 125n12, 128n15, 163, 182, 189, 203, 209, 263n7, 266; *see also* Consilium
communion, reception of, xvi, xix–xx, 7, 37, 56n8, 95n8, 162, 173, 178, 194n10, 239
communion of saints, 138, 151, 159, 217–18, 221, 224, 226–28; *see also* saints, veneration of
complexity, 11, 24–29, 90, 128, 199, 219–20
comprehension, 94–97, 100, 153–54, 187, 202, 253–54
confession, *see* penance
confirmation, xxv, 42, 111, 165
Confiteor, 34n2, 95n8, 126, 200, 216–17, 219, 221, 223, 236, 244, 257, 261n5, 262n6
congregation, xviii, xx, 46, 48, 68, 72–73, 90, 96, 131, 155, 185, 203, 204–5, 239, 243n14, 259
consecrated life, *see* religious life

Index of Proper Names

About the Author

Dr. Peter Kwasniewski earned his bachelor's degree in Liberal Arts at Thomas Aquinas College in California and his master's degree and doctorate in Philosophy at the Catholic University of America in Washington, DC. After teaching at the International Theological Institute and the Austrian Program of the Franciscan University of Steubenville in Gaming, Austria, he joined the founding team of Wyoming Catholic College, where he teaches theology, philosophy, music, and art history, and serves as choirmaster and curator of the library. He is a composer of sacred music and a prolific writer and speaker.